Planning Resilient Infrastructure Systems

Institution of Civil Engineers Publishing

Planning Resilient Infrastructure Systems

Alexander H Hay
PhD, CEng, PEng, FICE, RSES, CRM
Southern Harbour Ltd, Toronto, ON, Canada

Published by ICE Publishing, One Great George Street, Westminster, London SW1P 3AA

Full details of ICE Publishing representatives and distributors can be found at: www.icebookshop.com/bookshop_contact.asp

Other titles by ICE Publishing:

Doing it Differently: Systems for rethinking infrastructure, Second edition
David Blockley and Patrick Godfrey. ISBN 978-0-7277-6082-1
Financing Infrastructure Projects: A practical guide, Second edition
Tony Mema and Faisal F Al-Thani. ISBN 978-0-7277-6336-5
Rethinking Masterplanning: Creating Quality Places
Husam AlWaer and Barbara Illsley. ISBN 978-0-7277-6071-5

www.icebookshop.com
A catalogue record for this book is available from the British Library

ISBN 978-0-7277-6562-8

ICE Publishing is a division of Thomas Telford Ltd, a wholly owned subsidiary of the Institution of Civil Engineers (ICE).

Cover photo: From the bird's eye view of Alesund port town on the west coast of Norway, at the entrance to the Geirangerfjord. Colorful summer sunset at the Nord port. Andrew Mayovsky/Shutterstock

Commissioning Editor: Michael Fenton
Production Editor: Madhubanti Bhattacharyya
Marketing Specialist: April Nagy

Typeset by Academic + Technical, Bristol
Index created by Pierke Bosschieter
Printed and bound in Great Britain by TJ Books, Padstow

Contents

Preface

During the winter of 1992–1993, we hacked and blasted 76 km of two-lane road through the Dinaric Alps into the interior of Bosnia–Herzegovina. An expedient-military road, *Route Triangle* carried essential humanitarian relief during the Bosnian War. With each season that followed, the road was gradually enhanced, only to be abandoned following the 1995 Dayton Peace Accords. The experience and example of *Route Triangle* spurred in me a lifelong interest in infrastructure. I was particularly interested in how infrastructure use and value could change so completely. I also wanted to understand how a successful project could fail its intended beneficiaries.

Over three decades, I have had the distinct privilege of working in many countries, variously as client, consultant and contractor, with some of the most capable engineers, architects, financiers and planners. More recently, I had the opportunity to investigate how my observations and experiences compared with academic teachings and to conduct research. For me, infrastructure is, quite simply, fascinating. Water infrastructure has had a more profound and lasting effect on public health than any number of physicians. These infrastructure systems have allowed us to advance civilisation, densify cities and project trade. Improvements in communications and energy infrastructure systems have advanced economies around the world. Yet, it is often misunderstood and misapplied despite all that infrastructure is and enables us to do.

Hindsight is, as they say, 20/20. After navigating the complexities of planning and implementing a new infrastructure scheme, someone will identify the real and perceived failings in the delivered works. I have conducted audits of infrastructure schemes on behalf of underwriters, financiers and owners, and risk profiled development strategies. There would seem to be two consistent issues. The first is the lack of a common conceptual understanding of infrastructure and how it works in the broader socioeconomic environment. The second is an apparent lack of evidence or use of a common reference to inform planning and discussions.

The lack of a common conceptual understanding affects everything from the approach to planning, assessment of benefit and commonality of purpose, and our understanding of through-life value and how to finance it. None of the particular tools that we use is wrong, per se, but they may not be the most appropriate to the situation. By any definition, infrastructure is a system that draws together structures, protocols for use and environmental dynamics to enable a capability or function. This system affects other systems and is supported by and influenced by yet other systems. The whole is thoroughly interconnected. We cannot fully understand one system in isolation, much less a multiplicity of individual or component systems.

Similarly, when something exists to enable an activity or capability, its value is defined by the degree of activity it enables. We can spend millions on a utility infrastructure system, but it has no value if no one uses it. Valuing infrastructure by the service it enables can present a challenge for infrastructure financing. Investment models that use real property cost or market value at the time of investment cannot capture the value of the infrastructure's use throughout its life.

Institutional investment in infrastructure as an asset class is still establishing itself. Many investment decision support models still use real property asset class valuation. Such models require assumptions, generalisations and estimates based on experience to inform the decision. These models are not designed for infrastructure investment decision-making. Therefore, the investor must use subjective assessment that is calibrated by experience, rather than an objective judgement based on available evidence. This evidence in context is the basis for the common reference. Institutional investors still wrestle with this, specifically how to inform the decision to invest. We often default to familiar models, defining the question by what we know we can answer. Consequently, we base our decision on a projection of value at the time of the investment.

Through-life investment decision-making involves real change. Climate, technological and societal changes all directly influence socioeconomic behaviours and so the use of the infrastructure. These changes in use represent changes in value and risks. The material disclosures in the annual directors' reports for public corporations generally focus on corporate and compliance-type risks around these investments rather than the actual risks to continued operation and hence value change. In the absence of empirical data collected for the latter, the former relies more on estimate and subjective assessment. This issue extends beyond financial measures and speaks to the heart of corporate resilience. We can have the best corporate risk management and resilience package, but there is no business if we cease operating. The two are inseparable.

Similarly, infrastructure risk management and resilience are about both performance and contingent capability. We can align key risk indicators with our key performance indicators to present a real understanding of threats and opportunities to our infrastructure's value. The performance and capability of infrastructure will depend on how it is perceived and the broader community's sense of ownership. Infrastructure is one of the critical connectors between a corporation or municipality and the community. It is environmental, social and corporate governance in its very essence. Little wonder that it is or enables most of the 17 Sustainable Development Goals (SDGs).

The apparent lack of evidence used in planning and design is becoming a common refrain. Emphasised in the (UK) 2013 Armitt Review and in the 2016 National Infrastructure Commission report, *Connected Future*, the use of evidence allows us to establish a common reference. This common reference is a pure expression of fact, empirically based, associating an action with a series of consequences and an outcome. These connections are knowable and, in most regions, can be established using little more than satellite data and open-source references. Informed discussion informs perspective, collaborative problem identification and solving, and judgement-based decision-making.

In the absence of any (empirical) common reference, we necessarily rely on individual perceptions of the situation and deficiencies informed by our professional experience and bias. We are hardwired to infer an understanding of requirements from familiar fragments of patterns, which we then reinforce using curated corroborating evidence. This inevitably leads to optimism bias and failures in beneficial outcomes and cost management. If we can control the patterning of perceived deficiencies by better informing ourselves of what is, we can better define the actual problems. We must avoid defining the problem by the solution or tools we have to hand.

The willingness to study a situation and derive the problem requires a professional humility and patience that may be lacking, particularly when a time imperative drives the agenda. For example, following conflict or natural disaster, the reconstruction effort is frequently driven by an assumption of what pre-existed the catastrophe and how it worked, with a vision of what the solution should be based on what is familiar to the reconstruction engineers, planners and donors. Often, there is an apparent mismatch between what was intended and the delivered benefit to the local community in postconflict reconstruction. The better use of evidence can fundamentally change practice and, I believe, reduce needless confrontation and expense.

When professional practitioners draw on a common concept of infrastructure and situational evidence, they can devise and deliver infrastructure systems that maintain value through life, benefiting all stakeholders. To me, this is the most explicit articulation of engineering in society. Engineering practice in infrastructure is inseparable from value, financing and the socioeconomic and natural environment that it functions within. Infrastructure

is complex but needn't be complicated;
it is dynamic but inanimate.

With this book, I hope to inform a more cohesive, joined-up understanding of infrastructure from a first-principles perspective. Consequently, this is not jurisdictional or sector-specific. Though I am an engineer, writing predominantly for engineers, I do not feel that our language use always promotes understanding across all stakeholders. Why, for example, would we use different risk terminology from the finance and underwriting industries? That is not to say that technical definitions, codes and standards are necessarily wrong. We must understand these differences in interpretation and intelligently adjust if we are to speak with different audiences.

The emphasis of this book is understanding. I have endeavoured to keep it mercifully short, hoping that I may keep your interest through to the conclusion. I also hope to stimulate your further reading and exploration of the various topics covered. The concepts and practices are accessible. Where I have not been able to identify a commonly agreed theory or practice, I offer my perspective based on my research and experience. I annotate each instance where I do this, most notably around unifying purpose and beneficial capability. I use examples to illustrate points rather than whole case studies. I've avoided case studies because it is rare for the combination of conditions that led to the successful application of a particular practice in one location to replicate in another. Each situation (operation, location and context) is unique, even within the same city.

I begin by introducing infrastructure, exploring why it is essential and where the issues are and presenting my argument. I focus heavily on the theory of infrastructure. This theory leads to an exploration of value and the use of risk as both a tool and a language. I explore sustainability, resilience and protection in infrastructure systems before drawing all of these strands together to present infrastructure planning in theory. I balance this with a planning-in-practice perspective, exploring the noise and disconnects that can change the planned infrastructure's path and outcome. I conclude by exploring what the future holds for the infrastructure world.

Acknowledgements
I wish to acknowledge Federico Sittaro, Adonis Yatchew, Sanjay Khanna, Yannick Beaudoin, Yvonne Steiner, John Neily, Heather MacLean and Bryan Karney, with whom I have enjoyed many conversations about infrastructure's role and influence in society. I thank Michael Fenton, who encouraged and guided my development of this book. I particularly thank Carla, without whose support I would not have been able to write it. This book is for Joseph, Sophie and Alastair.

About the author

Alexander H Hay PhD CEng PEng FICE RSES is a civil engineer specialising in infrastructure systems risk. He is a graduate of the University of Edinburgh and the University of Toronto, where he is an adjunct professor. He has 35 years of international experience in infrastructure development and fortifications in regions as diverse as the High Arctic, Europe, North Africa, the Middle East and Central Asia. Commissioned into the (British) Royal Engineers in 1989, he released in 2013 to pursue a career in industry. He is the founding principal of Southern Harbour Ltd, an independent infrastructure risk advisory service operating globally, advising on the through-life risk profiles of sustainable economic development strategies, and infrastructure reconfiguration and development. His research interest at the University of Toronto's Centre for Resilience of Critical Infrastructure is postconflict and postdisaster community rehabilitation and the role of infrastructure in regional socioeconomic transition to a low carbon dioxide emissions world. He joined the ICE knowledge panel on capacity building from 2007 to 2009 and has remained keenly interested in professional formation and development since, particularly in how to develop the competencies that the next generation of professional engineers will need to deal with the world they inherit.

About the collaborators

Yannick C Beaudoin MA PhD is a senior economist and Director General for Ontario and Northern Canada with the David Suzuki Foundation. Previously, he was Chief Scientist with UNEP/GRID-Arendal in Norway. He brings an 'economics for transition' lens to the Foundation, aimed at helping to enable a socially thriving and ecologically sustainable Canada. He applies art of change and participatory social processes to a variety of themes that include: adaptation to uncertain climate futures; embedding of local, traditional and indigenous knowledge in policy-, decision- and choice-making; and promoting a transition to a sustainable relationship between society and Nature. From his decade with the United Nations to his return to Canada in 2018, he has been facilitating conversations around the world, highlighting various solution pathways towards a well-being centric, #beyondGDP economic system.

Sanjay Khanna BEd MFA GCB.D is a strategic advisor and foresight expert. Previously the futurist at global law firm Baker McKenzie, today Sanjay works with organisations to illuminate risks and opportunities associated with the converging crises of geopolitical fragmentation, socioeconomic reordering, population health issues, technological acceleration, and environmental and climate change. Sanjay has been interviewed by the *Financial Times*, *The Globe and Mail* and the Canadian Broadcasting Corporation, among others.

John Neily A/Commr (Retd) CEC PCIP is a strategic advisor in security and criminal intelligence, and a Certified Executive Coach. He served in the Royal Canadian Mounted Police for 35 years and as operations and operational support executive for specialised criminal investigations and operational readiness in the last 8 years. During this period, he was instrumental in organising the Canadian criminal intelligence–critical infrastructure interface with public and private sector partners. As Director of National Security and Emergency Management at the Conference

Board of Canada, his team informed the shift in approach from critical infrastructure protection to critical infrastructure resilience, and published several cross-border reports. He was a strategic advisor to the Defence Research and Development Canada's Centre for Security Science for 4 years to integrate the first responder community in science and technology programmes. He is a sought-after consultant, facilitator and coach, working with established and upcoming leaders in both public and private sectors.

List of abbreviations

AI	Artificial intelligence
AOI	Area of influence
AOO	Area of operations
BFCA	Builders for Climate Action
BLM	Black Lives Matter
BOMA	Building Owners and Managers Association
BRE	Building Research Establishment
CAF	Corporacion Andina de Fomento
CAPEX	Capital expenditure
CC	Carrying capacity
CDBB	Centre for Digital Built Britain
COP	Common operating picture
CP	Calculation plan
CPNI	Centre for the Protection of the National Infrastructure
CPTED	Crime Prevention Through Environmental Design
CRA	Canadian Revenue Agency
CRCI	Centre for Resilience of Critical Infrastructure
CSR	Corporate social responsibility
DCS	Distributed control system
DHS	Department of Homeland Security
ERM	Enterprise-wide risk management
ERSA	European Regional Science Association
ESDA	Exploratory spatial data analysis
ESG	Environment, social and governance
FMEA	Failure modes effects analysis
FMECA	Failure modes effects and criticality analysis
GDPR	General Data Protection Regulation
GPIF	Government Pension Investment Fund
GRMI	Global Risk Management Institute
GSD	Ground sample distance
HTT	Hazard travel time
IAO	Indicators of anticipated outcome
ICE	Institution of Civil Engineers
ICS	Industrial control systems
ICT	Information and communications technology
IDP	Infrastructure development plan
IMF	International Monetary Fund
ISO	International Standards Organization

LCA	Life-cycle analysis
LCI	Life-cycle inventory
LEED	Leadership in Energy and Environmental Design
LoP	Level of protection
LRA	Location risk assessment
MAR	Maximum acceptable risk
MDG	Millennium Development Goals
MOC	Minimum operating capability
MRTC	Maximum realisable threat capability
MSC	Minimum sustainable capability
NOAA	National Oceanic and Atmospheric Administration
OECD	Organization for Economic Cooperation and Development
OPEX	Operation and maintenance expenses
OSPA	Oxford Scenario Planning Approach
PP	Planning point
PRI	Principles for Responsible Investment
PTSD	Post-traumatic stress disorder
RAMP	Risk Analysis and Management for Projects
RIBA	Royal Institute of British Architects
RICS	Royal Institution of Chartered Surveyors
RIMS	Risk and Insurance Management Society
ROI	Return on investment
SAID	Systems approach to infrastructure delivery
SARS	Severe acute respiratory syndrome
SCADA	Supervisory control and data acquisition
SDG	Sustainable Development Goals
SPV	Special purpose vehicle
TCFD	Task Force on Climate-related Financial Disclosures
TRA	Threat & risk assessment
TUNA	Turbulence, uncertainty, novelty and ambiguity
UN	United Nations
UNDRR	UN Office for Disaster Risk Reduction
UNEP	UN Environment Programme
UNISDR	UN International Strategy for Disaster Reduction
UPS	Uninterruptable power supply
VaR	Value at risk

VBIED	Vehicle-borne improvised explosive device
VSOS	Vitae system of systems
WCED	World Commission on Environment and Development
WCR	Whole cost of risk
WEF	World Economic Forum
WHO	World Health Organization
WRI	World Resources Institute

ICE Publishing

Hay, Alexander H
ISBN 978-0-7277-6562-8
https://doi.org/10.1680/pris.65628.glossary

Glossary

Acceptable risk	The risk acceptability threshold is expressed in the organisation's risk criteria and represents the level of risk that the organisation is willing and capable of absorbing. Typically, the event's likelihood is minimal, and its adverse consequences are comfortably within the organisation's capacity to compensate, or the potential benefits are significantly large.
Area of influence (AOI)	The area beyond our immediate control in which we can exert some influence on the controlling authority. This is typically associated with areas in which systems that we critically depend on are located.
Area of interest	The area in which a specified threat or hazard can form and move towards our area of operations. The area of interest is defined by the precursors, preconditions and resources of the threat or hazard, and their associated indicators.
Area of operations (AOO)	The area that we control and within which we have complete freedom of action and resource allocation.
Asset-based planning	The redevelopment of an asset or facility based on its current functions and risk exposure.
Beneficial capability	The concept that for a change or initiative to have a sustainable benefit in a community, it must satisfy three requirements: that there is a facility from which the local community can benefit, that the local community can access the facility and that the local community members are capable of benefiting. It is associated with intelligent resourcing.
Black elephant	A term coined by environmentalist Adam Sweidan, a black elephant is a cross between a black swan

	event and the elephant in the room. In a departure from Taleb's definition of a black swan, Sweidan describes an event that is unlikely and unexpected with enormous impact yet is also quite apparent to everyone and is wilfully ignored.
Black swan	Though an ancient metaphor describing the presumption that something does not exist, its modern usage stemmed from Nassim Nicholas Taleb's 2010 book, The Black Swan*: The Impact of the Highly Improbable*. Taleb's black swan theory describes black swan events as being rare high-impact events that are beyond historical expectation; it's exceedingly hard to predict their probability or consequence, and they're subject to a cognitive bias that leads to 'the underestimation of the role of the Black Swan and occasional overestimation of a specific one' (Ibid., p. 301).
Calculation plan	An auditable record of analysis, from original data source references and citation to analyses, summaries of findings, synthesis and outputs, tags for further investigation and cross-referencing to other parts of the investigation. The calculation plan is opened at the start of the desktop study and closes when the project is decommissioned, and often includes a log of project decisions. It will have regular archive milestones, when the current version is recorded for archive with a date and time signature. The calculation plan forms the basis for audit.
Capability-based planning	The projection of a desired capability in space and time that anchors the desired end-state of a development strategy amid environmental uncertainty. It is closely associated with safe-to-fail and resilience planning.
Committee of Sponsoring Organizations of the Treadway Commission (COSO)	Formed in 1985, the Committee of Sponsoring Organizations of the Treadway Commission (www.coso.org) is a private sector initiative to inspect, analyse and make recommendations on fraudulent corporate financial reports. It provides financial guidance on enterprise risk management, internal controls and fraud deterrence.

Common operating picture (COP)	An organisation's interpretation of a common reference against its priorities, interests and goals.
Common reference	An objective evidence-based model that describes the current situation and can be used by all stakeholders as a common understanding of the existing configuration and composition of the vitae system of systems, and the potential consequences of a change. The common reference is free from any interpretation or organisational or interest bias; it is the basis for digital twin modelling.
Community engagement	The process of working collaboratively with a particular group, defined by geography, interest or shared circumstances. In infrastructure planning, it most typically, but not exclusively, refers to a geographic community's relationship with infrastructure systems.
Consequence	The effect that a change in the function of one entity has on another entity. Consequence is measured in terms of operational (or mission) performance, direct financial cost, and market, reputation or goodwill. Consequence is normally associated with a dependency relationship and, quantitatively and qualitatively, shows the effects of changes in one entity on another.
Cost–benefit analysis (CBA)	A decision support calculation that compares the costs of a particular option with its expected benefits. This can be presented as a ratio of benefit to cost or as a summation. The value and effectiveness of CBAs are determined by what costs and benefits to include in the calculation.
Demand management	The reduction and reallocation of resources to minimise overall consumption and improve operating efficiency.
Dependency management	The reduction in risks inherent in resource availability, by both source and quantity, through diversification and supply management.
Dependency model	A network representing functional dependency relationships between different entities defined by the consequence of function deterioration and

	interruption. The function of entity A may depend on the function of entities B and C. The function of B may deteriorate and affect the function of A. At some level of performance deterioration, B fails, with consequences for A. Entity B will depend on the function of entities X, Y and Z, and entity Z may depend on entities K and L. A manually built dependency model has a useful limit of three to four dependency relationships between entity A and the upstream entity K. Digital dependency models typically have longer dependency chains, of around nine distinct relationships. The dependency model forms part of the common reference.
Desktop study (DTS)	The first stage in any investigation or analytical process, it is the desk-based collation and analysis of the available data to produce an initial conceptual model of the situation. It will normally comprise a study of the subject organisation, operation and context, typically defined as PESTLE (political, economic, social, technological, legal and environment).
Digital twin	The data–model representation of a thing, person or process. More generally, it refers to a built asset, though is increasingly used in reference to infrastructure systems. As with others terms with expanding applications, one needs to be clear what it includes and its purpose. In infrastructure planning, the term typically includes both a common reference and a COP.
Distributed control system (DCS)	A computer application that autonomously adjusts a system's performance within defined parameters for a defined part of the system or its components. This can be locally automated or controlled by a local operator who is familiar with the defined part of the system and its role in the whole. The DCS may be connected to the Internet or function in isolation.
Enterprise-wide risk management (ERM); also enterprise risk management	'An approach to managing all of an organisation's key business risks and opportunities with the intent of maximizing [shareholder] value.' Enterprise Risk Management, 1st edn (Elliott MW (ed.)) The Institutes, Malvern, PA, USA, 2013.

Environment, social and governance (ESG)	The core criteria for measuring the sustainability and societal impact of an activity.
Equilibrium	An extension of Elinor Ostrom's studies on the self-organising collective management of a shared resource in a closed system; it is the relationship between communities and the higher authority sharing a common resource and bounded by the same infrastructure system.
Equity of access	A concept of adjusted access to common opportunities defined by the same possible outcome. It is distinct from the equal provision of access, resources and opportunities, instead reflecting the allocation of resources to enable an individual's capacity to realise the opportunity and benefit. It is commonly associated with the concept of fairness.
Exploratory spatial data analysis (ESDA)	A critical approach to investigating and interpreting spatial data from different sources, using tools and techniques that help gain insight and build better interpolation models.
Failure modes effects analysis (FMEA)	The systematic evaluation of component assets and subsystems to identify potential failure modes and their associated causes and effects.
Failure modes effects and criticality analysis (FMECA)	An extension of FMEA, incorporating the likelihood and consequences of failure, identifying which components are critical to the system, i.e., relatively high likelihood and consequence of failure.
Fragile, fragility	The inherent property of a system to fail or break, associated with its sensitivity to failure in one of its subsystems, components or enabling functions or resources.
Hazard	A hazard is something that can cause harm. Malicious hazards are often called threats.
Hazard travel time (HTT)	The time taken for a hazard to travel from first detection to its target or protected asset. The HTT is the basis for an analysis of response travel, interdiction and readiness against obstacles that cause delay. It is used to calculate the critical period

	in which a decision to respond must be made, as well as its supporting degree of confidence.
Holon	An entity that is both a whole in its own right and a part of one or more greater wholes.
Incident sequencing	The graphical representation of an operation's performance before, during, and following an incident. It includes the minimum operating capability (MOC) and minimum sustainable capability (MSC) thresholds. By expressing performance over time, one can determine resource requirements at each stage of an incident and the strict sequence of functional restoration for response and recovery, and ascribe a total cost of loss and interruption for each scenario and treatment proposal.
Influence model	A network representation of the virtual domain effects on the operation of a system and its infrastructure. It is the development of governance criteria to explain how an event of decision can influence the performance of an operation and the perspectives and interests of the entities involved. It is part of the common reference. Note: McKinsey & Co., a management consultancy, use the term to describe their change management framework, which helps the user navigate shifts in people and processes during organisational change.
Information and communications technology (ICT)	Technologies that provide access to diverse sources of data and information through telecommunications.
Infrastructure development plan (IDP)	The structured programme of infrastructure delivery to achieve a desired end-state capability and outcome. It is typically structured in three parts, comprising (1) strategy, (2) finance & benefit, contracting & risk allocation and (3) portfolio projects aligned to stage objectives.
Intelligent resourcing	A planning concept first described by a Roman architect, Vitruvius, which involves adapting a standard design to locally provided materials and services without compromising performance.

Level of protection (LoP)	The performance of protection measures up to and including an acceptable risk, i.e., the likelihood of the scale or severity of a hazard or threat exceeding the protection measures being acceptable. It is often articulated as the acceptable consequence of a threat event.
Level of protection, operational	The degree of risk treatment to achieve an acceptable or optimum risk, usually in the form of security measures that modify the likelihood and consequence of a range of hazards of threats.
Level of protection, structural	The physical security measures necessary to enable the full range of security postures (relational and procedural) to achieve the operational level of protection. A structural level of protection is defined by the operational level of protection that it enables. It is also known as the physical level of protection.
Likelihood	The chance of an occurrence. It is used as an estimate and in contrast to probability.
Location risk assessment (LRA)	The assessment of all hazards that are inherent to a specified location, and that can represent risk to operations conducted there.
Maximum acceptable risk (MAR)	The threshold level of threat or risk that the organisation is unwilling or unable to manage, accept or transfer. It is associated with the decision to cease operations or relocate away from the threat area, i.e., avoid the risk, and is articulated in the organisation's risk criteria.
Maximum realisable threat capability (MRTC)	The greatest possible threat to an operation or asset, irrespective of likelihood.
Minimum operating capability/capacity (MOC)	The threshold of performance of an operation, below which the operation ceases to exist.
Minimum sustainable capability/capacity (MSC)	The continuing stable level of performance of an operation in which there is no (market, financial or capability) loss and negligible gain.
PESTLE	PESTLE is a mnemonic for 'political, economic, social, technological, legal and environment'. (It is

	sometimes referred to as PEST or PESTEL). It represents the areas to be investigated in a macroscopic scan of the situation. It is commonly used in all forms of strategic management, and is a standard approach in desktop studies.
Principles for Responsible Investment (PRI)	A UN-supported independent network of investors, working to promote sustainable investment through environmental, social and governance practices. It has six defining principles (www.unpri.org).
Probability	The statistically calculated chance of an occurrence, based on a large number of identical past occurrences. Since infrastructure projects are, by definition, each unique, probability cannot be calculated and likelihood is used in preference.
Protection	The prevention of harm to an asset.
Public safety	The protection of a nation's people, communities and institutions against threats to their well-being.
Resilience	In its most general (ecological) sense, it is the persistence of a system. It is the ability to absorb and adapt to variabilities in the environment and persist.
Resilience, corporate	The ability of an organisation to absorb the impact of changes in circumstances, and assign resources for a timely and sustainable response. It is normally associated with contingency plans, governance structures and crisis management. Where corporate resilience is concerned with the organisation's relationship with its environment, the organisation is ineffective if the operations are not resilient.
Resilience of infrastructure systems	The configuration and design of infrastructure systems to enable a resilient operation or service.
Resilience of operations	The ability of an operation to sustainably adapt to changes in circumstance and rapidly self-recover routine performance. It is focused on the enabling functions of the operation and its supporting supply and distribution chains.
Resilience, operational	The 'essential ability of an operation to respond to and absorb the effects of shocks and stresses and to

	recover as rapidly as possible normal capacity and efficiency' (https://crci.utoronto.ca/about/faqs).
Resilience, social	'Social resilience is about social entities and their abilities to tolerate, absorb, cope with and adjust to environmental and social threats of various kinds. The development of the concept of social resilience started with a rather unspecific understanding of social resilience as the capacity to respond, which then evolved to incorporate notions of learning and adaptation to form a composite definition, which includes the acknowledgement of the importance of the roles played by power, politics, and participation in the context of increasing uncertainty and surprise.' (Sakdapolrak P, *What is Social Resilience?* http://www.transre.org/index.php/blog/what-social-resilience, 26/09/2018).
Risk	'The effect of uncertainty on objectives' (ISO 31000:2018 para. 3.1). For a risk to exist, there must be a hazard, an asset exposed to the hazard and a consequence of the hazard occurring. This is represented by the consequence and likelihood of the hazard occurrence.
Risk context	The changing context in which an operation exists, comprising its relationship with other operations and entities and all changes and hazards or threats that can affect the operation's performance and attainment of objectives. It comprises the operating context (all neighbouring operations that affect and are affected by the operation), the operating environment (all neighbouring operations that affect the operation but are not affected by it) and all hazards.
Risk horizon	A period in which a risk exists.
Safe-to-fail	Safe-to-fail is the property of a system in which the system's operational purpose is not interrupted by the failure of a component or subsystem. In practice, a safe-to-fail system's performance can be impeded, though is not considered interrupted unless that performance falls below a stable or minimum sustainable capability. This is different from a fail-safe procedure or design, where there is minimal

	harm to people, equipment and the environment in the component failure vicinity.
Security	The system of measures taken to keep an asset or capability safe and protected. It has three components: relational, procedural and physical. Relational security is the (human domain) relationship between the secured, the guard and the general public – changes in established patterns and behaviours can cue investigation and other measures. Procedural security is the (virtual domain) codified sequence of activities that reduce the exposure to, and the likelihood and consequence of, harm. Physical security encompasses measures in the natural and built domains that shield the secured from harm and contain the effects of the threat or hazard.
Social capital	The network of communications and interactions between members of a group or community, around shared identity, norms and understanding.
Stakeholder engagement	The planned interactions with individuals and organisations having a real or perceived interest in a proposed activity according to their ability to affect the activity. This involves understanding the respective stakeholder perspective, self-interest and influence. It has become a highly specialised field in its own right.
Supervisory control and data acquisition (SCADA) system	A computer application that (centrally) gathers and presents performance and other situational data in real time and allows the operator to adjust the industrial systems' settings, as part of a digital industrial control system.
Sustainability, dimensions of	Defined by the UN Environment Programme (UNEP), sustainability is represented by the integration of economic, environmental and social activities. Sustainability initiatives must exist across the three dimensions to be genuinely sustainable.
Sustainable development	Development that 'meets the needs of the present without compromising the ability of future generations to meet their own needs' (*Report of the World Commission on Environment and*

	Development: Our Common Future, Brundtland Commission, Oxford University Press, Oxford, UK, 1987).
Sustainable infrastructure	Infrastructure that enables sustainable services and operations. By extension, it is taken to mean financially sustainable infrastructure that does not have a net adverse impact on the environment, and that benefits society through equity of access and beneficial capability.
Tableau	The geospatial representation of the natural and built domains, used as a reference for other models in the common reference and COP.
Threat & risk assessment (TRA)	An assessment of the current threats to an operation or asset, the consequences and impact of the threat occurring, and the recommended measures that would bring the LoP within acceptable risk parameters.
Threat spectrum	The range in threat severity and likelihood from a minimum of the historic statistical threat to the lesser of the MAR and MRTC. It is usually represented on a scale of zero (statistical threat) to one (lesser of MAR or MRTC), so that it can be compared with other threats and hazards.
Through-life value	An entity's total functional benefits (infrastructure, operation, organisation) over its life, divided by its cost. This is different from the whole-life value, which will include externalities that are associated with the entity.
Use	The functional benefit that stakeholders gain for a purpose (by using the infrastructure system).
Value	The ratio of beneficial function and cost, typically represented as function divided by cost.
Value at risk (VaR)	The likelihood of losing more than a specified amount of money (investment) over a defined period (risk horizon).
Vitae system of systems (VSOS)	'A construct of operationally and managerially independent systems, distributed geographically,

	which as a whole and by parts evolves, adapts, self-organises and produces emergent behaviour around three related functions of survivability, vitality, and conviviality.'
	Bristow DN (2015) Asset system of systems resilience planning: the Toronto case. *Infrastructure Asset Management* 2(1): 15–22.
Whole cost of risk (WCR)	The sum cost of risk treatments and the residual risk, usually represented as the cost of risk treatment measures and the associated or revised consequence of loss.

ICE Publishing

Hay, Alexander H
ISBN 978-0-7277-6562-8
https://doi.org/10.1680/pris.65628.013

Chapter 1
Introduction

Infrastructure is the foundation of civilisation. It enables us to survive, thrive and advance both individually and socially. Roads, railways, navigations and airports connect us with our neighbours, facilitating our travel and exchanging goods and ideas. Utilities directly support our physical health and comfort, from the provision of clean water to the safe removal of foul water and the supply of electricity to keep our lives comfortable, illuminated and sustained. Yet, it is more than just the physical world we inhabit; infrastructure supports the social fabric that permits us to use it effectively, ranging from laws and regulations to money and institutions. In this, infrastructure spans our natural, built and societal frames of reference. Infrastructure enables the services that we depend on in our day-to-day endeavours.

Because our relationship with infrastructure is seldom direct, we are often blind to its presence and function. We are instead aware of its absence or when a vital service that it enables is interrupted. We can say confidently that all infrastructure has a role in enabling a service or capability. Each service and capability supports our society and economy. We rely on many services each day, even as those services rely on others. The relationships between infrastructure and the socioeconomic fabric of our lives are complex. The benefits are not directly attributable to any one part of the infrastructure, nor the services and capabilities that are enabled and, in turn, support each aspect of our lives. Such complexity influences our behaviours and perceptions of the world around us. How, then, do we unpick this complexity to identify what value infrastructure represents in our lives? Our blindness to it can mean that it doesn't attract the same priority for municipal funding that other public needs do. We need to be able to relate its role and value to our investment in it.

One of the extraordinary challenges of infrastructure is that it typically has a long operational life, during which much can change. Long recognised in the drafting of government policy and codes of practice, we tolerate infrastructure use changes to maintain the original investment's best societal value. In the last 30 years, climate and technological changes have accelerated, forcing a reappraisal of what we require of our infrastructure today and tomorrow. Advances in information and communications technology (ICT) have concentrated business in both time and space. Operations that might once have employed many people over several locations can now be conducted more effectively with far fewer, virtually connected through a single node. With the business efficiencies that this concentration represents comes an increased consequence of loss arising from a single catastrophic event.

This same concentration of value has influenced supply chains. The increased collocation of production means the collocation of risk. This is of particular concern when many operations rely on the same supply chain source. The recent COVID-19 pandemic experience exposed the fragility in supply chains with a common origin. For example, a number of manufacturers of electronic components and equipment have developed lean and efficient supply chains that increasingly rely on a single source of feedstock microchips. When production ceased in China during the initial COVID-19 outbreak, so did the supply chains. We had a similar experience in 2011, when the tsunami hit Japan and interrupted one of the principal electronic component manufacturers. The balance between fragility and efficiency is not a simple one.

Technological change is also making it possible for us to lead more environmentally sustainable lives without compromising comfort or cost. It presents questions about how we envision transportation over the next century, with the inevitable impact on our infrastructure development planning. Approaching this question with an idealised view of how the world should be would be costly to implement and challenging to force user behaviour changes. For example, the debate over whether advances in transportation should allow us to realise an enhanced public transit network with a road-building requirement to service 'the first and last mile'. The counterargument says that with the advent of autonomous electric vehicles, we can use our conventional highway system more efficiently with fewer accidents and, therefore, advance road development. The arguments can each present an optimised balance between sustainability goals and public convenience.

Depending on our perspective, both arguments are correct. However, which is most appropriate in the situation will be determined by the context over time. Any idealised vision of the future anchored by little more than a snapshot of the current circumstances will miss many of the complexities unique to any situation. The technological and climate change trends will also affect many parallel infrastructures and services that enable the infrastructure in question. We cannot look at any of these infrastructure questions in isolation. We need a more holistic understanding. It will also allow us to allocate risk to those best equipped to deal with it.

The Earth's climate is dynamic. It has always changed, with flora and fauna adapting to those changes incrementally with each successive generation. Today, the rate of climate change is more significant than ever before. It is this rate of change that causes concern. We have always experienced catastrophic natural events, and our codes of practice and economies have responded, adjusting to mitigate the impact of such events in the future. And so, we move on. In this, our codes of practice and regulations are necessarily behind our lived experiences.

Changes in the frequency and severity of extreme weather events outpace codification and policy development. How do we future-proof a regulation when we don't know how bad the damage will be, and so what level of risk to accept? How should we convince investors to pay to mitigate the effects of an event that has not yet been experienced? When we combine this increasing frequency and severity of hazards with the increased concentration of value in operations, we have an unanswerable risk problem. However, we can unpick the risk by treating the hazard separately from the failure of the operation. More than one hazard can cause a failure in operation, whether directly or indirectly.

Furthermore, we cannot predict when these hazards will occur or how severe they might be over the infrastructure's life. Conversely, we can control our exposure to the hazard to some extent. We can control what we depend on to manage our supply chain vulnerability to these hazards. Most importantly, we can manage how our operations are affected by a failure in one of the services on which we rely. It makes sense to manage what we can control. This focus is the basis of resilience planning. However, like sustainability, it depends on our understanding of our operations. How else do we make sense of the development needs when the infrastructure requirement and risks are in constant flux? We need to base this understanding on evidence. We need to look at the current situation, the current trends, and have a clear sense of what service or capability we wish to achieve. The need for informed contextual understanding echoes the UK National Infrastructure Commission's call for greater use of evidence in infrastructure planning and delivery.

Suppose it makes sense to look at infrastructures as an interconnected complex whole, enabling the services and capabilities that support our socioeconomic fabric and way of life. How is this different from current practice? It would be unreasonable to generalise infrastructure planning practice, since each nation, region or municipality, corporation and agency will have its unique approach. However, sector and engineering specialisation will apply hydraulic engineers to water supply infrastructure, transportation engineers to transport infrastructure and power engineers to electricity grid development. The question is more about how to account for systems integration and context rather than individual infrastructure delivery's technical specifics. Furthermore, as technology advances and takes on more of the routine that defined specialist engineering professional practice, we need to ask what we require of our infrastructure engineers in this changing world.

Much of my research has been in protracted and postconflict infrastructure reconstruction and development. I came across several technical exemplars of wastewater treatment works and water treatment plants, which could not operate because of a lack of electricity or skilled labour or local supply chain capacity. My observations match examples in postdisaster reconstruction efforts and even in developing countries, where the time imperative is not as acute. There are many reasons for these projects, each highly successful in their own right, yet delivering a wholly inadequate outcome for the local beneficiaries.

They typically centre on a combination of insufficient (evidence-based) understanding of the requirement in its context, donor self-interest and professional bias. Even in more established economies, I have observed examples where a road driven through a town bisects a poor community, resulting in a substantial increase in pedestrian deaths and injuries as residents attempt to get to work or visit family members across the road. The road certainly provided quick access to the town centre, but at a cost in human life.

Infrastructure changes the world around it. It influences human behaviour. Stakeholders will all perceive the infrastructure differently, according to how they individually benefit from it. Where there is substantial local engagement and a sense of ownership in the infrastructure, issues are identified and addressed before they can become problems. Where there is no sense of community ownership, there is no assistance in a crisis. This sense of local ownership is powerful. Social capital is a crucial component that, as will be discussed, Daniel Aldrich has shown to support or hinder infrastructure owners and operators during times of stress and shock.

Faced with such complexity, we need to look at the infrastructure (and the services and capabilities it enables) in its socioeconomic context. To paraphrase President Eisenhower, *if a problem is too complex, make it bigger*. The socioeconomic context and cross-disciplinary working are not the typical engineer's professional area of comfort, yet they are the essence of *engineering in society*, what engineering is all about. To make sense of this, to make this accessible, we will need to build our exploration of infrastructure on a fundamental first-principles understanding of what it is and how it works. The focus is, therefore, not on individual types of infrastructure but rather its entirety.

Suitably armed, we can explore different planning considerations and look at the generic approach to infrastructure development strategy. For this, we shall use the first stage of infrastructure development planning, 'strategy'. The subsequent stages, concerning networks, financing, contracting and individual projects, have become specialised in their own right, procedurally aligned with particular jurisdictions and owner or lender requirements. We are focused on what comes before the specialisation. We will look at how to work out what we need our infrastructure to achieve and identify project requirements. When we understand this, we can critically assess whether the proposed best practice is indeed applicable in our situation. We can also build a business case that looks at the infrastructure in its environmental, operational and socioeconomic context.

I am not writing for any particular jurisdiction. The aim is to present a comprehensive way of looking at infrastructure to adapt to jurisdictional constraints. When we understand how something works, we are better able to modify it to suit local requirements. This book is about understanding infrastructure. One of the concepts discussed at various stages in the book is *intelligent resourcing*. The label is relatively modern, but the Roman architect Vitruvius presented the idea some 2000 years ago. He wrote that our standard designs should adapt to the local materials and trades without compromising performance. He explains that buildings are better suited to the surroundings; this limits construction costs, makes timely maintenance and repair cost-effective and provides local employment.

This concept's wisdom remains, yet we still deliver projects that need an external workforce for construction and maintenance, exceed the local supply chain's capacity and do not benefit the local population. One need look no further than the membrane water treatment plants constructed in the West Indies by USAID; they cannot be maintained locally and so are bypassed. Projects intended to improve the local domestic water supply quality are replaced by simple chlorine dosing and lead to poorer health outcomes than the original sand bed filtration plants. On a larger scale, we might look at the 'Great Ditch' project in Libya, which cannot be operated or maintained by local resources. Our approach to infrastructure needs to be intelligently informed.

Therefore, in this book, we follow a simple exploration of the fundamental concepts, principles, related theories and illustrations of leading practice. We pull these various strands together to present the process of planning practice in delivering the first stage of an infrastructure development plan (IDP) – *strategy* – and examine how this process is affected by other influences. Finally, we have a look at what the future may hold for infrastructure engineering.

In *Chapter 2: A theory of infrastructure*, we explore how infrastructure works and how each infrastructure system reflects an operational system and a whole in itself, while also being part of many other operating systems or 'wholes'. This interconnectivity and multitude of roles and values lead us to question what we seek to achieve in project development and how we can link this to the system's impacts and effects on other services and operations. We explore the language of infrastructure, risk, and how we can use it with evidence to produce a common reference so that all stakeholders can work from the same framework knowledge. How they then perceive the project is particular to their interests, biases and strategic goals. The discussion of risk leads to questions around value and how to maintain it through life. Through-life value raises three aspects of infrastructure planning that merit further exploration.

In *Chapter 3: Sustainable infrastructure,* we explore what sustainable infrastructure is and what it means in practice, both during planning and delivery and in subsequent operation. We explore how the risks in sustainable infrastructure change with what is valued, and how to be genuinely successful demands a holistic perspective. What does this mean? Consider a simple example, a passive house. We can design a sustainable building from an energy perspective, but is it culturally appropriate? If not, the occupants may compromise many of the energy-saving measures through its use. Conversely, will our familiar material selection result in a carbon footprint for construction that exceeds any energy savings over the structure's life? We can still achieve the (sustainability) performance objectives but need to consider each project again in context. This example applies equally to infrastructure, just different parameters and scale.

Of course, to be truly sustainable, we need to be around tomorrow. In *Chapter 4: Resilient infrastructure,* we explore the concept of resilience applied to infrastructure systems and what this entails in practice. Today, resilience has become something of a fashionable term, much as sustainability was, and there are many interpretations and comments in circulation, not all of which are helpful. We use the Centre for Resilience of Critical Infrastructure (CRCI) definition of operational resilience, consider what resilience isn't before exploring further its application to infrastructure, and explore the idea of safe-to-fail and how infrastructure systems can adapt to hazards by measuring the hazard travel time (HTT). We also explore what this means for the community and the relationship between infrastructure resilience and community resilience in adapting, absorbing, responding to and recovering from shocks and stresses. However, it can become wearing to fail and recover from each hazard, both large and small, and we need to reduce the typical level of interference by hazards in our operations. In *Chapter 5: Protecting value*, we explore the idea of infrastructure protection to provide that baseline level of protection against routine or frequent shocks and stresses. We discuss how much is sufficient and the factors in balancing protection with resilience in sustainable infrastructure.

In *Chapter 6: Infrastructure planning in theory,* we draw these strands together around part 1 of the IDP, strategy. How do we plan infrastructure development, whether an expedient repair, reconstruction, repurposing or new development, while aligning to the desired outcomes over its life? However, practice is seldom as smooth as an ideal translation of theory. In *Chapter 7: Infrastructure planning in practice*, we explore how the IDP process must be adapted to these external domain influences rather than the externalities themselves. It all brings us back to the primary point that we must focus on what we can control and how it is affected by interruptions and failures, rather than addressing each disruption or failure. In *Chapter 8: 2020s and beyond*, we conclude by speculating about what the world will require of its infrastructure in the future and the next generation of engineers who will deliver it.

There are two consistent themes in any consideration of infrastructure. The first is the use of evidence. When we base our understanding on what exists and not on what we think is there, we can know the real issues and how changes to the existing situation affect outcomes. Evidence also forms the foundation for informed discourse and broader stakeholder engagement. We structure this evidence as a common reference. In understanding what is, we know what is possible and its consequences. This is the basis of informed risk management, the second theme. When we understand influence and consequence, we can actively manage risk and assess outcomes. The book includes evidence, *common reference* and risk as cross-cutting themes through each chapter.

FURTHER READING

Two ideas are worth exploring further. The first is the idea of value in the economy. Mazzucato's *The Value of Everything* (2020) examines the traditional construct that confuses price with value, resulting in social benefits being seen as net costs and losing sight of the real benefits that they bring. The second is the idea of a changing profession; we can either drive or be driven to change. On becoming president of the Institution of Civil Engineers, Rachel Skinner (2020) emphasised that, with 70% of global emissions caused by infrastructure delivery and operation, our approach needs to change. Infrastructure needs to be genuinely sustainable, economically, environmentally and socially. Technological change is also forcing professional change. Susskind and Susskind (father and son) point out in *The Future of the Professions* (2015) that the routine activities that defined the bulk of professional practice are increasingly conducted by computers, undermining the premise of what Susskind and Susskind term 'the grand bargain', as it were, the 'broad deal between the professions and society', and forcing a change to the way professions, including design professions, conduct themselves. These changes in approach and practice do bring added complexities, but such change is not itself new. Professor Paul Jowitt's paper 'Sustainability and the formation of the civil engineer' (2004) provides a useful reminder that, as we work to increase the complexities of professional understanding and practice that a holistic approach demands, it is not so different to past changes in professional practice. As he concludes, '*It just requires a more sophisticated calculus.*'

Jowitt PW (2004) Sustainability and the formation of the civil engineer. *Proceedings of the Institution of Civil Engineers – Engineering Sustainability* **157(ES2)**: 79–88, 10.1680/ensu.2004.157.2.79.

Mazzucato M (2020) *The Value of Everything: Making and Taking in the Global Economy*. Public Affairs, New York, NY, USA. (Previously published in 2018 as *The Value of Everything: Who Makes and Who Takes from the Real Economy*.)

Skinner R (2020) *ICE Presidential Address 2020*. Webinar 3/11/ 2020. https://www.ice.org.uk/eventarchive/ice-presidential-address-2020 (accessed 26/03/2021).

Susskind RE and Susskind D (2015) *The Future of the Professions: How Technology will Transform the Work of Human Experts*, 1st edn. Oxford University Press, Oxford, UK.

ICE Publishing

Hay, Alexander H
ISBN 978-0-7277-6562-8
https://doi.org/10.1680/pris.65628.021

Chapter 2
A theory of infrastructure: how does infrastructure work?

When we think of infrastructure, we typically think of roads, railways, airports, electricity lines, wastewater treatment plants and similar. Each is designed, operated and maintained by specialists in that type of infrastructure. Investors and underwriters might even specialise in particular types of infrastructure projects. Yet every kind of infrastructure is wholly linked to other infrastructure. The airport cannot be effective without road access, electricity and water supply, wastewater and garbage removal, or communications. Each piece of infrastructure is an entity in its own right, a whole, while also being a part of other infrastructures, other wholes. We need to be able to think of infrastructure in isolation. Still, we must also appreciate that it fulfils a number of roles and is part of many other infrastructures. A road is not just a road. It is the access to the airport and allows passengers and freight to continue their journey on land.

In 1967, Arthur Koestler wrote *The Ghost in the Machine*. He described holons and the idea that an entity can be a whole itself while also being a part of a number of other wholes. Holons are a handy way to look at infrastructure. The theory affords a conceptual understanding of how infrastructure connects, by operation and physically, and a handrail for reviewing infrastructure proposals. Building on Gilbert Ryle's 1949 challenge to a traditional philosophical dogma of dualism, Koestler wrote about how, through human evolution, our brains have developed ever-higher functions, building on more primitive ones. Because of this, we are capable of higher intellectual capacity. This evolved structure still carries the basic functions, which can, from time to time, overwhelm the higher logical functions, resulting in fear, anger and hate. Koestler uses this observation to explain what he sees as humanity's inevitable journey to self-destruction, made possible by nuclear weapons. Koestler's narrative was very much of its time.

A philosophical work warning of humanity's most self-destructive tendencies is not generally associated with infrastructure planning. However, it does serve as a useful simile. Our infrastructure has evolved. Each piece connects to something else, built on, adapted to other uses and entirely incorporated into other infrastructures. Cities rise on the ruins of their predecessors. Digging foundations in the City of London leads us on an extraordinary journey through history, revealing different river alignments, structures and materials, and how people lived. Each piece of infrastructure is a holon. Past functions re-emerge as relevant to a new configuration or provide a weakness in it. We see this with the repurposing of various facilities, such as railway lines rebuilt as cycle paths or street lamps adapted to provide electric vehicle charging. We particularly see this with frequent upgrades in industrial control systems (ICSs). The ICS operators have not yet become fully conversant with the application and its vulnerabilities before a new version overlays it. Sometimes these vulnerabilities are addressed in the upgrade; at other times, they are hidden from view until they contribute to a failure. It is useful to understand the whole situation beyond the immediate issue before us.

We have observed several properties of infrastructure, different parts working together as a whole, organised and controlled for a purpose. We are describing systems, and have also observed differences between what is built, how it is used and the world around it. It is reasonable to say that infrastructure is the physical manifestation of a system. Where we perceive the system conceptually, the infrastructure, its use and its relationship to the world around, is what we experience. A few ideas have emerged so far, so let's start with a systems view.

2.1. A system of systems

A system is a group of separate entities working together to commonly agreed procedures. Whether each entity has that systems view or understanding does not change the function that it contributes to the effectiveness of the system (Gall, 1977). This difference in perspective is important, and we explore this later. For now, let's focus on what the system looks like and how to describe it. We see the infrastructure in space and time. It is connected to other things that we have built and exists within the natural world. We may have incorporated natural features (facilities) into our infrastructure, such as a navigation along a river as part of a transport route. Infrastructure is used. Its use will be to a set of procedures. The general public will be affected by it, and they may even use it. Our infrastructure spans the built environment and the natural environment, complies with rules and customs, and interacts with people. We can structure this as the domains of infrastructure.

The natural domain is what is pre-existing, and we can incorporate it into our system. It also provides part of the physical context for our infrastructure system. The built domain is everything that we have built, from roads and railways to the Internet. The virtual domain is what we imagine and collectively agree. Money has no intrinsic value, yet we collectively agree that we can exchange a $20 banknote for $20 in services. Similarly, the laws and regulations, societal norms and organisational structures all exist in the virtual domain. It can control what is built, where and when, and how it is used. These three domains of infrastructure allow us to describe what the infrastructure is and how

Figure 2.1 The three domains of infrastructure and their interaction with the human domain to realise value

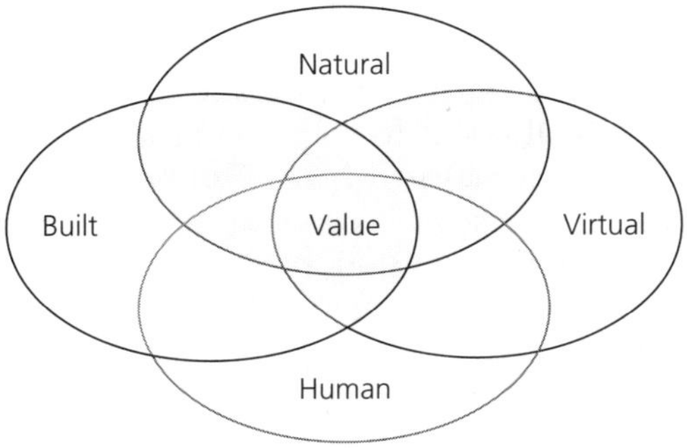

it is used. They also allow us to collect data about the infrastructure, its use and context, so that we can assess its value (Figure 2.1).

Infrastructure influences people's behaviour at many levels. A colour change can affect a person's mood. The presence of an industrial processing plant next to a residential area can influence the residents' physical health. The availability of employment that the infrastructure enables can benefit the mental and social well-being of the community. Access to the infrastructure will define opportunities for those with and without it – equity of access and inclusion are persistent planning issues. The presence of a wastewater treatment plant can affect property prices, and the residents of a community may resist the construction of a new adjacent railway line. Infrastructure is an emotive issue. It can bring significant benefits, and it can cause great harm. We must understand how it affects people. We say, therefore, that infrastructure has a relationship with the human domain. When infrastructure is in harmony with the human domain, that is, there is a stable relationship between the domains, we can say that the infrastructure value is optimised. Each aspect of the infrastructure system and its interaction with humanity is beneficial.

When we now look at these four domains together for each infrastructure system, we have a way of collecting data and associating it with other data and functions. We can make sense of the data and inform ourselves of how the infrastructure is performing. While we might seek to do this for each infrastructure system, we also recognise that the systems are interconnected. They may share the same site, or one may rely on the other to function. We can draw all of these infrastructure systems together within a *vitae* system of systems (VSOS). This is a conceptual model of how all of the different infrastructure systems interact for life. The concept is not confined to either urban or rural environments. Instead, it allows us to draw all of these systems together as a whole, enabling community vitality, survival and conviviality. This VSOS view allows us to see how the whole can be vulnerable to disaster and how to restore and maintain harmony between domains in each system and between systems.

The VSOS concept was developed by Kilgour (Hipel *et al.*, 2012) and initially used to understand disaster risk dynamics (Okada, 2006). We find that the concept is scalable and allows us to understand the dynamics of infrastructure systems and people at local, regional, provincial and national levels. Conceptually, it is not bounded, which makes it a potent tool. Using directed path modelling, the VSOS allows us to map the infrastructure functionality and its dependencies and influences (Bristow, 2015; O'Neil, 2013). We are now able to describe the infrastructure systems as a whole and the impact of change. The purpose of the model defines the nature of that impact. When we model something, we seek to understand how it works (Louie, 2010). That understanding depends on the question we ask. For example, we might build a model to understand the influence of the infrastructure system on carbon-based energy use. We should not expect that model to inform our understanding of how the same infrastructure influences stunting or bowel cancer in the population. So the purpose of the model is essential, just as the purpose of the infrastructure is.

2.2. Purpose

All infrastructure has a purpose. To put it another way, we don't build infrastructure without a purpose. Even follies, whimsical eighteenth-century buildings and ruins, had a mostly decorative purpose. Infrastructure takes such a large investment in time, materials and effort that the costs are prohibitive if there is no benefit. The alignment of benefit with demand will determine its use and value. If the purpose is misaligned with the demand, it has no value. We return to this issue when we explore value and carrying capacity. It is this idea of benefit that informs purpose. Why are we building this power transmission line through northern Ontario? A functional response may be that we are transmitting electrical power from A to B. That doesn't answer the question. An operational response may be that we transmit electrical power to provide grid connectivity to a remote community and alleviate their diesel dependency. This answer introduces the idea of reliability of supply and implies that the new infrastructure enables something better than the existing. It still begs the question of *why*. Without understanding why, we cannot measure whether the infrastructure is successful and represent a tangible benefit for the investment.

We need to define the purpose of the infrastructure system by the intended outcome. In creating a new infrastructure system to achieve the intended outcome, we are also changing the dynamics in the VSOS. With change comes risk and a shift in value from one system to another. The essential service may have been airlift fuel to ensure sufficient supply for the generators through the winter. With the provision of grid-supplied electricity, the demand for the airlift reduces, which may increase the airlift cost of foodstuffs. Before, we looked into the relative costs of building the transmission line and reducing the cost of airlifted fuel; now, we have to ask if we have changed the reliability of supply. The winter storms that prevent airlift are also known to cause downed transmission lines. So the unintended consequences of the proposed scheme may well result in a reduced benefit for the end user, less electricity supply reliability and more expensive groceries. One could also argue that the grid supply of electricity will reduce the carbon footprint of the community energy consumption. However, when we consider the infrastructure's carbon footprint, it may well exceed any savings in generator emissions over the expected life of the transmission line. We need to identify a higher purpose. We need to establish why we are changing the infrastructure systems.

Through research and experience, I have come to the inescapable conclusion that the unifying purpose of infrastructure is *health*. By health, I mean the 1948 definition of health used in the World Health Organization constitution (WHO, 2021): 'Health is a state of complete physical, mental and social well-being and not merely the absence of disease or infirmity.' It allows us to capture the complete range of the infrastructure's physiological, community and economic effects. It also means that we can create a measurable relationship between infrastructure, the services it enables and the society and economy that those services support; we are assessing the infrastructure development outcome against its unifying purpose. The advantage of this approach is that we can measure each stage and create an audit trail of evidence and analysis that allows us to say with confidence what a change in infrastructure means. We return to this point later in this chapter and in Chapters 3 and 6.

I would not claim that this is the only way to view the purpose of infrastructure; this is a discussion that I have had with various colleagues from time to time. In the absence of a reasoned and realistic alternative, it is a good starting point for infrastructure planning, and I use it throughout this book. Irrespective of whichever unifying purpose you use, it must be common to all infrastructure systems because they are interconnected and inseparable. We cannot identify the purpose of one infrastructure system that depends on another with a different purpose. They can have different functions and even operational uses. Still, the infrastructure system of systems, the VSOS, must have one common unifying purpose.

Furthermore, by defining the unifying purpose, we can say how it is affected by changes in its context, not just in the VSOS. For example, the changing climate will influence both the infrastructure's performance and the beneficiaries' demands. Electrical switches become less efficient at higher temperatures, while the demand for air conditioning also climbs. Technological changes will change the social expectations of reliability and the consequences of impaired reliability. The world about us continues to change. Many of those changes may occur 20 or 40 years after building the infrastructure. Without that understanding of the outcome (the unifying purpose), we cannot identify how these external changes, directly and indirectly, affect it through the VSOS. Without the defined outcome, we cannot identify whether some system adaptation or reconfiguration is needed to address risks unforeseen during the initial development. We explore what these changes over the life of the infrastructure mean in Chapter 3 and 4. When we are clear on what we wish to achieve, we can define its (intended) beneficial outcome. This means that we can also say whether the infrastructure will continue to enable the beneficial outcome when something changes.

This idea of unifying purpose is useful in contingency planning. When a bridge fails in an incident, natural or malicious, is the broader VSOS infrastructure able to deliver the same outcome, say? Perhaps there are other bridges, and so the outcome is unaffected. Operationally, the loss of the bridge will change the evacuee traffic flows across the other bridges. Functionally, the bridge may simply be unable to take vehicular traffic but remains open to pedestrians. Knowing what the bridge does (functional), the service it enables (operational), and its unifying purpose (desired outcome), allows us to predict its changing role under different stresses, shocks and with age. Now apply this approach to evacuation planning for Abu Dhabi, say. If the Emirate had to evacuate the islands, for whatever reason, how would you evaluate the infrastructure needed? The infrastructure enables a service, and those services enable the evacuation. We can identify gradations of performance and capacities. Can we still conduct the evacuation, resulting in a common beneficial outcome? What now is the value of that bridge development or other infrastructure realignment? It depends on the value of the evacuation to the responsible authority. Purpose allows us to define value under a variety of conditions over a development's life.

2.3. Value

The value of anything is proportionate to its usefulness. The engineering term 'value' is a relationship of function over cost. The calculation only has meaning if the functions are useful to us. Value is something defined by the beneficiary, and so is relative to each user's perspective. Considering the usefulness criterion for value, we can say that the northern Ontario electricity transmission line only has value if it is used. This is one of the peculiarities of infrastructure. Its value lies in the services and capabilities that it enables. If those services aren't needed or aren't used because they are too expensive, the infrastructure that enables the service has no value. Consider, for example, a high-speed rail link from the airport to the downtown core, the Toronto Union Pearson Express, say. Irrespective of the cost of building the link, it has no value if there are no riders. The link doesn't attract the anticipated ridership, so the operator reduces the ticket price to a level comparable to other forms of public transit. The result is that ridership increases, as does its value with increased use. The question that will then face the rail link's owner-operator is how much the ridership are willing to pay for the value that the (now established) link represents to them. The cost of building the rail link and running the service is the same whether a rider uses it or not. The ticket revenue must cover these costs if the service is to be financially viable. If it is to be a sustainable service, the revenue should also cover the upgrade and eventual replacement cost, but we are getting ahead of ourselves.

This relationship between the value of infrastructure and its use is an important one. It allows us to look at how changes in the infrastructure's use and context

Figure 2.2 The service or operation and its enabling components in context: each component is an extension of the context

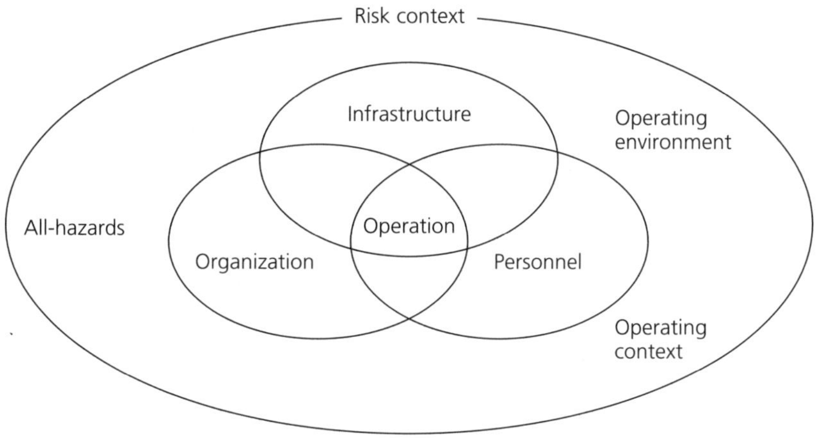

over its life will affect its through-life value. There's a lot here to unpack, so let's start by defining the context in which the infrastructure is used.

The service or operation that the infrastructure enables is also enabled by the operating organisation and people (both staff and users). This is shown in Figure 2.2. The organisation provides the virtual construct in which the operation is conducted, coordinating resources and activity with outputs. The infrastructure, organisation and people are also part of the context in which the operation exists. The infrastructure connects to other infrastructure and services. The people are also in the community. Their view of the operation is reflected in how the local community views the operation and organisation. (File this thought for later, as it crops up again in Chapter 3 to 5).

Similarly, the organisation connects with its stakeholders, local regulations, municipal activity, and so on. The operation is also affected by its context. We call this, for lack of a more imaginative term, the risk context. It comprises three parts: operating context, operating environment and all hazards. The operating context encompasses all those other operations that influence the operation and are also influenced by the operation's actions. Conversely, the operating environment encompasses all those other operations that affect the operation but are unaffected by it. This is a useful distinction because it informs stakeholder management analysis and the calculation of socioeconomic impact when there is a change.

To illustrate the difference between operating context and operating environment, let's consider the Varsity Stadium at the University of Toronto (Figure 2.3). The Varsity Stadium is the focal point for university athletics. Some members of Team Canada also use it in preparation for major

Figure 2.3 The University of Toronto's Varsity Stadium operational relationships and risk contexts

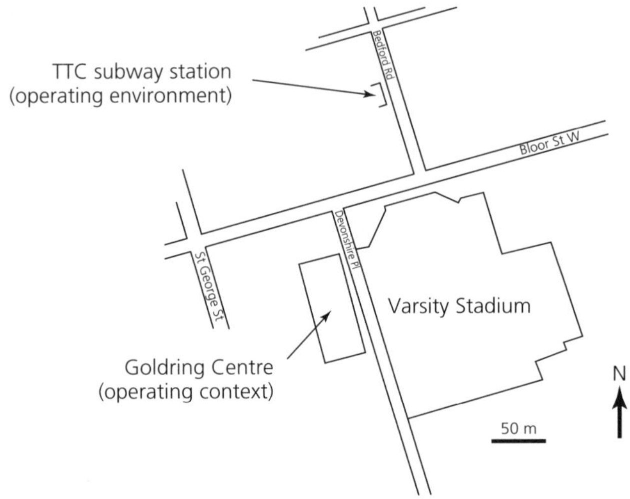

competitions, such as the Olympics. Adjacent to the stadium is the Goldring Centre for High Performance Sport. The two venues are linked in both function and use. One enables and enhances the other. Across Bloor Street West is the St. George subway station, which athletes and spectators use to get to both venues. When there is a big Varsity football match or competition with many spectators, the subway's efficient operation directly affects ticket revenue at the turnstiles. In this case, the Goldring Centre is the operating context, while the subway station is the operating environment. The subway will continue to run whether the stadium is there or not, but the use of the stadium and the Goldring Centre will be directly affected by any change in each other's operation. The third part of the risk context is all-hazards risks. We'll come back to this in Chapter 4.

So let's now look at this relationship over the life of the infrastructure. The planning and discussion of infrastructure development will already have a socio-economic impact through investor speculation. Some will see an opportunity to buy land affected by the proposed infrastructure in the expectation that it will increase in market value. They may intend to sell it for far more or develop it to catch secondary use by those using the infrastructure. For example, a discussion about a subway line extension prompts property developers to buy land adjacent to the proposed stations; they plan to build apartments as the stations are built. These apartments would need to appeal to a higher disposable income demographic unless the capital costs are subsidised. Such speculation can lead to housing insecurity, denying affordable housing to local families. At this stage, we have yet to build anything. Still, the value is perceived through the virtual domain, affecting real property values in the natural and built domains. This value increases as the planning and design progresses. When the infrastructure

Figure 2.4 Infrastructure value change through life

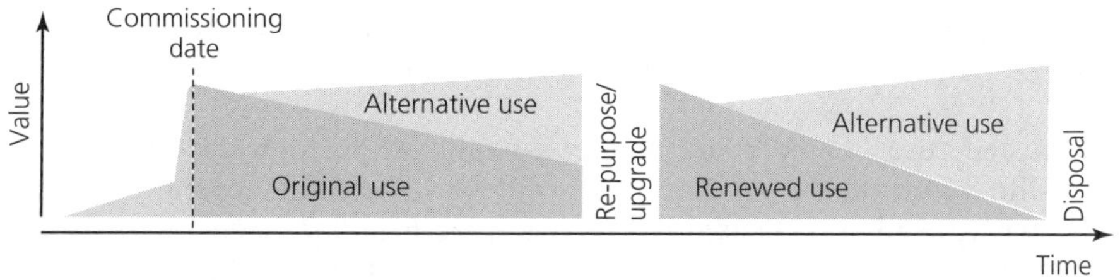

is delivered and commissioned, the value is already high and increases steadily for a period. As technology changes working and living patterns, that value plateaus and begins to decline. The users gradually see less of that original value in the infrastructure.

However, by its existence, the infrastructure has influenced other operations, and changes in the risk context result in new and alternative uses for the infrastructure (Figure 2.4). There will come a point where the value of alternative uses exceeds the original use value. The alternative uses can be incorporated during a midlife upgrade or enhancement, and then the dynamic resumes. Eventually, the original use will have no or minimal value, and the infrastructure will be serving an entirely different user. It is repurposed. It is a change in operational use while still supporting the unifying purpose. This evolution in use and value is more apparent in urban settings. However, we can also see it in rural industrial facilities, such as the big woollen mills of the nineteenth century becoming twentieth-century apartments and light industry workshops.

An example might be useful to illustrate this. In Alexandria, Virginia, USA, the old torpedo factory was a crucial part of the US defence industry for some time. Eventually, as a drive for greater industrial efficiency replaced the need for dispersed manufacturing, the torpedo factory was closed and vacated. It became an unofficial artists' commune and began to attract tourists and other artists to the area. The city formally repurposed the premises into an artists' centre, and the surrounding waterside area greatly improved. The result was a substantial improvement in local area tourism and associated small business revenues. Elsewhere, we see old water pumping stations and water towers that have become obsolete through system demand and technology changes. These are repurposed as businesses, residences and community facilities. All of these represent a shift in value according to use.

In many cases, this means removing the asset from an infrastructure system and repurposing the system as a real property asset. In other cases, it can mean adapting the infrastructure system to serve supplementary demands. For example, a hydroelectric dam built to power an aluminium smelter enabled the development of a small town when the smelter closed down. The operational or functional use of the infrastructure changes, but the unifying purpose remains. By seeing the net effect on the unifying purpose, the outcome, we can say what the total value of these changes is. It doesn't matter if we are driving those changes or they are happening in the world around us.

The infrastructure engineer or planner's challenge is to work out what the through-life value of the infrastructure will be. There are several approaches to infrastructure planning, explored in Chapter 6 and 7. Generally, there are asset-based and capability-based approaches. The asset-based approaches view infrastructure as a network of individual assets. Each asset is maintained and enhanced or adapted according to the relevant policy, regulation or other direction. This approach is particularly suited to a stable operation, where the demand for the service will not change faster than the infrastructure is capable of responding or adapting. A capability-based approach sees the infrastructure as a vehicle to achieving a particular capability or market position at a set time and place in the future.

Capability-based planning follows one of two models. The first is an expanding vision model, where we have an idea of the end-state and develop the infrastructure in self-contained increments. The revenue arising from each incremental development funds the next increment, and so on. This was a common approach for colonial railway development, for example. The other model is projection. The idea is that one projects a desired capability to a time and space in the future. By analysing current trends in climate, technological, economic and social change, we identify what can most influence this projected capability. Selecting the two most influential trends, we create a 2×2 matrix of four possible futures. We determine what the infrastructure requirement is to support the projected capability in each of these alternative futures. The point at which the infrastructure requirements diverge is the point of investment. That is what we build. After some time, we review the model, validate the trends and repeat the process. This new iteration would typically indicate the next generation of infrastructure development towards the projected capability end-state.

The point is that, whichever approach or model we use, we can identify the anticipated value over each period in time. These successive periods in which we identify the infrastructure's value are known as risk horizons because they define a period of known or consistent risk profile (discussed later). In so doing, we can estimate the minimum duration that we know the infrastructure will have value, that is, the time until the point of investment. We can also say what the value will be up to this point with some confidence. After that, it will depend on how the risk context changes. Therefore, it is curious that we often tend to look only at the value at the time of investment and treat the infrastructure as real property assets. However, if the infrastructure can have a known value, it begs the question of whose valuation. The corollary is to ask who pays for it and the service that it enables.

The standard principle of any public service is that the beneficiary pays. Central government functions, such as defence, will be paid for through taxes because everybody benefits from defence. Similarly, municipal services are relatively easy to attribute to beneficiaries. Fire service coverage in a district costs a certain amount of money, and the taxpaying residents of that district benefit from the coverage. Hence, municipal taxes cover the costs. The challenge comes when the beneficiaries are not local to the service's cost or the infrastructure that enables it.

Consider a river system that passes through many jurisdictions. One or two of these jurisdictions may be vulnerable to flooding. It might even be that the imperilled jurisdiction is a significant employer in the area, attracting commuters from upstream jurisdictions to its financial centre. To reduce the likelihood and socioeconomic impact of a catastrophic flood, river management measures need to be implemented upstream in another jurisdiction not directly affected by the flooding. Is the cost borne by the upstream municipality or the downstream one? These river management measures will impede the development opportunities and potential of the upstream jurisdiction. If we say that the downstream jurisdiction should pay for the river management, does that mean that it will need to compensate the upstream jurisdiction for opportunity costs? Taxpayers and voters have short memories when it comes to the benefits of risk mitigation, and it is difficult to see a sustainable political resolution.

In many cases, we see treaties and formal agreements for precisely this situation, or the province or state stepping in to resolve the sustainable allocation of responsibility between municipalities. The challenge with such arrangements is that they are only valid as long as the signatories are willing to be bound by them. We have international examples where populist leaders abandon treaties with impunity. We need to understand the authority relationship with infrastructure to make sense of where self-interest resides. If all parties' self-interest can be satisfied, the agreement has a better chance of being effective.

2.4. Equilibrium

In 1990, Elinor Ostrom published *Governing the Commons*. Drawing on her study of a community water-table management scheme in southern California set up by its stakeholders, she directly challenged the orthodoxy of Garett Hardin's 1968 essay 'The tragedy of the commons'. Hardin tells the story of farmers keeping cows on common pasture, until one adds an extra cow to gain an advantage over the other farmers and instead harms everyone through overgrazing. Ostrom's study and subsequent research indicated that diverse stakeholder groups could avoid this *tragedy* without imposed top-down regulation. She developed eight principles for designing effective management of a shared resource pool:

1. Clearly defined group boundaries of both stakeholders and the resource pool.

2. The rules governing the use of common goods must be appropriate to local needs and conditions.
3. Ensure that those affected by the rules have a say in modifying the rules.
4. Ensure that external authorities respect the rights of the stakeholder group to make their own rules.
5. Enable stakeholders to monitor each other's behaviour.
6. Have a system of graduated sanctions or penalties for violations of the group rules.
7. Dispute resolution must be transparent and readily accessible at minimal cost.
8. There needs to be tiered responsibility for governance that connects with other authorities.

In 2009, Ostrom was awarded the Nobel Prize for Economics and, the same year, published *A Polycentric Approach for Coping with Climate Change* for the World Bank. Her insight has a direct bearing on shared infrastructure systems. Remember that infrastructure enables a service. It doesn't provide the service. When we consider utilities, for example, the infrastructure carries the water or electricity; it isn't the resource. This distinction is important because the infrastructure can still exist when the service has ceased. This is known as a stranded asset. It is the zero-value infrastructure described earlier, which no one is using. One would hope that the fall in use occurred after the cost of creating the infrastructure system was covered.

Where several jurisdictions use the same infrastructure system, they are all drawing on a shared resource. The limits of the infrastructure bound the group. Remember that the infrastructure may be a lake or river that provides a water source. The total extraction from the lake must be less than or equal to the rate of replenishment. If not, water availability will steadily reduce until no one has any. We can see this in the development aspirations of desert communities drawing off a seasonal aquifer. If the shared resource governance is not respected, the whole development scheme will fail, along with the neighbouring communities. We see this situation in quite a few development initiatives.

Let's consider once more the isolated northern Ontario communities, dependent on a finite airlift for the resupply of commodities. The generator farm that supplies the community has a finite capacity, limited by the availability of fuel. Fuel is the shared resource, reflected in the availability of electrical power. Initiatives that promote improved health, such as the construction of a clinic and a water treatment plant, will demand a more significant share of electricity. This needs to be rationalised to ensure that others aren't compromised for the pursuit of one health outcome. Perhaps this is part of the justification for that electricity transmission line. Ostrom's eight principles apply more widely across infrastructure systems. We can see how neighbouring communities connect public transit systems to ensure a shared benefit from employment, both in the municipality where people are employed and the municipality where the employees live. This leads to a dynamic relationship between communities around shared infrastructure, known as equilibrium.

The infrastructure enables the community vitality, conviviality and survival. The community is dynamic, and there are continually shifting concentrations of demand for services as businesses start-up, neighbourhoods transition and areas densify. The infrastructure cannot change so readily, resulting in a consistent background level of stress. Furthermore, we generally do not like paying for the services once we've become used to them. The priorities for municipal spending reflect this and help explain the extraordinary municipal infrastructure deficit worldwide. This lack of maintenance adds another layer of background stress but rarely enough to cause failure. The critical dynamic becomes a balance of service receipts being equal to or greater than the cost of operating and maintaining the service and its supporting infrastructure. When tax receipts fall below the basic cost of operating and essential maintenance of the service (and infrastructure), we would expect to see a withdrawal of service and associated depopulation of neighbourhoods. Detroit's experience following its financial crisis is such an example (Saunders, 2018; Turbeville, 2013). The community–infrastructure relationship forms a delicate balance. Each community will have its delicate balance and so is sensitive to changes in stress and shocks.

Shocks are sudden. They affect infrastructure systems and cause a failure in flow. When the power transmission line collapses in an ice storm, say, the electricity stops flowing. When the culvert washes out, fracturing the water main and natural gas main, both services are interrupted. However, the stresses associated with a gradual reduction in infrastructure performance, through an unwillingness to pay taxes or the effects of climate change, are felt across the community. It is unusual for the community to suffer a shock from an event unless it is genuinely catastrophic. The 2005 flooding of New Orleans caused by Hurricane Katrina shocked the city. The Christmas 2013 ice storm that cut power to much of Toronto only reduced community performance. It did not interrupt it. It means that there are thresholds of stress that can trip failure, which are discussed further in Chapter 4.

Each community that draws on common infrastructure carrying a shared resource needs to find a balance with its neighbours. The balance extends beyond the infrastructure system or even the service that the infrastructure enables. Because of the nature of infrastructure systems, many aspects of community and municipality routine are affected. The relationship between municipalities may or may not be codified but needs to be recognised by the higher authority (regional or provincial). So what? Quite simply, we need to be acutely aware of the consequences of any change to the infrastructure laydown, governance and rezoning of areas for development. Assessing the impact of such changes through individual infrastructure systems or services is rarely successful, resulting in less beneficial outcomes. Using the VSOS construct allows us to understand the dynamics, and Ostrom's principles inform how to adjust the governance and maintain balance between the infrastructure domains.

2.5. The role of risk

One feature of specialisation is that it takes on its unique jargon. A specialist language evolves around shared ideas and concepts that provide a professional shorthand for communication between peers in the same specialisation. The longer this specialist language evolves, the more arcane it becomes, and the further it will be from common understanding. We can see this in the professions, trade groups and closed organisations. The challenge comes when the specialist has to communicate particular complexities of an issue with laypersons unfamiliar with the specialisation's language or practice. It can be frustrating when the specialist cannot make the public understand the need for a particular decision or behaviour. The specialist can be seen as irrelevant when the public feel that their perspective is not *understood*. We are communicating in the same language, but the meaning for each participant is different.

The idea of a shared understanding and the role of language has been a philosophical focus for some time. Most notable among these thinkers was Wittgenstein, who famously presented the 'beetle in the box' analogy in 1953 (Wittgenstein, 2009). Each person has a beetle in a box. They each believe that they know what a beetle is and describe the beetle to the others without letting them see it. The shared knowledge of what a beetle is arises from the different explanations of the various beetles. It is possible that one or more people don't have a beetle at all. The role of language in forming common knowledge is significant. Our understanding, or what that knowledge means, will be informed by our perspective. The shared knowledge of the beetle may mean something threatening to one and benign to another.

The language of science is mathematics. However, the language of applied science and engineering is risk. Risk management is the fundamental business of the civil engineer (ICE, 2014; Steels, 2011). Risk is also the language that links professions, from law to finance and medicine. Risk informs each practitioner's approach to the project, identification and solution of problems. It will inform our contracting structure, financing models and cost of finance, by-law development, user pricing structures, and so on. Therefore, it is important to communicate in clear and unambiguous terms about risk with other professions working on the same project. Easier said than done.

Risk is a discipline in itself, and it isn't possible to do such a subject any real justice here. Our focus is on the role that risk plays in infrastructure engineering and how we communicate about it. There is no better introduction for those interested in exploring the subject of risk in greater depth than Peter Bernstein's *Against the Gods: The Remarkable Story of Risk* (1996). It is, however, useful to look at a few definitions that seem to trip up engineers.

Probability is often used casually to say what the chances of something happening are. The word has an exact meaning based on statistical evidence. When we have a large number of events with differing results, we can calculate the probability of a specified result as, say, 0.25 or 25% or 1 in 4. The risk is calculated using past experiences. We invoke the *law of large numbers*, saying with some confidence that the probability of a particular result is x, because that is what experience tells us. It is particularly useful in calculating the mean time to failure for engine components, for example, and is the basis for various preventative maintenance schemes. It is also the basis for actuarial tables, used to calculate insurance risk exposures. We don't have a wealth of past data to calculate probability in infrastructure projects, since each is unique. Furthermore, the premise that the future will reflect the past presents us with a problem.

Amid accelerating climate change and rapid technological change, it is difficult to see how the future will resemble the past. Remember that we are discussing infrastructure performance in the future, not an engine part under defined conditions. Today doesn't resemble the past. We see the effects of climate change in more frequent and severe extreme weather events. Whether you believe that climate change is accelerated through humanity's actions in the Anthropocene period or not, it is difficult to deny that extreme weather is becoming more frequent (Kolbert, 2014). The so-called 1 : 200 year event is occurring several times in the same decade. When we don't have a stable history of extreme weather events to support our prediction of expected frequency in the future, how can we calculate the probability of a particular event occurring over the infrastructure system's life? At best, we can estimate the current likelihood of an extreme event and the accompanying trends that influence this estimate. Therefore, when we discuss infrastructure risk, it is more accurate to refer to the likelihood. Likelihood is also the preferred terminology used by both lenders and underwriters, for whom probability has a precise meaning.

We also need to consider why this is important. After all, we have always had extreme events, catastrophes, and we are just having more of them. Technological advances, particularly in information and communications technology (ICT), have fundamentally changed the way we live and work, challenging the very nature of professional practice (Susskind and Susskind, 2015). This has concentrated the value of our operations. Operations that were conducted by hundreds of people over many sites can now be completed faster by fewer in one location. The concentration of that operation in both time and space means that the consequence of an extreme event affecting the site of an operation is more significant than previously. We discuss how we might manage this in Chapter 4, but it means that we have an increased exposure to and consequence of loss. This upward trend in likelihood and consequence has led to consistently higher losses by underwriters, both insurers and reinsurers (III, 2020). The impact on both their capital reserves (investments) and their book of business (insurance policies) precipitated the hard market that began in 2019.

To add a further level of uncertainty, it would seem that the evolutionary advances in ICT are leading to a revolution in technology. In North America, the widespread assumption is that technology will provide solutions to our current worries, such as climate change. However, technology also changes the risk context; hence, the risks to our operations and services and the infrastructure that supports it. Engineering balances the effect of technology. A significant shift in transportation needs and means could result in stranded assets, as infrastructure is no longer needed for the originally intended operational purpose.

When we speak of a constant flux in the risk context, we are typically referring to the continual change in the all-hazards risks, operating context and operating environment. It is useful to approximate the periods of consistent risk profile in each of these components. These periods are known as risk horizons. When we conduct a risk evaluation for infrastructure planning, we forecast the risks over the infrastructure's intended life. We seek to minimise the risk profile in each risk horizon through adjustments in the design brief and even sequencing of the project objectives or deliverables. Each risk horizon is used to categorise the risk profile over that period. This makes it manageable in planning terms, and often informs the investment decision-making process. When we know that we have a particular risk over a fixed period, a risk horizon, we can say what our loss exposure is. Remember that use determines value, and revenue for the operator and owner. In this case, we equate value to the anticipated revenue that will service the debt raised to build the relevant part of the works. We recognise that there can be losses, and the debt is underwritten. Still, there will always remain a slim chance that we lose everything, or at least more than we have set aside as a contingency. In this instance, we would use 'value at risk' (VaR). This is a simple expression of the likelihood that we will lose more than a certain amount of value over a given period.

For example, we might calculate a 0.5% chance of $225 million over 3 months from 1 May. If the threshold amount or likelihood is too high, that is, more than our risk appetite, we might explore a resequencing or redesign of works. For example, let's say that we are building bridge piers across a seasonal river bed, a wadi, in Oman. The wadi is dry for 10 months of the year, but when the *Khareef*, the monsoon, arrives, the wadi is a raging torrent and will wash away anything that is not designed to withstand the flash flood. Early in the dry period, we take the chance by not putting expensive flood protection measures in place. The closer we get to the rains, the higher the likelihood of losing any incomplete works. Eventually, the likelihood exceeds our risk appetite, and we resequence the project to avoid the risk of losing an incomplete pier. Alternatively, we may use the same calculation to justify installing flood protection at the construction site.

This example raises an interesting point about the calculation and, more specifically, how we decide when a risk treatment is worth the cost. Our most straightforward tool is the 'whole cost of risk' (WCR). This is the cost of any risk treatment measures and the cost of the risk after those treatment measures have been implemented. It has a couple of uses. When we need to select a design option, we can compare the WCR, the cost of the design option and the associated risk profile. The lower WCR option is typically a better investment. There may be some contextual nuances around this comparison, but the principle holds. The other use is to compare risk treatments when a quantification of likelihood has been impossible. For example, let's say that we have a minimal likelihood of a catastrophic event, yet the consequences are existential for the community. We can conduct our WCR comparison, but the calculation only includes the cost of loss plus the treatment cost. The likelihood of the event is constant. You will have noted by now that risk is more than money. Risk encompasses all aspects of an operation and infrastructure. It encompasses how the infrastructure is built, operated, regulated and maintained, environmental changes, community influences, funding, technological change and more. We draw all this together under the mantle of enterprise-wide risk management (ERM).

Having spoken about risk and how it is used, it might be worth refreshing our memories on what risk is. Risk is change. Risk in infrastructure can be a gain or a loss, depending on the value of the infrastructure's alternative use when change occurs. For risk to exist, there needs to be a hazard that threatens an operation or assets, which must be exposed to the hazard, and there must be a consequence, arising from the hazard. The finance industry uses one ERM standard, COSO, while others will typically comply with ISO 31000:2018 risk management standards.

The COSO standard (COSO, 2004) sees the consequences of risk as only negative, so any gains arising from change are benefits that aren't included in the calculation. The ISO 31000 approach (ISO, 2018) sees consequences as either positive or negative. It is useful to agree early on which standard the project will use. In ERM, we consider four quadrants of risk: *strategic* and *financial*, which are external to the operation, and *true* and *operational*, which are internal. External hazards we have no control over, whereas internal ones we do. Strategic risk includes changes in regulations, changes in political policy, political instability, wars and similar national and international events. Financial risks are changes in the foreign exchange rates, or interest rates for lending. They are changes in the value of money, as it affects our operation. You cannot affect whether the changes will happen or your exposure to them. True risks are the fluvial and pluvial floods, earthquakes, wildfires and similar. They are typically natural events. You can control your exposure to them by your location. Operational risks are the risks arising from your actions. You can change the existence of these risks by how you operate and your exposure by how the operation is arranged or spaced.

The one thing that you can control for all risks is the consequence of a risk occurring. We can control our own operation, and we can therefore control how we fail. Irrespective of what causes a system failure in something we depend on, we can always change how it affects our operation and how much we lose. This is explored in detail in Chapter 4.

Risk treatments fall into five categories:

- avoidance, by not having anything that you depend upon exposed to the hazard
- acceptance, by judging the risk to be within your risk appetite
- management, by reducing the likelihood and consequence of the risk
- transfer, whether financially by insurance or setting aside a contingency fund, or non-financially or contractually, by assigning the liability to another party
- exploitation, where you see a relative advantage for your operation in the risk occurring, and so you are ready to exploit it should the risk occur.

Let us return to the question of language. We need to be able to speak with other engineers and professions, so we use the language of risk, as it is internationally recognised. The Global Risk Management Institute (GRMI) provides a useful reference lexicon if there is doubt (Elliott, 2012). However, we must also communicate with people who have neither a systems understanding nor a professional or specialist understanding of the subject matter. They are laypersons. We must have a sufficient understanding of infrastructure and our scheme to be able to explain it in clear, simple language. Many of the people you are communicating with may not share your education level, and English may not be their first language. A useful rule of thumb is to aim for CEFR level B2.2/Grade 8 (CEFR, 2021; Trinity College London, 2021). Grade 12, or college entry, would be suitable for diverse professionals working in English as a first language. In several conflict zones, we have even been encouraged to use Grade 5 English to ensure understanding across a multinational staff and local interpreters, who may translate the same message several times and not from the original. Communications and risk communication will be explored in more detail in Chapter 7. Our focus here is on understanding.

2.6. Common reference

It is one thing to have a sense of what infrastructure is and how it works, but we need to know where it is, how it is used and how the risk context affects it. If we can base our knowledge on evidence, we become all the more credible when communicating with other stakeholders. The availability of modern data collection and analytics means that there is no reason not to use evidence. Even in protracted and postconflict areas and the aftermath of disasters, we can know from the evidence what the situation is. Often, it comes down to knowing about the resources available to us, and whether we are willing to look holistically. When designers focus on a single system, they assume a deficiency and collect data to support a concept of what is needed to address that deficiency. When you look holistically, you collect data to know what the situation is. You derive a requirement, which is then investigated and addressed. The difference is an important one.

Let's say that the issue in some villages is water supply; we might pursue an improved water supply initiative, following the UN Millennium Development Goals (MDGs), as they were. We collect the supporting data for this work and connect each house to the water distribution system. We have met an MDG and have ostensibly achieved a great thing. However, by removing the well from the daily household routine, we have also removed the one opportunity that the village women had to meet and socialise. We have isolated them further and, in some cases, undermined other MDGs. The UN Sustainable Development Goals (SDGs), which replaced the MDGs in 2015, go a considerable way towards rectifying such misleading goals and metrics, but still depend on an evidence-based understanding of the situation (discussed further in Chapter 3 and 6). We see the same effects in developed regions. When we research data to support a development policy, we are collecting data that assists in that policy implementation. When we collect data to know what the policy should be, we are more likely to have a balanced approach around a unifying purpose with predictable consequences. Our apparent preference for performance metrics and targets can drive policy that is blind to its context and collateral impact (Muller, 2018).

We need to base our knowledge on evidence. We need a holistic perspective that places the infrastructure in context, recognising the influences on it as much as how it will affect the natural environment and the population's behaviours and well-being. When this knowledge is the product of evidence that is collected and analysed with transparency and free from bias, we have the basis of a common reference for communicating with all stakeholders. All stakeholders must come to the same situational awareness – recognising that their interpretation is specific to their perspectives and interests. The common reference informs our understanding of the dynamics of the infrastructure in its context. Given our concept of infrastructure and its role within the VSOS, how best to build a common reference?

There is no common reference without trust: trust in the data collection, its objective analysis and synthesis. Therefore, the foundation of a common reference is a calculation plan (CP). The CP is an auditable record of data collection, analysis and synthesis, drawing a *red thread of logic* from data to model. There are many versions of CP, and none is better than the others. There are only two criteria for an effective CP.

- Can another engineer pick up the project after you and be able to read-in efficiently?
- Can an independent auditor trace your reasoning to the satisfaction of other professions?

An underwriter is going to want to know what you have based your risk assessment on, for example. The CP must be written in clear language.

There are two stages to data collection. The first stage is the general overview, sometimes referred to as a desktop study (DTS). The idea is to get an appreciation of what the project is about. Consequently, the format is simple. There are three parts: operation, organisation and context. We start with the proposed operation (or mission) or change. What is it, and what does it need to function? Next is the organisation proposing the capability development, specifically its risk criteria, mission, decision-making structure, resources or capacities and culture. Finally, we look at the context. This isn't the risk context, but merely the context in which the proposed infrastructure will function. There are various ways to approach this initial exploration of the context, but generally, PESTLE is adequate. PESTLE is a mnemonic: P = political; E = economic; S = social or societal; T = technology; L = legal and E = environmental. We don't need to conduct a DTS when we're working with a familiar organisation and region. However, it can be useful to conduct a refresh every once in a while to ensure that we don't start making assumptions based on when we last looked at an issue. For example, a dramatic shift in government policy, such as exiting an established carbon trading scheme or an economic union, will influence changes beyond that specific policy. The significant advantage of a DTS is that it informs your approach to planning. It also means that you can have an intelligent discussion with the end user or client from the outset. The practicalities of the DTS are explored in Chapter 6.

The second stage is the collection of data to build our models. You will recall that the VSOS sits across four domains: natural, built, virtual and human. These usefully define the data categories for our models. The base models of the VSOS and common reference are the tableau, dependency model and influence model. Each is distinct yet synchronised in time and space. Let's explore what each model is and how it relates to the others.

(*a*) *Tableau*
The tableau is a geospatial model of what physically exists. It is like the Lego base plate that we use to build dioramas, in that it spatially defines relationships between assets, systems and actions. Everything georeferences to this model. There are many data sources; where possible, we would collect laydown maps from utilities and other authorities. It is also good practice to use a satellite overlay to confirm locations, as the larger authorities may have incomplete asset registers. Of course, in more austere environments, we would typically start with satellite data. However, the tableau is more than merely a collation of data. We need to relate the data to its context and actions and effects. This is the realm of exploratory spatial data analysis (ESDA) (Bivand, 2010), which was first articulated in 1983 (Good, 1983) but came into its own following Michael Goodchild's call to action (Goodchild, 1987). More typically associated with crime

Figure 2.5 Near infrared band 1 (NIR1) spectrum image of the sewage treatment plant and coastal water at the Wadi Gaza estuary, indicating similar dissolved solids signatures; this image was extracted from the 2016 Airbus 4 Band 50 cm ground sample distance (GSD) imagery. (Full colour image available on ICE Virtual Library)

Stand off Observation 2: NDVI Profile of WWTP and near coastal water

WWTP at Wadi Gaza returns similar NDVI Signature to Near Sore coastal water indicating high nutrient content

1000ft

Esri, HERE, Garmin, USGS, METI/NASA | Esri, HERE, Garmin, USGS | DigitalGlobe

trends analysis (Murray *et al.*, 2001) and poverty and health studies, it has excellent utility in investigating land use, agriculture and environmental contamination. It is not so much that ESDA provides an answer, but that it exposes a lead for further investigation, based on human interaction with the natural and built environments.

For example, using multispectral satellite imagery of the Gaza Strip, from 2018, we found that the coastal water returned a similar signature to that of the adjacent wastewater treatment lagoons (Figure 2.5). This observation cued an investigation of sewage release, which identified the possible discharge of untreated sewage into the Mediterranean. Such a discharge might have contributed to the algae blooms that forced the mayor of nearby Ashkelon to close the intakes for his desalination plants. The reason for raw sewage discharge wouldn't be a lack of capacity in the wastewater treatment facilities, but a lack of power supply.

The CP meticulously records each step in the investigation. The gradual shift to hyperspectral imaging and machine learning for anomaly detection brings the processing time down rapidly, without compromising the audit trail.

A working tableau that can identify disparities between demand and the carrying capacity of infrastructure (and physical disconnects in infrastructure laydown in protracted-conflict areas) can be assembled in around 2 weeks by a team of three. The task is quicker in more stable regions.

(*b*) *Dependency model*

The dependency model uses directed graphs to trace the relationship between the operation and its support supply lines, services and infrastructure. Each operational dependency links to everything that it, in turn, depends on. Theoretically, this can go on ad infinitum, and some digital models can do that. When tracing manually, we can map most operational dependencies using three orders of removal: three iterations of dependency mapping. This approach is generally known as causal chain mapping. We can trace the consequences (operational, financial and political) of a failure in one asset or subsystem through the model to calculate the overall impact.

This dependency model is georeferenced to the tableau. We can say that the flooding that affects a specific area will cause a failure in certain assets located in that area. This failure, in turn, results in a discernible impact on the operation. We can map the chain of consequence in both time and space. Understanding this chain of consequence is invaluable for contingency planning, resilience assessments, security integration and a host of other risk management activities. Of particular value to planners is the exposure of inherent risks in the existing VSOS and each proposed treatment. This is the basis for studying fragility in both infrastructure systems and the wider VSOS.

Using tools like incident sequencing, we can work out the combination of stresses and failures that will cause a VSOS-wide impact, a crisis. It matters less what causes failure, as how we respond to it and what resources that response requires. Our adaptation to sustained stress will also shift our balance of resource capacity. For a period, the resources available to respond to a failure will reduce, as they are committed. How we live and work will similarly change the demand for our response resources. If we have to focus our resources on providing shelter during a prolonged winter power outage, they are not available for recovery until the crisis passes. The impact of the crisis will, therefore, be that much more significant. Providing adequate housing for the vulnerable often proves to be the most cost-efficient municipal risk treatment.

Another exciting aspect is that we can extract the indicators of anticipated outcomes for a particular development plan. These indicators are more pertinent to using a *common operating picture*, discussed later. These are all the 'tells' that the VSOS is moving towards a specific outcome. This means that we can monitor our infrastructure development's socioeconomic and health impact as it is being implemented instead of retrospectively. We'll come back to this idea in Chapter 6.

Modern applications of these models use hypergraphs to capture some of the contextual influences of system failures, even when there is no direct relationship. Like ESDA, this is a rapidly evolving field. Today, we can know how failure will propagate through a complex system of systems after a few weeks of study. In 2013, it took a team of six analysts over 6 months to conduct a similar analysis of the City of Toronto to just three degrees of dependency. Emerging developments in machine learning promise to bring the same processes down to about 3 weeks for a team of three and many more degrees of dependency.

(*c*) *Influence model*

Like the dependency model, the influence model maps relationships between organisations, decision-makers and influences with operational functions. These relationships are georeferenced, where applicable. This allows us to see the inconsistencies between response or decision times and the time for the failure in a dependency to impact the operation. Influence models are also sometimes known as governance models. They are not the same. Governance models are representative of how things should be, *de jure*, not how they are, *de facto*. The difference is the mental model that organisations and individuals carry, which informs their decision-making and perceptions. It explains where the distinction lies between opinion and judgement. This distinction is an important one and has been the basis of extensive research into risk perception and risk-based decision-making, most notably by Baruch Fischhoff (Fischhoff *et al.*, 2011; Morgan *et al.*, 2001). The main difference between an opinion-based decision and a judgement-based decision is that the judgement-based decision is impartially informed and deliberately considered. However, moving to judgement-based decision-making across all stakeholders requires a detailed knowledge of these mental models and perceptions. It is all the more relevant in an increasingly post-truth world.

It is useful to look at Turkey Point Nuclear Generating Station's relicensing to understand the influence model value. Florida Power & Light sought US Nuclear Regulatory Commission approval to extend the operating life of two 1970s 729 MW_e pressurised water reactors from 2002. Of the influences on this decision, the Sierra Club and Greenpeace were most notably against renewing the licence. A risk communications company investigated stakeholders' mental models to understand what was relevant to their respective decision-making considerations. This understanding formed a basis for informing the decision process to reach an impartial judgement-based decision. The operating licenses were extended for 20 years, and in 2019 for a further 20 years (US NRC, 2021).

When we integrate these three models, we can say that we know what the infrastructure does and how it compares with demand across the region. This is the common reference and forms the basis for informed discussion between stakeholders. It also forms a valuable basis for issue-based policy and capability-based infrastructure development. How we interpret the common reference depends on our perspectives, interests and priorities. This interpretation is our understanding of how the situation affects us, and is, unhelpfully, known as the common operating picture (COP). The COP is specific to an organisation's interests and goals, and not representative of all stakeholder understanding.

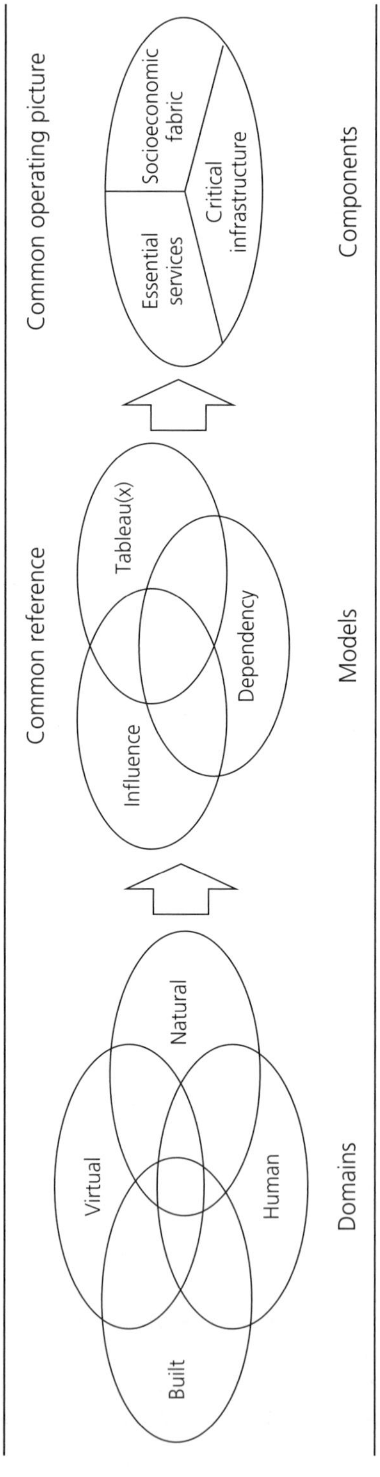

Figure 2.6 Service operation and its enabling components in context: each component is an extension of the context

Since we have interpreted the common reference to understand the effects and impact of different options to achieve our strategic goals, we need to represent that understanding in the components of the VSOS. These are critical infrastructure, essential services and the socioeconomic fabric (Figure 2.6). Each directly relates to the other. The infrastructure is critical because it supports an essential service. The service is essential because it enables the socioeconomic fabric of the community. When we specify health as the unifying purpose of the VSOS and align the COP to this outcome, we see substantial disparities in how we choose to live as a society. This takes us into the realm of social justice and equity of access, which is touched on through the book. Both are bound intimately with our infrastructure choices, as well as our societal ones.

The common reference informs stakeholder engagement. It can significantly improve local population engagement in the infrastructure planning process, raising public engagement towards community *ownership*, or *control*, in Arnstein's levels of stakeholder engagement (Arnstein, 1969). The COP informs the infrastructure development strategy. Both are useful, but they are not interchangeable and not to be confused with each other. The common reference and COP are also known collectively as the 'digital twin' in some countries. Once again, when discussing digital twins, we need to be very clear about their purpose. Do we wish to inform all stakeholders or understand the impacts of specific actions on our interests? I keep the capabilities and uses separate as common reference and COP in this book to avoid confusion.

2.7. Chapter summary

In this chapter, we explored a basic theory of infrastructure. Infrastructure is the physical manifestation of a system that serves a purpose, and its use defines its value. The infrastructure incurs development, operation and maintenance costs but, without demand for and use of the service that it enables, it has no value. Infrastructure is bound intimately to its context. One cannot fully understand its function and influence on the region's socioeconomic fabric without understanding the system of systems that it is part of. We call this the *vitae* system of systems (VSOS), and it allows us to understand the many roles that infrastructure may play in different systems. In this, we expose the unifying purpose that the infrastructure supports, which I have suggested is the physical, mental and social well-being of the population, as well as its operational and functional roles. The VSOS allows us to understand how changes to one system can translate through other systems and cause an effect to the VSOS as a whole.

When we collect data to study the VSOS in practice, we build from a foundation of the three infrastructure domains (natural, built and virtual) and the human domain. This data collection has been helped tremendously by technological advances in recent years. It is collated and analysed as a common reference.

The common reference comprises three basic models, each georeferenced to the others. They are the *tableau*, a spatial representation of what exists, the *dependency model*, a representation of how the operation works, and the *influence model*, a representation of governance, perception and decision-making. Together, these models inform our situational awareness and systems understanding using only evidence, providing a factual representation of the infrastructure system's cause-and-effect that is common to all stakeholders. Each organisation will interpret the common reference differently, reflecting its priorities, operations, risk criteria and objectives. Each interpretation of the common reference is known as the common operating picture (COP). Depending on the context, both the common reference and the COP are sometimes referred to as the *digital twin*, though they are treated separately in this book.

The common reference allows all stakeholders to draw on the same evidence-based knowledge of the current situation. It allows each stakeholder to trace the consequences of change, creating an awareness of how change affects others and changes the context in which they work. It also means that one can calibrate expertise to the current situation instead of drawing on experiences of a world that no longer exists.

There is a persistent communication theme, based on our confidence in evidence and the awareness of risk. More specifically, it is the need for evidence to inform our knowledge of the current situation and the shared consequences of changes. Similarly, our understanding of what change means to our operations, business and bottom line depends on our understanding of the risks associated with our operations. We must communicate in a way that best suits the audience. We need to ensure that we use both evidence and risk correctly. When we do, we understand the current situation and so may know what is possible.

BIBLIOGRAPHY

Arnstein SR (1969) A ladder of citizen participation. *Journal of the American Planning Association* **35(4)**: 216–224.

Bernstein PL (1996) *Against the Gods: The Remarkable Story of Risk*. Wiley, New York, NY, USA.

Bivand RS (2010) Exploratory spatial data analysis. In *Handbook of Applied Spatial Analysis: Software Tools, Methods and Applications* (Fischer MM and Getis A (eds)). Springer, Berlin, Germany, pp. 219–254.

Bristow DN (2015) Asset system of systems resilience planning: the Toronto case. *Infrastructure Asset Management* **2(1)**:15–22.

CEFR (Common European Framework of Reference for Language) (2021) The CEFR Levels. Council of Europe, Strasbourg, France. https://www.coe.int/en/web/common-european-framework-reference-languages/level-descriptions (accessed 30/03/2021).

COSO (Committee of Sponsoring Organizations of the Treadway Commission) (2004) *Enterprise Risk Management – Integrated Framework*. Pricewaterhouse-Coopers, New York, NY, USA.

Elliott MW (ed.) (2012) *Risk Assessment and Treatment*, 1st edn. The Institutes, Malvern, PA, USA.

Fischhoff B, Brewer N and Downs JS (eds) (2011) *Communicating Risks and Benefits: An Evidence-based User's Guide*. Food and Drug Administration, Washington, DC, USA.

Gall J (1977) *Systemantics: How Systems Work and Especially How They Fail*. Quadrangle/*New York Times* Books, New York, NY, USA.

Good IJ (1983) The philosophy of exploratory data analysis. *Philosophy of Science* **50(2)**: 283–295.

Goodchild MF (1987) A spatial analytical perspective on geographical information systems. *International Journal of Geographical Information Systems* **1(4)**: 327–334.

Hardin G (1968) The tragedy of the commons. *Science* **162(3859)**: 1243–1248.

Hipel KW, Kilgour DM and Fang L (2012) Systems methodologies in *vitae* systems of systems. *Journal of Natural Disaster Sci*ence **32(2)**: 63–77.

ICE (Institution of Civil Engineers) (2014) *RAMP: Risk Analysis and Management for Projects*, 3rd edn. ICE Publishing, London, UK.

III (Insurance Information Institute) (2020) Facts + Statistics: Global Catastrophes. https://www.iii.org/fact-statistic/facts-statistics-global-catastrophes (accessed 02/07/2020).

ISO (International Standards Organization) (2018) 31000 Risk management. ISO, Geneva, Switzerland.

Koestler A (1967) *The Ghost in the Machine*. Hutchinson, London, UK.

Kolbert E (2014) *The Sixth Extinction: An Unnatural History*, 1st edn. Henry Holt, New York, NY, USA.

Louie A (2010) Robert Rosen's anticipatory systems. *Foresight* **12**: 18–29. https://www.researchgate.net/publication/228091658_Robert_Rosen's_anticipatory_systems (accessed 11/02/2020).

Morgan MG, Fischhoff B, Bostrom A and Atman CJ (2001) *Risk Communication – A Mental Models Approach*. Cambridge University Press, New York, NY, USA.

Muller JZ (2018) *The Tyranny of Metrics*. Princeton University Press, Princeton, NJ, USA.

Murray AT, McGuffog I, Western JS and Mullins P (2001) Exploratory spatial data analysis techniques for examining urban crime: implications for evaluating treatment. *The British Journal of Criminology* **41(2)**: 309–329, 10.1093/bjc/41.2.309.

Okada N (2006) City and region viewed as *vitae* system for integrated disaster risk management. *Annuals of Disaster Prevention Research Institute* **49(B)**: 131–136.

O'Neill P (2013) Protecting critical infrastructure by identifying pathways of exposure to risk. *Technology Innovation Management Review* **3(8)**: 34–40.

Ostrom E (1990) *Governing the Commons: The Evolution of Institutions for Collective Action*. Cambridge University Press, New York, NY, USA.

Ostrom E (2009) *A Polycentric Approach for Coping with Climate Change*. Policy Research Working Paper 5095, World Bank, Washington, DC, USA.

Ryle G (1949) *The Concept of Mind*. Hutchinson, London, UK.

Saunders P (2018) Detroit, five years after bankruptcy. *Forbes*, 19 July. https://www.forbes.com/sites/petesaunders1/2018/07/19/detroit-five-years-after-bankruptcy/?sh=59801f6fcfeb (accessed 29/03/2021).

Steels HM (ed.) (2011) *Initial Professional Development for Civil Engineers*. ICE Publishing, London, UK.

Susskind RE and Susskind D (2015) *The Future of the Professions: How Technology will Transform the Work of Human Experts*, 1st edn. Oxford University Press, Oxford, UK.

Trinity College London (2021) GESE – Graded Examinations in Spoken English. Trinity College London, London, UK. https://www.trinitycollege.com/qualifications/english-language/GESE (accessed 30/03/2021).

Turbeville W (2013) *The Detroit Bankruptcy: The Causes of Detroit's Bankruptcy and what the City's Emergency Manager Can Do to Turn It Around*. Dçmos, New York, NY, USA.

US NRC (2020) Turkey Point Nuclear Plant, Units 3 & 4 – Subsequent License Renewal Application. https://www.nrc.gov/reactors/operating/licensing/renewal/applications/turkey-point-subsequent.html (accessed 30/03/2021).

WHO (World Health Organisation) (2021) Constitution. http://www.who.int/about/mission/en/ (accessed 11/05/2018).

Wittgenstein L, Anscombe GEM, Hacker PMS and Schulte J (2009) *Philosophische Untersuchungen – Philosophical Investigations*, revised 4th edn. Wiley Blackwell, Malden, MA, USA.

FURTHER READING

Our understanding of infrastructure, both conceptually and in practice, continues to evolve. In some ways, it has been the impetus of climate change that encouraged us to relearn past generations' lessons and think critically about what we want to achieve and how it will affect the world around us. The Institution of Civil Engineers (2020), among others, has drawn on this past knowledge and projected forward in systems thinking to make it relevant to today and into the future. The Centre for Digital Built Britain (CDBB) has produced helpful guidance on building digital twins with the Gemini Principles and presents a vision for infrastructure that is both systems-based and people-focused (Schooling *et al.*, 2020). There are interesting papers in the *Proceedings of the Institution of Civil Engineers*, such as 'Towards the future-proofing of UK infrastructure' (Masood *et al.*, 2016). Of course, you can always find examples in the business papers describing a misalignment between an infrastructure purpose and the demand for the enabled service, though I don't point to one article in particular. Disappointingly, it is much harder to find articles examining successful project outputs with unsuccessful outcomes. For those curious about the virtual domain and how it affects us, Yuval Harari provides an excellent description in *Sapiens* (2015).

Harari YN (2015) *Sapiens: A Brief History of Humankind* (Purcell J and Watzman H (trans.)). Vintage Classics, London, UK.

ICE (Institution of Civil Engineers) (2020) *A Systems Approach to Infrastructure Delivery: A Review of how Systems Thinking Can Be Used to Improve the Delivery of Complex Infrastructure Projects*. ICE, London, UK.

Masood T, McFarlane D, Parlikad AK *et al.* (2016) Towards the future-proofing of UK infrastructure. *Infrastructure Asset Management* **3(1)**: 28–41, 10.1680/jinam.15.00006.

Schooling J, Burgess G and Enzer M (2020) *Flourishing Systems: Re-Envisioning Infrastructure as a Platform for Human Flourishing*. Centre for Digital Built Britain, Cambridge, UK.

ICE Publishing

Hay, Alexander H
ISBN 978-0-7277-6562-8
https://doi.org/10.1680/pris.65628.051

Chapter 3
Sustainable infrastructure: who do we build infrastructure for?

With Yannick Beaudoin

Sustainability is, in itself, a relatively simple concept. Human beings have always instinctively understood it. The conventional interpretation of what it means in practical terms, as sustainable development, was first articulated in the Brundtland Commission's report *Our Common Future* (WCED, 1987). The commission defined sustainable development as 'development that meets the needs of the present without compromising the ability of future generations to meet their own needs.'

Despite being such a simple concept, it is often misrepresented. The popular impression of sustainability and sustainable living was associated with alternative lifestyles until this century. It wasn't taken seriously by the mainstream of the design and planning professions, who often saw it as an added cost to projects for an intangible benefit. Christof Miska *et al.* (2018) argue that the adoption of sustainability and sustainable practices reflects corporate or institutional culture. It may seem obvious from today's perspective, but it does explain why many developments in this century have proclaimed accredited sustainable characteristics while not being sustainable. The rising demand among activist shareholders and voters for a more environmentally responsible and ethical approach has developed corporate social responsibility (CSR) accountability into greater environmental, social and governance (ESG) measurement and reporting. There was a growing expectation for corporations and governments to show that they are responsible citizens, and ESG criteria offer a way of demonstrating that. Wary of the perceived increase in cost that sustainability might represent, checklists became a popular way of calculating which measures were worth incorporating to demonstrate a sustainable approach.

One popular certification programme in North America is the Leadership in Energy and Environmental Design (LEED) programme offered by the Green Building Council (Canada Green Building Council, 2021; US Green Building Council, 2021). Depending on the green building measures incorporated in the design and the subsequent operating practices, facilities can be certified at four levels from *certified* to *platinum* by allocating points, which are distributed between a number of categories or credits 'based on the potential environmental impacts and human benefits of each credit.' When applied as part of an integrated design philosophy, this programme leads to more efficient and sustainable facilities. When used as a checklist, less so. This is a real shame because the latter can foster cynicism and reinforce some negative corporate prejudices.

In 2009, an article in the *Harvard Business Review* described a stand-off between governments representing the demands of a sustainability-aware electorate and corporations concerned that sustainability investment would disadvantage them (Nidumolu *et al.*, 2009). As the world was starting its recovery following the 2007–2008 global financial crisis, it was felt by many that sustainable operations would disadvantage business. In the absence of real accountability, CSR remained divorced from business objectives. By the time the UN Millennium Development Goals (MDGs) were formulated, sustainability was perhaps better accepted. However, it was still seen as a series of stand-alone deliverables and outputs (UN, 2015). It was not applied holistically – it was not seen as a system property. For example, one might *improve* the water supply by connecting each house to a piped water supply network but not distribute clean water. By 2015, there was extraordinary progress across all of the eight MDGs, but the outcome wasn't sustainable or equitable. The UN Sustainable Development Goals (SDGs) address these shortcomings and have enjoyed greater uptake. Similarly, transparent ESG criteria were used to inform more socially aware investors.

It is interesting that when we look at what sustainability is, the more sustainable organisations are typically more resilient to these strategic changes, like the 2007–2008 global financial crisis or the 2020–2021 pandemic. When sustainability is a philosophy – an approach to planning and design – we see tangible improvements in business and community. This chapter explores what sustainability is, starting with how the concept came about and how it is applied. The discussion leads into what it means for infrastructure planners and the community, including its cultural impediments. We explore the social aspect with a discussion about social justice and the role of community ownership in infrastructure development, which leads to intelligent resourcing and the role of risk.

3.1. Origins

It is worth exploring the origins of the Brundtland Commission to understand the influences at play. The 1972 UN Conference on the Human Environment, held in Sweden, was intended to focus on human interaction with the environment. However, geopolitical interests drove much of the conference, from a boycott by the Warsaw Pact nations over the exclusion of East Germany (not a member state of the UN), to Chinese objections to US policies in Indochina, to continuing postcolonial arguments from several developing countries.

However, it did result in the UN Environment Programme (UNEP), established in Nairobi, Kenya. It is probably this aspect that allowed some general agreement at the conference, at a time when few saw environmental protection as a priority. One of the most notable events at the conference was a speech by Indira Gandhi, India's Prime Minister, associating environmental protection with poverty alleviation (LASU, 2000). This link has been repeatedly demonstrated since. The Conference agreed on 26 principles of environmental protection, together with an action plan. These principles are collectively known as the Stockholm Declaration and ranged from the condemnation of colonialism and apartheid to protection of the oceans, banning weapons of mass destruction and ensuring planned settlement.

The UNEP did enjoy some modest successes over the following decade, though national adoption was inconsistent. In 1983, the UN asked former Norwegian Prime Minister, Gro Harlem Brundtland, to set up an independent World Commission on Environment and Development (WCED). It became known as the Brundtland Commission. The commission sought to find a balance between global economic growth and environmental protection. The solution was to associate economic development with 'sustainable development' and introduced as a concept in the 1987 report. It centres on the idea of intergenerational equity, arguably shifting the emphasis from economic growth to economic development.

So why is this relevant to infrastructure? Infrastructure is how we adapt the world around us to enable our socioeconomic fabric. If that infrastructure, which typically spans several generations, compromises future generations' ability to continue their economic development, we leave our children a liability instead of a legacy. Therefore, if we are to have sustainable development, our infrastructure must also be sustainable. If we can plan our sustainable infrastructure intelligently, we can significantly impact poverty and the broader physical, mental and social well-being of the population. If we accept this relationship, we must now ask what this means in practice. How do we deliver sustainable development and sustainable infrastructure?

The UN initiatives address the first part of the question, specifically the MDGs that set specific targets by 2015 and the SDGs that continued progress more holistically (UNHCR, 2017). These SDGs feature in many large institutions' investment policies, notably the larger pension funds and the multilateral development banks. Pension funds, including the Japanese Government Pension Investment Fund (GPIF), which is possibly the largest investor by assets globally, make up one of the most prominent groups of investors in infrastructure development. The Asian Infrastructure Development Bank has the fastest growing infrastructure investment portfolio. Both advance the UN's Principles for Responsible Investment (PRI) and use the SDGs as part of their investment selection criteria. Other institutions are using similar investment selection criteria to emphasise net socioeconomic benefit or focus more on the (human) physical, mental and social well-being outcomes of the investment. For some institutions, this has meant a divestment in fossil fuels. In contrast, following the UN PRI, others actively assist energy companies in transitioning to a low carbon dioxide business. These policy changes place ever greater emphasis on infrastructure engineers and planners to demonstrate, with evidence, how infrastructure development proposals meet these goals.

The second part of the question is more nuanced. There are already several excellent explanations of sustainable infrastructure, and the aim is not to replicate any of it here. Instead, we will examine how we set the context and requirements for our sustainable infrastructure within the broader VSOS. A focus on the infrastructure systems would present a convenient framework for our examination. However, exploring a shifting context is more nebulous, and there is no discernible starting point for our journey. We need to consider how our understanding and interpretation change with the context, including the market perspectives and expectations. To do this, we must recognise the sometimes conflicting priorities in what sustainable infrastructure means in practice. There are three dimensions to sustainability: economic, environmental and social (UN ESCAP, 2015). We can approach these dimensions from their own perspectives.

The first perspective is a financial one. If we are to invest in sustainable infrastructure, the infrastructure can self-sustain from the revenues generated by the service it enables. At the very minimum, these revenues will cover the operation and maintenance expenses (OPEX) over its design life. In this model, our calculation removes capital expenditure (CAPEX). We would see this model where there is a political interest in keeping service fees low and the associated acceptance that the treasury will continue to pay for each CAPEX demand.

This approach works well, as long as the CAPEX fund is ring-fenced and not diverted to other priorities. The weakness is often that the public does not recognise the service's real value and can pressure the continued reduction in fees, resulting in growing deficiencies in the infrastructure. In some extreme cases, it can result in a complete failure in supply, owing to a lack of maintenance. This public perception of service value is seen in providing water and electricity to Canadian households, for example. The municipal infrastructure deficit in Canada exceeds its capacity to remedy, necessitating a new national strategy (Mirza and Shafqat, 2017). They aren't alone. Underinvestment in the maintenance of existing infrastructure is a widespread problem.

When we include CAPEX in the calculation, we can see the requirement for the service fees to generate the CAPEX for eventual infrastructure replacement and cover the full OPEX. Queensland, Australia, has such a model, for example. When private finance provides the initial CAPEX, it must be repaid, with interest, to the investors from the service revenue. Some projects' cash flows cannot cover CAPEX and OPEX, which has led to some of the recent innovations in public–private partnership contracts. A purely financial perspective can be limiting, leading to decisions that make financial sense and still result in unsustainable infrastructure, such as the wastewater treatment plant example in Chapter 2.

The second perspective is an environmental one. Unlike the economic and social dimensions, the environmental dimension is defined by the laws of physics. Adopting an environmental perspective depends on whether we accept those laws or we don't. We can print more money and change the economic dimension. We can restructure communities and relocate them or change the nature of their institutions, changing the social dimension. However, we cannot change the laws of physics, and the environmental dimension is fixed and immutable. More than any other way of looking at infrastructure, the environmental sustainability perspective is about the triple bottom line. That is, doing what makes financial sense, doing what is socially and ethically right, and ensuring that our operations will continue. During the COVID-19 pandemic, our experience reminds us of the need to consider the triple bottom line holistically and not allow each aspect to be reduced to a financial metric. Movement restrictions impeded many services, including essential ones. A loss of service reflects a loss of infrastructure value. Some services that had pursued an efficiency drive based on financial metrics were compromised by the pandemic response and needed external intervention to continue functioning. Vulnerabilities such as key-worker access and food distribution were exposed. The issue of metrics limiting our understanding rather than informing it is a critical concern, and we return to this issue.

3.2. Informing sustainability decisions

Some refer to the triple bottom line as head, heart and gut. We do what makes business sense, supports market goodwill and preserves our place in the future. In one respect, we might look at the financial part as the overall efficient consumption of resources, designing infrastructure to more efficiently consume those resources. However, can the consumption of resources be, by definition, sustainable? We might build on this and look at the effects of our infrastructure on the natural world. If we squander those same resources now, they won't be economically available for the next generation, if at all. Of course, that would suggest that being in business tomorrow matters more than maximising profit today. We shall return to this later.

The effect we have on the natural world, from deforestation and the destruction of natural habitats to polluting soil and water, reduces what will be available to support our children. There is a social imperative to act responsibly in our stewardship of the finite world entrusted to us. Our physical, mental and social well-being are directly linked to the health of the natural world. Each action we take must consider this relationship (UNEP, 2019). The challenge is that while we may seek technological solutions to address the imbalance between our immediate interests and the health of the natural world, it has more to do with our behaviour and attitudes. Infrastructure is the expression of those behaviours and attitudes, as much as it shapes them. Our view of sustainability becomes necessarily more ecological, recognising a single shared ecosystem that is our world.

There is a current drive, internationally, to reduce levels of carbon dioxide in the atmosphere and, ideally, sequester more. The excess carbon dioxide released since the start of the Anthropocene has greatly accelerated what would probably be a normal warming of the planet. It presents a problem in that the accelerated warming is faster than ecosystems can adapt (Kolbert, 2014). A significant part of excess carbon dioxide release is in dwellings, and their construction in particular. We gradually embrace energy conservation, demand reduction and transition the grid supply of electricity away from coal towards natural gas and, eventually, renewables. These changes have not been easy, and various countries are making slow, steady progress. However, the carbon dioxide released in the manufacture of the materials used for energy conservation, traditional construction techniques and the supply chain, in addition to the carbon dioxide released in operating and maintaining the structure, are part of the carbon footprint. This carbon footprint can tell us the real impact on carbon dioxide emissions of the choices we make.

Interestingly, the capital release of carbon dioxide, which is the part of the carbon footprint that represents a structure's construction, remains the more significant part. We can construct net negative-carbon footprint dwellings without compromising on cost, comfort or efficiency (Racusin and Magwood, 2020). This means that before we even start to occupy and operate the dwellings, we have already sequestered carbon. Nothing in the negative footprint, also known as a handprint (Norris, 2015), is new. However, it does require a change in attitude and conduct. Human beings don't appear to be good at that.

Some years ago, we investigated the risk profiles for a major dairy. This investigation was prompted by the accidental death of a technician conducting routine maintenance on the ammonia refrigeration system. For this size of dairy, the refrigeration system would carry more than 10 000 lb (4500 kg) of ammonia (NH_3). If there were a catastrophic release, the factory and surrounding town would have to be evacuated, with no authority to reoccupy until cleared by the local fire chief. The insurance only covered the refrigeration system's repair under their 'boilers and pressure vessels' provisions. There was no coverage for the liability of mass evacuations and casualties. The consequences of such an event at just one of their factories would have been sufficient to fail the whole international business. In this particular case, we found that a carbon dioxide (CO_2) transcritical system would not carry the same liability though operating at higher pressures. When we compared the WCRs for the ammonia and carbon dioxide, the difference exceeded by orders of magnitude the full cost of replacing the existing refrigeration systems with transcritical ones. The case for change was overwhelming, yet the retained consulting engineers strongly argued that ammonia was safe, dismissing the client's broader risk picture. Their main argument was that there was no reason to change because they had always designed ammonia systems for this dairy. They were unwilling, perhaps incapable, of seeing the bigger picture from their client's perspective.

Actual change took a few years, and the death of another maintenance technician elsewhere in the sector. In the end, the consulting engineers were let go, and others were retained who were willing to work within the dairy's risk criteria. The urgency for evidence-based material disclosure of risks would probably have provided the final impetus. At each stage, the argument would always be, what was the 'probability [sic] of a catastrophic release', to which one need only refer to the catastrophic Union Carbide incident in Bhopal, India, in 1984. Dow Chemical acquired Union Carbide in 2001. Union Carbide was found liable in 1989 for US $470 million in damages for the incident, and in 2010 Indian courts convicted seven former executives at the plant for criminal negligence and sentenced them to 2 years in prison plus fines. High-consequence, low-likelihood risks still need to be taken seriously. This dairy example illustrates how our technical perspective can sometimes lose context. We can tend towards the familiar, blind to a change in requirement and the whole metric. Often, delivering on true sustainability can be just beyond our familiar professional frame of reference. It takes effort and humility to perceive our work differently.

These examples bring us to the third bottom line, the visceral one. How important is it to know that you will survive? We will explore this in greater detail in the next chapter, but behaviour and perspective have significant influence. If we continually put off dealing with issues because they will require an investment of effort and resources to maximise our immediate benefits, we will always procrastinate. When we are mandated to deal with our survivability, we tend to make a checklist to demonstrate compliance. Whether there is any substance to the checklist of actions is neither here nor there. The Task Force on Climate-related Financial Disclosures (TCFD) commented on the lack of material reporting in 2019, effectively encouraging listed companies to take material disclosure more seriously for their shareholders. The Financial Stability Board established the TCFD in 2015 to develop recommendations for more effective climate-related disclosures that could promote better-informed financial decisions and stakeholder understanding of climate-related risk. The TCFD presented its recommendations in 2017. The emphasis is firmly on an evidence-based understanding of risk.

The recent COVID-19 pandemic has also provided a significant shock to businesses. Several businesses had prepared their pandemic contingency plans following the severe acute respiratory syndrome (SARS) epidemic in 2003. Whether they had subsequently rehearsed or reviewed them is a matter for debate. Still, many found their contingency plans inadequate because the coronavirus that causes COVID-19 did not behave as SARS did. These *retrospective* plans focused on the cause, rather than the effect of the epidemic or pandemic on our operations. If we know how our operation must adapt to failures in any of the systems that it comprises and depends on, then we know what our infrastructure must enable. Much of the requirement for sustainable infrastructure is determined by the operation's resilience requirements that it enables. That is why sustainability and resilience are often referred to as two faces of the same coin. The UN International Strategy for Disaster Reduction (UNISDR), the precursor to the UN Office for Disaster Risk Reduction (UNDRR), declared in 2014 that resilience was the prerequisite of sustainability. They certainly feature jointly throughout the SDGs.

Suppose we wish our operation or business to be (ecologically) sustainable and to be confident that we will be around tomorrow. In that case, we must ensure that we don't compromise the supplies of resources that we depend on today and in the future. There is no need for intellectual acrobatics or complicated reasoning. It is little more than the extension of naked self-interest. So, if taking a future view of our business and maximising profit today are both in our self-interest, how might we encourage a shift in corporate priorities? We seek to shift a director's principal responsibility from the Milton Friedman school of thought (maximise returns for shareholders) to the Peter Drucker school (to protect against loss). Interestingly, we are seeing such a shift, arising from the experience of the COVID-19 pandemic.

This challenges the idea that economic development still relies on growth and consumption. *Our Common Future* (WCED, 1987) changed the label from 'economic growth' to 'economic development'. Yet the dominant (Western) economic development frameworks define success in terms of growth. Recognising that UN policies and guidance are born out of geopolitical compromise, informed by scientific benchmarks, our definition of what successful sustainable infrastructure is should be aligned with the (local) beneficiaries' economic culture. Might 'sufficiency of service' define success, or health, or social equity, rather than return on invested capital? It is important not to impose our definition of success on the intended beneficiaries, who may have other values. This revision in thinking drives the circular economy concept and an increased desire to harness economic success to the 'frugal consumption of resources'. When the City of Toronto introduced recycling, the quantity of waste per capita increased. People's self-restraint was released. A similar rebound effect is seen in the increased carbon efficiencies in building and a wide variety of services and operations, yet total carbon dioxide emissions continue to rise. Perhaps real sustainability is only achievable through a sense of sufficiency? It is little wonder that ambiguity remains the preferred use of 'sustainability'.

The third perspective is a societal one that looks at the whole VSOS impact, generation on generation. When we take a VSOS or holistic view of our operations and the infrastructure that enables it, we encompass both the financial and environmental perspective. Within the UN definitions, the three dimensions of sustainability must be in harmony to deliver sustainability. From a more narrow infrastructure perspective, we are integrating the economic and environmental within the social. We see this increasingly reflected in multilateral development funding for infrastructure projects conditional on social outcomes. Until we find another means of exchange, our actions must be financially supportable. As long as we have children, we must be willing to provide for their world. Both perspectives directly influence the physical, mental and social well-being of the current and future generations. Rather than seeing only a particular aspect of the infrastructure's operational function, we must understand how it interacts with the world, from conception to final destruction.

A useful acid test of an idea is to apply it to a postconflict situation. We can see whether it enables the stable rehabilitation of that region as rapidly as possible without raising the spectre of postconflict poverty. We might argue that such things don't apply in a developed setting because needs are different. On the contrary, self-interest in a postconflict area is naked because it is existential with prejudice born out of experience. To satisfy the unifying purpose in such a setting is to have a more developed, less unstable economy. We will continue this perspective in this chapter.

One thing that always seems to come to the fore is the importance of a local sense of ownership of what is built. There are several building blocks to this, but local ownership ties directly to the tangible local benefit now and over the foreseeable future. It involves local engagement, even *partnership*, as defined in the Arnstein ladder (Arnstein 1969), shown in Figure 3.1. It also means using the infrastructure to enable local development as an operating context, such as building local supply chains and resource capacity. It means making the benefits accessible. In my postconflict infrastructure rehabilitation research, I termed this *beneficial capability*. This is a relatively simple idea but provides a useful indicator of the 'stickiness' of an infrastructure project, as one colleague put it. She was referring to whether the sustainable infrastructure would be socio-economically sustainable in practice. Beneficial capability has three conditions: that a facility can benefit the local population and designated beneficiaries, that the local and designated beneficiaries have equity of access to the facility, and

Figure 3.1 Arnstein's ladder of citizen participation

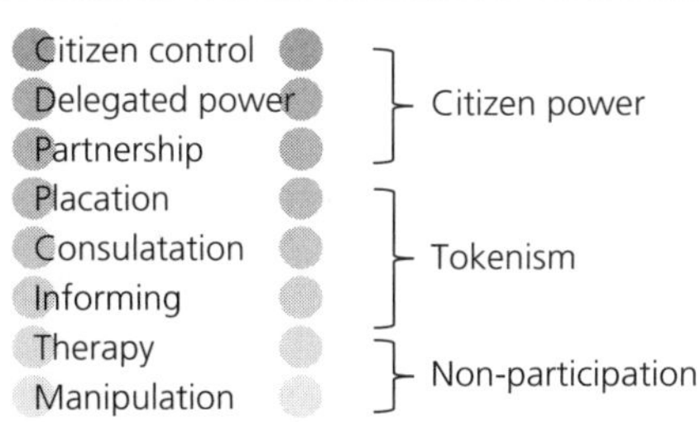

that local and designated beneficiaries are capable of benefiting. We'll come back to this in Chapter 4.

3.3. Sustainability, influencing change

Having said that sustainability is an inherently simple concept, instinctively understood by many, and provided a fundamental description, I would be remiss if I didn't acknowledge other perspectives. The differences in definitions are more a reflection of scale, context and purpose than anything else. For example, sustainability in practice for many people describes energy efficiency in buildings and appliances because that reflects the associated marketing. More recently, this interpretation has extended to 'green' and 'smart' buildings. So while the essence of the concept is, by definition, holistic, it can be popularly interpreted as a functional characteristic. This can be a problem when discussing a proposed development with a lay audience. It is more of a problem when dealing with developers and contractors used to working in silos and reverting to the familiar.

Some time ago, I designed an expedient ballistic barrier. The design included sandbags filled with a particular type of gravel. When I inspected the partially completed works, I found beautifully laid sandbags filled with sand. It wouldn't work in this design. I asked the contractor what had happened and was told that this is how one lays sandbags. The specification seemed to be secondary to *the way things are done*. It took some persuasion to strip out the work and rebuild using gravel.

More recently, I had the great pleasure of collaborating with Chris Magwood of the Endeavour Centre Sustainable Building School. He had demonstrated that one could build a family dwelling that sequestered carbon without compromising cost or comfort (BFCA, 2019). I was quite inspired by this and discussed the necessary building choices and approach with contractors for an affordable housing scheme. They were reluctant to work with different building materials. Even when presented with a compelling argument that we could demonstrate a through-life (construction and operation) handprint design and deliver on council policies, and attract supplementary grants, they remained reticent. The concept of a handprint design is that it leaves a positive effect on the world instead of a footprint that leaves an indent. These handprint houses sequester more carbon dioxide than is expended in their construction and have very low to zero carbon signatures in their operation. A conventional house will release a significant amount of carbon dioxide into the atmosphere through its construction and operation.

This hesitation to change the way we do things is not limited to contractors. The reluctance to change exists in every stage of the infrastructure planning process, every trade and profession. This doesn't mean that change is not possible. It means that we have to understand why there is hesitation and ensure that we can inform change. Interestingly, the pressure to change is building across institutions, countries and investors. UNEP produces a global environmental assessment. The sixth report, *GEO 6: Healthy Planet Healthy People* (UNEP, 2019), is a compelling document and often referenced in conjunction with the COP21 (Paris) Agreement on greenhouse gas (GHG) emissions, World Economic Forum (WEF, Davos) reports and the ubiquitous UN SDGs. These reports and agreements provide an impetus for change, and conferences such as ICE's Global Engineering Congress in 2018 share awareness of what change is possible.

However, substantive change is being driven more effectively today by institutional investors, including BlackRock and the Japanese GPIF, as the two largest by assets held. The requirement to demonstrate improved environmental, economic and social outcomes is forcing change. Some lenders require a beneficial social outcome as a condition of infrastructure investment, above and beyond the operational and economic justification (CAF, 2020). These interests can sometimes compete, depending on stakeholder interest, and present the infrastructure planner with some challenges, discussed in Chapter 6. However, it is the question of demonstrating sustainability outcomes that is key. It's not enough to be a sustainable infrastructure project; it must be seen and understood to be as well.

The challenge of measuring sustainability will influence infrastructure planning and design. We've explored the question of purpose and what it means functionally, operationally and strategically. This was illustrated using the example of a northern Ontario power transmission line extension to remote communities. We need to look at this holistically. We discuss the influence of risk on these through-life calculations later and in the next chapter. Let us focus for now on these three components of sustainability (environment, social and economic) and what they mean in practice.

Environmentally, we seek to enable an operation with minimal, if any, adverse impact on the environment. This would mean ensuring that our infrastructure and its enabled services do not pollute or contaminate the natural world, and provide a safe and healthy atmosphere for users, operators and the general public. Some would argue for infrastructure that depollutes; infrastructure that captures carbon dioxide and incorporates waste. While some countries might repeal or avoid the legislation that mandates such outcomes, it is increasingly the ability to secure financing that drives the requirement. A tangible metric that is gaining popularity is the GHG signature of the project. This ostensibly provides a means of comparing projects and informing investment decisions. The standard GHG emissions calculation uses the international GHG Protocol (WRI, 2004). This protocol applies a life-cycle approach for the commodity, activity or asset in question.

The first challenge is to establish the boundaries of what will be included. The GHG calculation per unit is assigned to the source. This is known as the life-cycle inventory (LCI). It can be a challenge. Say you are planning a pipeline to transport oil from the wells to the refinery. The final GHG calculation will refer to the crude oil extracted at the well. In this case, we have no control over refining, because it is in another country, or what is subsequently done with the refined products. Do we calculate the GHG emissions from *well to wheels* to compare it with other operations? We are comparing ourselves with operations that have control over their refining and product distribution. They control the full *well to wheels* chain, and we don't, say. Our refiners refuse to invest in a more efficient distillation plant because there is no incentive to do so. Consequently, our crude oil will always compare poorly with other sources of oil. We may not attract the necessary investment.

The second part is the calculation itself, and which sources of GHG emissions should be included. These are categorised as Scopes 1, 2 and 3 and accounted for as equivalent carbon dioxide. Scope 1 comprises all direct GHG emissions 'from sources that are owned or controlled by the company'. Scope 2 comprises all emissions 'from the generation of purchased electricity consumed by the company'. Scope 3 is a catch-all that comprises all other indirect emissions, which is optional accounting, if increasingly required. 'Scope 3 emissions are a consequence of the activities of the company, but occur from sources not owned or controlled by the company' (WRI, 2004). This approach is also used to account for GHG emissions through the corporate value chain (WRI, 2011). Why does this matter to us?

When the owner, operator, and user organisations are judged by their carbon footprints, the infrastructure's design and delivery matter. Some organisations do brush off any criticism of their carbon footprint, but they are becoming fewer. We must therefore consider our infrastructure in two ways. The first is the capability that it delivers and its associated sustainability characteristics. The second concerns the transition of the organisation and its operations to a more sustainable performance. The process of transition means change and, therefore, risk. It is a key focus of the TCFD reporting, discussed further in the next chapter. Some organisations have chosen to consider only the physical characteristics of the operation and its enabling infrastructure. In these cases, we can see divestment in big GHG-emitting companies and industries. The growing divestment in the fossil fuels industry is a case in point. The challenge that many societies face is that fossil fuels remain the means to deliver that transition.

Many institutional investors subscribe to the UN PRI and recognise the value in engaging with a company's transition to a better GHG emissions profile. These investors are conscious of the social impact of abrupt change, specifically on the mental and social health of people and communities that depend on these industries for their livelihoods. This means that the infrastructure requirement is necessarily more extensive than merely supporting a specified operation. The requirement will recognise that the use of the infrastructure will change, and some enabling provisions may be incorporated to enable that change during its working life. For example, a new community development recognises that there will be an eventual transition to electric vehicles. Charging stations are fitted into new houses as a matter of course, as well as the conduits and enabling infrastructure for future public charging stations. This will also include considerations of how the infrastructure is delivered and can even extend to apprenticeships and specialised training to facilitate the transition.

More recently, we have become able to measure the effects of infrastructure use on public health directly. This allows us to say how the proposed service or operation and its enabling infrastructure will affect the population's physical well-being and the associated impact on healthcare costs and economic productivity. This affects the rural environment's carrying capacity and, therefore, the population that it can directly support. Recall Indira Gandhi's speech to the UN Stockholm Conference in 1972 (LASU, 2000). We can also say how infrastructure and the wider built environment impact mental health (BC CDC, 2019). However, the economic costs of this are more difficult to calculate. We also know how infrastructure affects social well-being and function (Aicher, 1998). This extends to how the infrastructure performs and influences the social fabric during periods of stress and crisis, affecting crime (Weil, 2020) and social capital (Aldrich, 2012).

Sustainability and sustainable infrastructure are much more than reduced carbon footprints, efficient operation and financial viability. It is a concept for living in a world of finite capital, natural and human. We are rediscovering practices, such as intelligent resourcing, that were commonplace 2000 years ago and were inherently more in tune with what we seek to achieve than the world we have created. Today, the concept of a circular economy is demonstrating real value. Municipalities are collaborating with Circle Economy, a not-for-profit organisation based in the Netherlands, to improve the environment for citizens while reducing costs significantly. Their reports and partnerships range from cities (Vienna, Dublin, Glasgow, Toronto) to regions and countries (Cornwall and Devon, Austria) and industry sectors that range from garments to construction waste and construction financing. The World Economic Forum (WEF) is also showcasing examples of environmental stewardship and improved sustainable infrastructure, such as the use of waste plastics to build more durable urban road surfaces or the planting of micro-forests in and around industrial and transportation infrastructure.

3.4. Ownership and social justice

There can be very few publications that look at the relationship between people and the built environment better than AlWaer and Illsley's *Rethinking Masterplanning: Creating Quality Places* (2017). It gets to the essence of what the built environment is for, providing pragmatic guidance in delivering it both as product and process. Many publications focus on a particular issue and pronounce how things should be. The danger is that they detach from context and oversimplify a message – they become political. To be genuinely effective, the infrastructure engineer or planner must be apolitical in all professional practice and understand the situational realities. We cannot impose solutions; they must be organic to the local community. This is a theme that we return to frequently because it is critical.

When we look at our infrastructure as a system in its context, it leads us down a particular approach to planning that recognises the impact of what we plan and how it is delivered. This is a pragmatic systems approach; the planner can approach the mechanics of sustainable development with confidence. This section explores the nature of the community connection to the infrastructure because we need to understand what the evidence tells us.

Arnstein (1969) guided us in stakeholder engagement for infrastructure development projects, and Anholt (2010) explains the value of place and location identity. What makes the difference in how the local community perceives the infrastructure? We can have a well and water treatment facility that is the sole source of clean water in an area and yet is left untouched by the local community when it fails, despite the immediate health impact. Conversely, we can have water pumping stations in the Gaza Strip that are repaired and serviced, even during periods of conflict, by technicians with local volunteers assisting. Whether we can conclude with absolute certainty how and why these different perceptions come about, there is a common thread around the concept of social equity and, more generally, social justice (Rawls 1999).

The idea of equity is not to be confused with equality. Equity advances the idea of equal outcome through appropriate opportunity or access, rather than equal allocation of resources or reward. To illustrate, consider a situation where three children wish to watch a football game. The tallest can look over the fence and watch the game. The shorter one stands on a box and looks over the fence. The one in the wheelchair looks through a hole in the fence. Each watches the game but from different vantage points.

The World Bank, in December 2019, launched their 'Reference Tool on Inclusive Infrastructure and Social Equity' with its six action areas:

- stakeholder identification, engagement and empowerment
- governance and capacity building
- policy, regulation and standards
- project planning, development and delivery
- private sector roles and participation
- affordability and optimising finance.

The idea of the value of infrastructure being realised through the sense of its local ownership remains a recurrent theme. It is implicit in the UK's Equality Act 2010, with its nine protected characteristics that connect the current generation's needs. Yet the need for inclusive infrastructure and social equity sometimes needs to be more explicit to guide development towards this sense of local ownership and genuinely sustainable infrastructure. There is always a risk of creating a built environment that is not inclusive or accessible, with limited access to services and barriers to inclusion in society, closing off opportunities and shutting people out of the labour market. The World Bank framework guides governments on accelerating the development and implementation of inclusive infrastructure. But why this emphasis on inclusion as an enabler of sustainability? It is getting to the heart of where that local sense of ownership comes from, inclusive institutions. Also, it perhaps explains how such tools can fail to benefit locals sustainably.

One critical aspect of equity that it does not address is the existing power imbalance between 'global North' and 'global South'. The contemporary economic operating system requires deep capital subsidies from the 'global South' to 'North' (Hickel, 2017) to function. This perversion has not been acknowledged by the World Bank or the International Monetary Fund (IMF). The relocalisation of key parts of the economic cycle would drastically shift that imbalance, though it runs counter to a *Bretton Woods* institutional belief. For example, the Grand Ethiopian Renaissance Dam is deemed a worthy infrastructure development, despite more sustainable options. So despite the six action areas being applied, the dam construction went ahead, to the benefit of 'global North' corporations, while locally the next generation may well be mired in conflict.

Daron Acemoglu and James Robinson (2012) present a compelling argument that inclusive institutions lie behind wealthy nations' success. From colonial examples to modern times, the difference in socioeconomic impact between inclusive institutions and exploitative ones is stark. Inclusive institutions demonstrate this sense of social ownership and equity. In contrast, exploitative ones serve a defined group or particular interest. In some Western countries, the recent political trend to undermine popular trust in public institutions and informed discourse would challenge progress towards social equity.

It's a strong argument, amplified indirectly by Angus Deaton's discussion of the balance between progress and inequality (2013). In essence, when there is an opportunity that a community can realise, there can be progress. This is a blend of recognising the opportunity available, a willingness to seize it and the capacity to benefit from it. The delivery of infrastructure is intimately bound up with this, both enabling access and providing benefit.

This relationship between equity and prosperity, access and poverty, has been at the heart of heated debate for decades. There are essentially two polarised views. The first, promoted by Jeffery Sachs (2005) and championed by the singer Bono, is that increased development spending will address the conditions that give rise to poverty. The other, promoted by Bill Easterly (2006), is that aid corrupts the recipient and produces a dependency culture. Easterly argues that at its heart is the hubris of wealthy nations that they know better than poorer nations. There are no successful demonstrations of either argument. Like all such debates, these positions are passionate and have merit, while the supporting evidence is seemingly curated to fit the argument. Within this spectrum, we find the work of Desha Girod (2015) in the destabilising influence of outside interests (strategic and resource rent) in postconflict rehabilitation, Deaton's examination of inequality (2013) and Lake's examination of state-building (2016).

The challenge that the infrastructure engineer faces in all of this is not whether the infrastructure development will directly impact the economy; it is how to adjust to the local culture and norms. We cannot take a successful model from one project and repeat it in a new location. Each situation is unique, even in the same country. We need to understand the socioeconomic context in which we are working and deliver infrastructure that enables sustainability. We can influence how the infrastructure is delivered and the local benefit, which leads us to the next challenge. How do we engage with the community when community-wide awareness is increasingly fragmented? Sometimes we need to actively enable social capital (Aldrich, 2012) through our planning and delivery.

Exploring community cohesion, John McKnight (1996) found that the incremental professionalisation of traditional community functions in developed countries has weakened the fabric of the community and eroded social capital. He draws on the example of the bereavement counsellor, who has increasingly replaced family and neighbours in care for the bereaved; this forms isolation within the community by removing shared experience. We see similar effects in the zoning of neighbourhoods rather than mixed use, and the design of spaces around the car rather than bicycles and pedestrians. Aldrich (2012) showed that the essence of social capital is communication, and its value during periods of stress and crisis. In many ways, this was the essence of Jane Jacobs' battle with Robert Moses and her fears for the future (Jacobs, 1961).

The relationship between economy and society defines the built environment, even as the same infrastructure enables the functions and services they depend on (Jacobs, 2000; Piketty, 2015). I would not suggest that we must be economists to plan infrastructure. Still, we must understand our role within the economic fabric and influences if we are to deliver sustainable infrastructure. Our interest remains the through-life value of the infrastructure that underpins its sustainability. The *dismal science*, as Thomas Carlyle called economics, is an inexact one, and we must account for these effects in our risk calculations.

3.5. Intelligent resourcing

Remaining with the theme of community ownership and adopting the infrastructure, mindful of the economic context, we return to the idea that the delivery is as important as the service we seek to enable. Vitruvius, the Roman architect, understood this inherently. His simple argument is that if we use local materials and skills, construction, maintenance and repair will be cheaper and quicker to execute (Vitruvius, 2001). The Roman legions realised this principle with standard designs that could be readily adapted to local materials without compromising their function or effectiveness. The principles remain valid 2000 years later, though we might nuance this by using what can be locally resourced. A substantial part of community ownership is a tangible benefit across the community, including developing supply chains and the demand for enhanced capabilities (both professionals and trades). We see local community engagement in the more successful projects. The community engagement around the Thames Tideway Tunnel, London, UK, is such an example in a developed and diversified economy. The USAID-sponsored membrane water treatment plants in the West Indies illustrate the absence of intelligent resourcing in the planning and design of new infrastructure. Intelligent resourcing also means adapting schemes and solutions to local governance.

A 2007 outbreak of Guinea worm infections in Buipe, Ghana, prompted a UNICEF-enabled taskforce with the local district government and regional water agency to construct a small-town water system fed from a high-yield borehole 5 km away. A local water board was established and trained in the system's operation and maintenance, which provided immediate benefit to the residents. After 6 months, one of the pump controls failed. The water board had not collected the user fees and could not pay the external contractor to replace the faulty part. The contractor claimed poor local maintenance and operation. When asked for further funding, UNICEF said that continued funding was the water board's responsibility. The rainy season arrived and the water plant, including the generators, controls and pump house, flooded. The local population reverted to the original infected water supply. Ghana has a decentralised form of government; this task force, with its MDG-funding, was structured top-down through the central government. Elsewhere, smaller non-governmental (aid) organisations had more success developing improved water supplies through local-level project development. We can analyse this project in exquisite detail. The essence remains a lack of intelligent resourcing, both in contractor delivery and in governance structure.

Let's look again at the concept of equity within the concept of intelligent resourcing. We see a direct link to poverty. In their Nobel Prize-winning work on the economics of poverty, Banerjee and Duflo (2011) highlighted the household priorities of putting food on the table today over the children's future health. When we can negate the necessity for such a decision, we can break the generational cycle of poverty. By providing the children of working households with vaccinations, early-years education or care and a nutritious meal each day, the next generation's prospects do not become compromised for today's existence. Within the context of intelligent resourcing, we can expand the local labour pool that we can draw on, particularly after conflict or disaster. In planning our infrastructure's delivery, we can include community measures that draw the community together and invest them in the infrastructure and the subsequently enabled service. When we look holistically, our infrastructure project spans many of the SDGs.

Our infrastructure project can provide local access and benefit through its delivery and operation. How we deliver infrastructure influences the local economy and broader local benefit because of the increased local access through the delivery process from consultation to employment. This economic and social benefit goes beyond addressing poverty (SDG 1) and improving the population's physical, mental and social well-being (SDG 3). It presents an opportunity for local training and development (SDGs 4 and 10) for all people in the community (SDG 5) within a self-sustaining model that builds local supply chains and capabilities (SDGs 8 and 9). Combined, these contribute to a more sustainable and just society (SDG 16). That is in addition to the benefits that the infrastructure is designed to provide. As engineers, we have the opportunity to do enormous good for the community while controlling our costs in infrastructure delivery. That has to be a good thing.

3.6. Acceptable risk

With all that we understand about infrastructure's relationship with the community and how to enhance its overall sustainability (environmental, economic and social), it begs the question of why we don't deliver more sustainable infrastructure. I think this is about a reluctance to do things differently and the associated perception of risk, founded on an arrogance that *we* know better. When I had the opportunity to ask organisations why an infrastructure project didn't pursue a more holistic outcome, the answer always seemed to be about familiarity with the metrics being used, even if they were not correct. When we manage by metrics, we measure what we are familiar with and bias our management decisions (Muller, 2018).

Kahneman (2013) famously described our human preference for assuming familiar patterns over critical analysis. However, organisations' impetus to implement environment, social and governance (ESG) policies and, increasingly, to demonstrate their activities is changing the discussion. For many, particularly given their experience of the COVID-19 pandemic, the desire to know where the fragilities are in an operation is forcing greater interest in evidence over opinion, however expert it might be. We explore the idea of fragility in the next chapter. The issue here is that the frame of reference is changing.

Reporting requirements, initially voluntary, are increasingly becoming mandatory. The most notable among these is TCFD reporting. The need to show how climate change will affect business operations and value, and what the company is doing about it, is driving a reappraisal of how infrastructure can enable that risk treatment. It means that we must think of infrastructure as more than merely an asset. We see this influencing institutions' investment decision-making and how they apply their ESG policies. So when we look at the environmental, economic and social value of the infrastructure, we are immediately exposed to the unexpected consequences that could previously be ignored when it was merely an asset. Does the material selection for our new passive house development have an increased GHG emissions signature that negates any savings in its through-life operation? Will our new road increase the number of traffic casualties and reduce residents' effective life span and health profile along its alignment? Will our investment in capacity building to enable a development project result in a *brain-drain* following project delivery?

The type of hazard no longer compartmentalises our view of risk, which is necessarily holistic, as we trace the direct and indirect consequences of our infrastructure development. For organisations, this will mean having robust and consistent risk criteria that inform decision-making and trusted situational information that can provide business-relevant leading indicators of an approaching hazard. When we know our fragilities and what failure or change can mean for us in context, we can articulate our risk treatment requirements, what we need to measure, a treatment strategy and the governance to ensure that it delivers. There is no coincidence that these are the four categories of TCFD reporting.

3.7. Chapter summary

Formerly considered through a single environmental lens or a financial lens, sustainable development in general, and sustainable infrastructure in particular, is a holistic concept based on an environmental, economic and social framework. It brings our understanding of infrastructure full circle to its purpose and its role and impact on communities over its life. We see sustainable infrastructure as an enabler of services and operations that underpin our society without compromising the ability of future generations. It considers together the effects, direct and indirect, on human health and the natural world and whether it can be financially self-sufficient. It has an essential value defined by its use, but that can be denuded by the harm it can cause.

Sustainable infrastructure cannot be delivered by single-issue concepts of complete streets, abundant access, urban densification, prioritised transit development, and so on. Sustainability in infrastructure is a unifying concept to optimise the environmental, economic and social value of the infrastructure's through-life use in context. Success is as individual as the community, location and situation. It demands a holistic understanding of influences and effects through planning and delivery, and continued operation.

Infrastructure development is judged by stakeholders using evidence and objective metrics that are increasingly accessible by the general public. We can see the effectiveness of sewage treatment systems from satellite imagery, and the owners of the infrastructure are being held to account. Institutional investors and multilateral development lenders are acutely aware of this and the broader social imperative to benefit society with our infrastructure choices. There is a real understanding and desire to use (natural, built and virtual) infrastructure for social good. Infrastructure delivery truly can improve physical, mental and social well-being, advance social equity and improve the world that the next generation will inherit. We have the understanding and the opportunity to deliver such sustainable infrastructure. The only thing holding us back is our intelligent imagination.

An ecological approach demands a thorough understanding of the VSOS, one based on evidence. When we use our familiar models to collect this evidence, we project our bias onto the world around us and only measure what is familiar. We need to create a common reference that is blind to what we think the answer should be. From common reference, we can engage with all stakeholders to identify capabilities, issues, concerns and risks. Our understanding of what this means for our operations and mission can inform our sustainable development strategy, which is ecologically balanced and locally sensitive. Informed risk treatment is inherent to that sustainable development strategy, which is necessarily informed by the common reference.

It is worth noting that our contemporary understanding of economics is dominated by one cultural group representing a small percentage of the global population. Perhaps, the reason that we have found it so challenging to become more (ecologically) sustainable, as a society, and deliver more sustainable infrastructure, as engineers, is that we are locked in the same mindset. It may be time for us to reconsider how we relate to Nature and other peoples, have the humility to accept other perspectives and deliver real improvements in (physical, mental and social) well-being rather than material benefit. Engineers cannot make that change, but we can enable it through the infrastructure we plan and deliver.

BIBLIOGRAPHY

Acemoglu D and Robinson JA (2012) *Why Nations Fail: The Origins of Power, Prosperity and Poverty*. Profile Books, London, UK.

Aicher J (1998) *Designing Healthy Cities: Prescriptions, Principles and Practice*. Krieger Publishing, Malabar, FL, USA.

Ainger C and Fenner R (2014) *Sustainable Infrastructure: Principles into Practice*. ICE Publishing, London, UK.

Aldrich DP (2012) *Building Resilience: Social Capital in Post-disaster Recovery*. University of Chicago Press, Chicago, IL, USA.

AlWaer H and Illsley B (eds) (2017) *Rethinking Master Planning: Creating Quality Places*. ICE Publishing, London, UK.

Anholt S (2010) Definitions of place branding – working towards a resolution. *Place Branding and Public Diplomacy* **6(1)**: 1–10.

Arnstein SR (1969) A ladder of citizen participation. *Journal of the American Planning Association* **35(4)**: 216–224.

Ashford NA and Hall RP (2018) *Technology, Globalization, and Sustainable Development: Transforming the Industrial State*. Routledge, Abingdon, UK.

Banerjee AV and Duflo E (2011) *Poor Economics: A Radical Rethinking of the Way to Fight Global Poverty*. Public Affairs, New York, NY, USA.

BC CDC (British Columbia Centre for Disease Control) (2019) *Mental Health & Well-being: Considerations for the Built Environment*. Provincial Health Services Authority, Vancouver, BC, Canada.

BFCA (Builders for Climate Action) (2019) *Low-Rise Buildings as a Climate Change Solution*. BFCA. https://www.buildersforclimateaction.org/whitepaper1.html (accessed 31/03/2021).

Blockley DI and Godfrey P (2017) *Doing it Differently: Systems for Rethinking Infrastructure*, 2nd edn. ICE Publishing, London, UK.

Brandon PS, Lombardi P and Shen GQ (2017) *Future Challenges in Evaluating and Managing Sustainable Development in the Built Environment*. Wiley Blackwell, Chichester, UK.

CAF (Corporacion Andina de Fomento) (2020) *Management Policies*. CAF, Caracas, Venezuela. https://www.caf.com/media/2244161/caf-management-policies-sep2019.pdf (accessed 14/07/2020).

Canada Green Building Council (2021) https://www.cagbc.org/ (accessed 30/03/2021).

Capra F and Luisi PL (2014) *The Systems View of Life: A Unifying Vision*. Cambridge University Press, Cambridge, UK.

Deaton A (2013) *The Great Escape: Health, Wealth and the Origins of Inequality*. Princeton University Press, Princeton, NJ, USA.

Dixon T, Connaughton J and Green S (eds) (2018) *Sustainable Futures in the Built Environment to 2050: A Foresight Approach to Construction and Development*. Wiley, Hoboken, NJ, USA.

Easterly W (2006) *The White Man's Burden: Why the West's Efforts to Aid the Rest Have Done So Much Ill and So Little Good*. Oxford University Press, Oxford, UK.

Girod DM (2015) *Explaining Post-Conflict Reconstruction*. Oxford University Press, Oxford, UK.

Hickel J (2017) Aid in reverse: how poor countries develop rich countries. *The Guardian*, 14 Jan. https://www.theguardian.com/global-development-professionals-network/2017/jan/14/aid-in-reverse-how-poor-countries-develop-rich-countries (accessed 30/03/2021).

HMG (Her Majesty's Government) (2010) Equality Act 2010. The Stationery Office, London, UK.

Jacobs J (1961) *The Death and Life of Great American Cities*. Random House, Toronto, ON, Canada. (Republished 1993.)

Jacobs J (2000) *The Nature of Economies*. Random House, Toronto, ON, Canada.

Kahneman D (2013) *Thinking, Fast and Slow*. Anchor Canada, Toronto, ON, Canada.

Kolbert E (2014) *The Sixth Extinction: An Unnatural History*, 1st edn. Henry Holt, New York, NY, USA.

Lake DA (2016) *The Statebuilder's Dilemma: On the Limits of Foreign Intervention*. Cornell University Press, Ithica, NY, USA.

LASU (Lagos State University) (2000) Indira Gandhi's Speech at the Stockholm. Conference in 1972. *LASU-LAWS Environmental Blog*. http://lasulawsenvironmental.blogspot.com/2012/07/indira-gandhis-speech-at-stockholm.html (accessed 31/03/2021).

McKnight J (1996) *The Careless Society: Community and its Counterfeits*. Basic Books, New York, NY, USA.

Merna T and Al-Thani FF (2018) *Financing Infrastructure Projects: A Practical Guide*, 2nd edn. ICE Publishing, London, UK.

Mirza M and Shafqat A (2017) Infrastructure crisis – a proposed national infrastructure policy for Canada. *Canadian Journal of Civil Engineering* **44(7)**: 539–548.

Miska C, Szöcs I and Schiffinger M (2018) Culture's effects on corporate sustainability practices: a multi-domain and multi-level view. *Journal of World Business* **53(2)**: 263–279.

Muller JZ (2018) *The Tyranny of Metrics*. Princeton University Press, Princeton, NJ, USA.

Nidumolu R, Prahalad CK and Rangaswami MR (2009) Why sustainability is now the key driver of innovation. *Harvard Business Review*, Sept. 2009. https://hbr.org/2009/09/why-sustainability-is-now-the-key-driver-of-innovation (accessed 30/03/2021).

Norris G (2015) *Handprint-Based NetPositive Assessment*. Centre for Health and the Global Environment, Harvard TH Chan School of Public Health, Boston, MA, USA.

Piketty T (2015) *The Economics of Inequality*. Belknap Press of Harvard University Press, Cambridge, MA, USA.

Racusin JD and Magwood C (2020) *Low-Rise Buildings as a Climate Change Solution*. BFCA. https://www.nehers.org/Data/Sites/1/media/training/webinars/presentations/embodied-carbon-2020.pdf (accessed 31/03/2021).

Rawls J (1999) *A Theory of Justice*, revised edn. Belknap Press of Harvard University Press, Cambridge, MA, USA.

Sachs J (2005) *The End of Poverty: Economic Possibilities for Our Time*. Penguin, New York, NY, USA.

Sanneh ES (2018) *Systems Thinking for Sustainable Development: Climate Change and the Environment*. Springer, Cham, Switzerland.

TCFD (Task Force on Climate-related Financial Disclosures) (2019) *Status Report*. TCFD, Basel, Switzerland.

Thiele LP (2016) *Sustainability*. Polity, Cambridge, UK.

UN (United Nations) (2015) *The Millennium Development Goals Report 2015*. United Nations Publication, New York, NY, USA.

UNEP (UN Environment Programme) (2006) Principles for Responsible Investment. https://www.unpri.org/pri/ (accessed 14/07/2020).

UNEP (2019) *Global Environment Outlook 6: Healthy Planet, Healthy People (GEO 6)*. Cambridge University Press, UK.

UN ESCAP (UN Economic and Social Commission for Asia and the Pacific) (2015) *Integrating the Three Dimensions of Sustainable Development: A Framework and Tools*. UN ESCAP, Bangkok, Thailand.

UNHCR (UN High Commissioner for Refugees) (2017) *The Sustainable Development Goals and Addressing Statelessness*. https://www.refworld.org/docid/58b6e3364.html (accessed 14/07/2020).

US Green Building Council (2021) https://www.usgbc.org/ (accessed 30/03/2021).

Vitruvius (2001) *Ten Books on Architecture*. Cambridge University Press, Cambridge, UK. (New translation by Rowland ID with commentary by Howe TN.)

WCED (World Commission on Environment and Development) (1987) *Report of the World Commission on Environment and Development: Our Common Future*. Oxford University Press, Oxford, UK.

Weil FD (2020) Researching crime after a disaster: what we can learn from a large survey in New Orleans after Hurricane Katrina. *American Behavioral Scientist*. **64(8)**: 1111–1128, 10.1177/0002764220938107.

World Bank (2019) Inclusive Infrastructure. https://inclusiveinfra.gihub.org/overview/ (accessed 31/03/2021).

WRI (World Resources Institute) (2004) *The Greenhouse Gas Protocol: A Corporate Accounting and Reporting Standard*, revised edn. WRI, Washington, DC, USA. https://ghgprotocol.org/sites/default/files/standards/ghg-protocol-revised.pdf (accessed 14/07/2020).

WRI (2011) *Greenhouse Gas (GHG) Protocol: Corporate Value Chain (Scope 3) Accounting and Reporting Standard*. WRI, Washington, DC, USA. https://ghgprotocol.org/sites/default/files/standards/Corporate-Value-Chain-Accounting-Reporing-Standard_041613_2.pdf (accessed 14/07/2020).

Yates JK and Castro-Lacouture D (2016) *Sustainability in Engineering Design and Construction*. CRC, Boca Raton, FL, USA.

FURTHER READING

Unsurprisingly, there is an extraordinary amount written on sustainability and sustainable infrastructure, from government policies and visioning to critical examinations of the minutiae. There are few better explanations of sustainable infrastructure than Charles Ainger and Richard Fenner's *Sustainable Infrastructure: Principles into Practice* (2014). It has a more structured approach to the subject matter than has been possible with this chapter. In the same vein, those wishing to explore the variety of financial tools available for infrastructure financing would do well with Merna and Al-Thani's *Financing Infrastructure Projects* (2018). More generally, you may wish to refresh your perspective of a systems approach with *Doing it Differently* by Blockley and Godfrey (2017). I find it complementary to the Gemini Principles suggested in the further reading section of Chapter 2.

The question of acceptable risk – acceptable to whom? – is a fascinating one. It connects intimately with the challenge of unintended consequences, foreseeability and planned outcomes, which is rarely objective. There are many examinations of such issues with the benefit of hindsight, though few seem capable of not taking a position on the issues. Opinion pieces of planned and recent developments can provide a useful insight into other perspectives that are sometimes lost in the planning process, such as the High Line in New York (Moss, 2012). However, it is also useful to see what others are saying and doing about making things better, influencing substantive change. The World Economic Forum (WEF, 2021) produces a steady stream of video clips showing small and large-scale examples of what can be done, while organisations like Circle Economy (2021) are enabling these changes.

Finally, I strongly recommend that you read the SDGs; read the goals and their component indicators (UN, 2021). Many can quote them and refer to them, but few can actually say what they mean. There is so much more to them than is immediately apparent. I have touched on the goals in this chapter, but their true value in infrastructure planning is how we apply our imaginations to delivering them. How we plan and deliver infrastructure is as important as what we deliver. A sound understanding of the SDGs and intelligent imagination in applying them to your next project will guide the most satisfying further reading.

Ainger C and Fenner R (2014) *Sustainable Infrastructure: Principles into Practice.* ICE Publishing, London, UK.

Blockley DI and Godfrey P (2017) *Doing it Differently: Systems for Rethinking Infrastructure*, 2nd edn. ICE Publishing, London, UK.

Circle Economy (2021) www.circle-economy.com (accessed 31/03/2021).

Merna T and Al-Thani FF (2018) *Financing Infrastructure Projects: A Practical Guide*, 2nd edn. ICE Publishing, London, UK.

Moss J (2012) Disney World on the Hudson. *The New York Times* 21 Aug. https://www.nytimes.com/2012/08/22/opinion/in-the-shadows-of-the-high-line.html (accessed 31/03/2021).

UN (United Nations) (2021) Make the SDGs a Reality. www.sdgs.un.org (accessed 31/03/2021).

WEF (World Economic Forum) (2021) www.weforum.org (accessed 31/03/2021).

ice Publishing

Hay, Alexander H
ISBN 978-0-7277-6562-8
https://doi.org/10.1680/pris.65628.075

Chapter 4
Resilient infrastructure: adapting to an uncertain future?

Much has been written and said about resilience over the last couple of decades. It is one of those concepts that users each adapt to their message. Sadly, the result is that it means everything and nothing to many. Yet, it is fundamental to our understanding of infrastructure systems. As with sustainability, it may be useful to look at its origins and the foundational concepts that gave rise to its application.

In 1973, Buzz Holling published a paper in the *Annual Review of Ecology and Systematics* entitled 'Resilience and stability of ecological systems'. He distinguished between resilience and stability. Stability, he explained, 'represents the ability of a system to return to an equilibrium state after a temporary disturbance; the more rapidly it returns and the less it fluctuates, the more stable it would be.' Conversely, resilience is a 'measure of the persistence of systems and of their ability to absorb change and disturbance and still maintain the same relationships between populations or state variables.' This idea can be developed to reflect a system's ability to self-organise, learn and adapt (Gunderson and Holling 2002).

As we see it applied more broadly to socioeconomic systems, the essentials remain valid in that the concept applies to the systems' ability to absorb, learn, adjust and adapt. It is wrong to describe inanimate objects as resilient. Until structures are capable of self-healing and adaptation, they are not resilient. They can be robust. Robustness and resilience are not the same; they are not interchangeable.

However, the concept of resilience resonates very closely with infrastructure because infrastructure is merely the physical manifestation of a system, and it is the system that can be resilient. The infrastructure enables its system resilience. We will explore this in detail. The concept also resonates with the idea of fortifications. Fortifications are not about the physical hardening of a structure, although that is undoubtedly one of the many tools used. Fortifications are about the protection of a capability. If we build a castle that requires many soldiers to defend it, we limit the military force capacity and impede its original purpose. An effective fortification does not hinder the operating efficiency of its purpose. It is capable of adapting to changing stresses and shocks. This idea is explored in Chapter 5.

The idea of infrastructure being resilient because the system that it manifests is resilient reflects the peculiarity of infrastructure value. You will recall from Chapter 2 that its use determines the value of infrastructure, the service that it enables. The infrastructure has no value if the service is not used. Similarly, the reliability of the service reflects the reliability of the infrastructure (system). That is not the same as the asset or structure being reliable.

This chapter explores how infrastructure enables a resilient operation. In doing so, the infrastructure is resilient, as the physical property of the system that is made resilient. We begin by examining the concept of operational resilience and how it is spatially and functionally defined. This examination leads into the core concept of resilient systems being safe-to-fail and how we can understand the threats to a system's reliable operation and purpose. Continuity of purpose is discussed in more detail, drawing on previously introduced incident sequencing and carrying capacity, and the relationship between the infrastructure and the human domain, specifically community resilience, is examined. The chapter concludes with an examination of consequence and black swans around the concept of reasonable foreseeability.

4.1. Operational resilience

When we look at resilience as a system property, an active property or capability, it begs the question, 'How do we measure it?' Before answering this directly, it is useful to note how resilience was progressively applied to infrastructure. The link is through the services that the infrastructure enables. The then president of the Rockefeller Foundation and architect of the Rockefeller 100 Resilient Cities, Judith Rodin, articulated her views in *The Resilience Dividend* (2014). She explored the increasing interconnectedness of our world and expressed the urgent need to build resilience, defining it as the ability to bounce back quickly and efficiently.

Such calls for resilience in society were not new (Flynn, 2007). This is something that humanity has inherently understood for centuries. Resilience principles are evident in how Cyrus the Great laid out the Persian Empire (Xenophon, 2000). We can see them in the Spanish Court's direction on designing cities in the New World (Butzer, 1992), the layout of frontier towns in the wilderness of the North American prairies and the British domestic war effort from 1940 to 1944. For whatever reason, they were broadly absent in the American model of town planning following World War II, and, when applied, then only in 'mission-critical facilities' design. Following the end of the Cold War, around 1990, they had seemingly disappeared from planning and design practice, even as the world began to change in unpredictable ways.

As the consequences and frequency of catastrophic events increase and their predictability decreases, we can no longer rely on past experiences to indicate the future, much less the hazards that our infrastructure will face over its life. This lack of predictability in the risk context means that we must know what we wish to be capable of at a defined point in the future and design our systems to adapt and respond to disruptions. We must focus on how our operations, both the essential services and the infrastructure's functions that enable them, will reliably continue in the face of hazards unknown at the design stage. This isn't as great a challenge as it might at first appear.

When we look at case studies of disasters and identify our lessons, it is remarkable how often these studies focus on the event rather than the operation. If we plan to perform better against a repeat of the last event, we're unlikely to be prepared for the next catastrophic event. However, suppose we plan our operation to cope with disruptions and failures in the subsystems that it depends on to stay in business. In that case, we are better prepared for the next unknown catastrophic event. We can predict and control our operation, while it would seem that the thing that we expend most effort on is often the very thing that we cannot control. As human beings, we tend to pattern our thoughts and jump to conclusions when observing familiar elements. It takes a somewhat more conscious effort to operate in a nebulous risk context and explore how the intangible will cause failure in our systems (Kahneman, 2013).

For infrastructure, we need to focus on operational resilience, which the University of Toronto Centre for Resilience of Critical Infrastructure (CRCI, 2021) defines as the 'essential ability of an operation to respond to and absorb the effects of shocks and stresses and to recover as rapidly as possible normal capacity and efficiency.' The CRCI's working definition of operational resilience allows us to separate the resilience of infrastructure systems and the essential services they support from the socioeconomic fabric of the communities in the VSOS. This is important because the nature of social resilience, and what it takes to make a city or region resilient, is not operational; it's behavioural. We shouldn't confuse the two. Instead, we need to recognise and work with both.

Resilience is about balance and the capacity for components to compensate for deficiencies in others. Resilience is about the operation; the infrastructure must enable a resilient operation. This means that our infrastructure system must be safe-to-fail, even as the essential service that it enables must be safe-to-fail, if it is to support community resilience. The same goes for corporations, as it does for communities. For a corporation to be resilient, its operations must be resilient. Put simply, if it isn't operating, it isn't in business. This relationship between the operational systems and the socioeconomic fabric they enable is represented by the VSOS and lies at the core of effective infrastructure planning. We explore this in detail in Chapter 6.

The most tangible and standard application of resilience practice is through demand and dependency management. This is seen in many of the procedural approaches we might find in various jurisdictions and is readily codified. The idea is to manage how much of a particular resource we need (demand management) to have more source diversification options (dependency management).

This simplified approach works when we consider our operation in context. When we lose sight of the context, we can miss the correlation of risks, the convergence in supply chain origin and resource competition during a crisis. In our risk audits, these are common issues. We also find that many forget that human beings make mistakes, particularly under stress, and don't always act as they are supposed to. Few expect the local authority to requisition their diesel during a prolonged power outage, despite published emergency management protocols. The point is that if we wish to conduct demand and dependency management as part of our resilience planning, we must consider our operation in context and carefully test our solutions against most likely and worst-case scenarios. This only works if we understand our operation in context, not assumed, and therefore the inherent risks and vulnerabilities. Some examples will probably help here.

A river overflows its banks, flooding a retail park, along with part of the neighbourhood. The flooding affects an electrical substation that supplies the retail park, as well as the park itself. The substation is shut down as a precaution as the floodwaters approach. The retail park has the mandated emergency measures and transfers to diesel generator electricity supply for safe and complete close-down. The standby supply lasts 2 h, as required in the by-laws, but there is no diesel replenishment when the header tanks run out. Later that night, some individuals help themselves to some of the stock. The retail park is fully compliant, but the stock was not adequately secure. If there is a need for security, it doesn't disappear in a crisis. There is a business continuity plan, yet the skills and leadership necessary to respond responsibly and minimise losses are absent. In this example, the emergency service response was also impeded, owing to the flooding, because the local division or precinct house was on the wrong side of the flooded area, as were the stationary engineers contracted to keep the place running in an emergency.

A supermarket lost its electricity supply on the hottest day of the year when a fire at the local substation resulted in a 4 day blackout to part of the city. The supermarket had considered reducing their energy consumption but decided not to, as it was felt that the options would have impeded the customer experience. Instead, they invested in a standby generator with a 12 h tank to keep the whole operation running. On the day, no stationary engineer was available to synchronise the standby generator, and so the manager started it. The standby power supply failed. In the 6 h that it took for the stationary engineer to respond, all refrigerated foods had to be removed from the chests and destroyed. Much of the frozen produce was also destroyed. The contingency plans considered only a power failure in isolation. They hadn't allowed for other calls on their contracted engineering services. The supermarket was then closed for cleaning and could only restock and open once cleared by the municipal inspector. The losses in stock and trading were severe.

A professional services firm in a commercial office space lost power, among other services, during an ice storm. They had invested in standby power systems to protect the electricity supply to their servers, which held all client files and their telecoms system. The data vault had standby cooling and an uninterruptable power supply (UPS) that more than adequately covered the 10 min agreed with the property manager before their *contracted* standby generator would be brought online. All reserve diesel was precontracted to ensure roughly 2 weeks of supply at minimum load. The firm's risk engineers had identified how to manage down demand to keep the firm operating in a crisis. The first contracted diesel resupply could not get to the property because the same ice storm that had brought down the electricity pylons had left sufficient ice accretion on the roads to prevent tanker truck deliveries. At this point, the authority requisitioned all fuel supplies to distribute to hospitals and emergency services. The business interruption for this firm was significant since many of their (international) clients were unmoved by the firm's challenges and expected a timely service.

In each of these cases, the insured's argument was that the business income losses were not reasonably foreseeable. This argument will depend on the jurisdiction and what a judge considers 'reasonable'. However, if we distil out these cases' core elements, we can say that the reasonably foreseeable threshold needn't be very high. If we build in a floodplain, whether primary or secondary, we can expect to be flooded at some point. This includes the loss of anything below the flood level that is not suitably protected. Furthermore, if we depend on a substation located in the floodplain for our electricity supply, it is reasonable to assume that we will lose that supply if it is flooded. While that may be a syllogism, it still isn't unreasonable for laypersons to recognise. We can also say that if we are flooded, then our neighbours are likely to be too. None of these associations is particularly challenging, but each one looks beyond the business area at the evolving risk context, as it affects us. So much of this comes down to critical thinking, a holistic perspective and some deductive reasoning. We can better understand these contextual risks by conducting a location risk assessment (LRA), and we can also look at clustering the operational resilience of a resource dependency.

4.2. A spatial concept

An LRA is a simple geospatial analysis tool that establishes what is known as a *tableau*. This archaic label is little more than an acknowledgement that the documented origins of the process are Sébastien la Prestre Vauban's terrain intelligence (Barros *et al.*, 2007). The tableau spatially describes the site of the operation in its context. It identifies what hazards can affect the site directly and indirectly through its operational dependencies. There are conventions around the designation of space. Our operating area, which we can directly control, is designated the area of operations (AOO). It is surrounded by the area in which we have influence but no control. For example, this might be the public roads around our sports stadium. We influence the management of that space because of the crowds that will traverse the area during match days.

Similarly, we may have a busy industrial site and need to maintain unimpeded heavy goods vehicle access and laybys along the approach. We would negotiate these with the local authority. This area is known as the area of influence (AOI). Beyond that is the area in which a hazard forms, and we would monitor it to provide us with a warning of an approaching danger. Known as the area of interest, this can extend over vast distances to include the water catchment for the river that runs beside our site or the resource supply chain for our works, or simply the areas in which our staff live. The operational laydown – our works and dependency chains – is overlaid on the tableau. The LRA includes the geology, hydrology, topography and hydrography, and the meteorology of the site. These provide context for the identified sources and vectors of natural and human-made hazards. The LRA is an evidence-only analysis. This is not the time for opinions about likelihood. The most significant value is when the analysis identifies possible hazards, directly and indirectly affecting our AOO. Most of the time, one can conduct an LRA using only open-source information.

While the LRA identifies where possible flood levels may come to and what third-party control systems our risk exposure depend on, we still need to limit the consequence of a failure as it affects our operation. This gets to the heart of the question around the reliability of service. In Canada, as in many other jurisdictions, the local electricity utility will not guarantee supply. As we discussed, the increasing concentration of value is accompanied by an increased sensitivity to supply interruptions, and reliability has become a critical consideration in operational risk management. For some high-value operations, a simple financial analysis of the supply risk has led to independent generation and the ability to *island*. Islanding is when a site separates itself from the main supply grid.

In some cases, corporations have decided to island altogether. While this may make pure risk-financial sense, it doesn't make sense operationally because there can be no partnership with the utility and redundancy of supply – islanding exchanges one single point of failure for another. Better, therefore, to be able to island, as necessary. Some utilities, sensitive to these issues, are reconfiguring their infrastructure to create customer clusters in which there is some generation, storage and load sharing. This concept involves more than micro-grids and can apply at different levels of laydown.

For example, we might designate a block in a residential neighbourhood as a *panel*. Houses may have photovoltaic arrays, type-3 electric vehicle charging stations and smart energy management within the *panel*. This means that electric vehicles provide home and *panel* storage. The smart energy management system assigns energy as it is needed, so when the grid connection is interrupted, users across the *panel* are prioritised. We'll explore how we calculate the reduced levels of demand when we look at incident sequencing. Inherently, the *panel* area has a minimum duration of continued, albeit reduced, energy usage should the main supply be lost. A similar arrangement would exist at the *cluster* level, which would group like *panels* together with some centralised storage. Each *panel* area is a single consumer-generator in the *cluster*. The utility infrastructure will allow the automated 'trading' of energy between *panels*. We group a number of *clusters* into *districts* under similar arrangements, the difference being that while *panels* and *districts* are geographically bounded, *clusters* don't need to be. There are any number of variations on this basic theme, depending on the local regulations. What is particularly interesting, though, is that it provides a useful model for a more efficient initial laydown of electricity infrastructure than the traditional mass transmission and *push* of energy to consumers – something to consider in new development and reconstruction.

4.3. A functional concept

All of this brings us to the core relationship between a service and its enabling infrastructure. It is the relationship between the concentration of demand for a service and the infrastructure's capacity to support it. This is known as the demand density and carrying capacity. A surprisingly simple concept, it has remained at the centre of infrastructure systems research for several years. It promises to stay there for many years to come. Demand density is the concentration of demand for a resource or service per unit area, typically measured per square kilometre or hectare. The demand density has a profile that reflects changes over the routine of the day, week and season. The carrying capacity of infrastructure is measured in terms of resource or service supply and capability. This dual measurement of carrying capacity is similar to the double metric of resilience, performance and capability. The resilience metric states the normal range of supply and what it falls back to when one of its dependencies is compromised.

For example, consider a fire hydrant system, recognising that the hydrant is part of the potable water supply in some jurisdictions. The carrying capacity of the system provides x m^3 at y kPa under normal conditions. However, there will be a period when the surcharge pumps stop in a grid power failure until standby power starts. The system carrying capacity reduces to a m^3 at b kPa. Therefore, the fire hydrant system's carrying capacity would be described as 'Serviceable: x m^3 @ y kPa; Emergency a m^3 @ b kPa', at a designated node. This metric would show an emergency capacity of zero for a traditional monolithic electricity network, yet there would still be a functional capacity under the clustering configuration. We will return to this idea later. Note also that when emergency capacities are time-limited, that is, they draw on a finite emergency store, the emergency capacity will carry a time qualifier or risk horizon. We'll explore this further in Chapter 6.

We've talked about the reliability of supply, managing our operation to reduce our exposure to loss and recover efficient functionality quickly, and the idea of reducing to a lower sustainable level of performance in a crisis. This begs the question of how we calculate these different levels of performance and the operation's time tolerance at a reduced level of performance. The method is a relatively simple one, known as incident sequencing. It is a graphical tool that relates an operation's performance over time through an incident to its eventual recovery. The area under the graph can be used for WCR calculations and comparisons, and resources can be identified for each designated level of performance by duration.

First, let's orientate ourselves to the incident sequence graph (Figure 4.1). The vertical (y) axis is the performance of the operation. We can designate the operation that the incident sequence describes at any level, from an individual function to the operation of a municipal service or fractional distillation column in a refinery. The organisation's risk criteria will determine how performance is measured. This can range from pairs of shoes made per day to MWh energy consumed to tonnes of steel produced. We can also use it for a capability, such as providing fire response coverage in a municipality, using a population percentage within 10 min response. The horizontal (x) axis is time, typically measured in hours and days, though, for some operations, such as data centres, it is measured in seconds or minutes.

Refer to Figure 4.1. Tracing from left to right, an operation's standard profile begins at its routine level of performance. At t_0, an incident occurs, and the

Figure 4.1 The incident sequence (graph adapted from Hay (2016a))

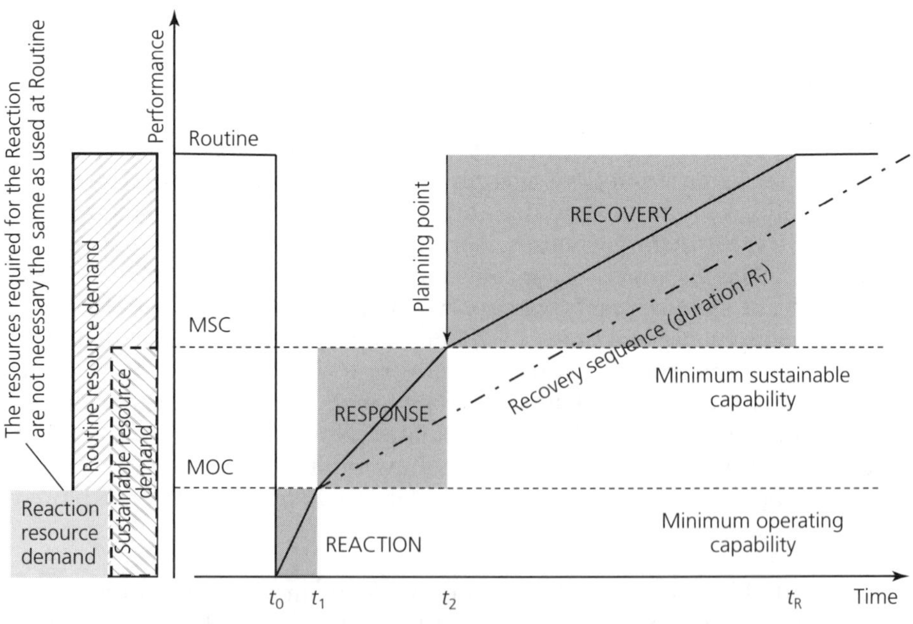

performance drops to zero, or very nearly zero. There then follows an automatic reaction, irrespective of what has caused the failure. This reaction may be the continued supply from a UPS unit, an emergency generator kicking in or an automated secondary function shutdown. The reaction period is an important one, and we will explore this both in this chapter and the next. This reaction brings us to the minimum operating capability (MOC), which is the minimum level of performance associated with staying *alive* and has a time limit. There then follows a period of deliberate response. The response is situation-specific, with resources allocated to restore function as necessary to achieve a stable level of performance. The response brings us to the minimum sustainable capability (MSC), which refers to a stable level of performance that can be maintained indefinitely (theoretically). At the MSC, the operation is not making money or growing, but it isn't losing money or shrinking either. A useful initial calculation of MSC is the net-zero cash flow level of performance, for example. Once the operation is stable, it can then begin recovery, a strictly sequenced restoration of functions.

A paramedic colleague of mine objects vehemently to this following analogy, but I think it serves our purposes here. Consider a serious accident in which the victim is bleeding, and the victim's heart stops. There is little point in patching up the bleeding if there is no heartbeat. The MOC is the heartbeat; however, it cannot be sustained long if the patient bleeds out. There needs to be a systematic response to bring the patient to a stable condition, the MSC, before anything else can be done, including recovery. There is an all-important planning point (PP) in any incident. It is the time tolerance of the operation or market. It denotes the time that we have available to us to restore stable operations, specifically the MSC. The PP can be as short as 10 s for information and communication technology (ICT) operations. However, the default today would appear to be 8 a.m. the next business day for most applications. Market tolerance of service interruption has steadily reduced over the last decade, as we become accustomed to near-instant access to information and service response around the clock. The PP will be specific to the operation, jurisdiction and risk context in which it exists.

4.4. Safe-to-fail

Consider a key asset in an infrastructure system, such as a bridge that connects an island with the mainland. The bridge is part of a broader transport system that may include ferries and other bridges and a network of roads on either side of the crossing. What would a closure of that bridge mean, a failure of the subsystem that the bridge represents? This failure could be structural, owing to a span collapsing or a major accident that closes both carriageways. It might be a precaution, in response to an extreme weather forecast. In the case of a structural failure, we will be keen to know that the failure does not cause immediate harm. This is termed 'fail-safe'. However, what about the operational consequences of the bridge closure? There is a system failure. Operationally, it means that the bridge crossing is no longer available, affecting the traffic flow between the island and the mainland.

In terms of the transport system's purpose, it may represent a complete loss of connection and hence a loss of emergency services access, other than by air. When we look at the broader system that the bridge is a part of, we can determine whether the bridge failure's impact means a loss of operational capability or purpose. Perhaps it compromises the unifying (strategic) purpose of the transport system. If the loss of a component system does not compromise the system's operational or unifying purpose, we can say that it is safe-to-fail. The functional purpose may be compromised, but the operational purpose is unaffected. However, the purpose is both the capability to do something and the carrying capacity to meet demand. In an emergency, we recognise that there will be a reduced demand centred on essential needs only. Therefore, if our transport system can continue its operational purpose when the bridge fails, safe-to-fail becomes a question of whether the continued functionality is sufficient to meet the essential operational demands. Safe-to-fail means that the island–mainland transport system can continue to provide the crossing capability at the volume required to meet essential demands if the bridge fails. Note that in evacuation planning, this emergency demand may well represent peak capacity.

Safe-to-fail is necessarily a systems view. Fail-safe is typically the basis for industry standards concerned with protecting workers, consumers and the public from any harm arising from an asset or process failure. Fail-safe will not result in a resilient system because it is blind to the purpose of the system. The first step in any resilience planning is the systems view of purpose and how to assure, as far as reasonably practicable, the continuity of purpose in the event of a failure.

This concept of continuity of purpose is being incorporated into the Canadian National Master Specification (National Research Council Canada, 2020) as a characteristic of system performance and residual capacity in the event of a component or subsystem failure. It will eventually cascade down to local building codes and specifications. It is also reflected in the commissioning process for completed systems.

There are five commissioning levels for completed works.

1. *Factory witness testing*. Factory testing of components or pre-assembled systems.
2. *Component start-up*. The field testing of installed component function and compliance with standards.
3. *Equipment testing*. The functional testing of an equipment package to the design performance specification as part of the operating systems.
4. *System and interface testing*. The operational testing of a complete system, its efficiency of operation and its connectivity with other systems.
5. *Integrated systems testing*. The performance and capacity testing of the system of systems through a series of predetermined failure scenarios.

Level 5 commissioning is more commonly associated with mission-critical facilities. However, it was more common in infrastructure planning for much of the twentieth century, until the end of the Cold War (about 1989 to 1990). Today, as the consequences of failure are becoming more pronounced, with impacts reaching far beyond a failed system's immediate context, owners require a higher degree of assurance that the completed system of systems will perform as designed. Consider a new general hospital. The local health authority has clearly stated the hospital's service criteria: patient care, patient safety and staff safety. In the event of a crisis, none of these criteria may be compromised. Proceeding through the different levels of commissioning during the project, beneficial occupancy is conditional on successful level 5 commissioning of the integrated hospital systems against these three criteria. If any of the test scenarios causes a possible compromise of these criteria, beneficial occupancy does not occur. The commissioning of the Oakville Trafalgar Memorial Hospital in Ontario, Canada, 2016–2017, is a particularly good example. Level 5 commissioning is the test for safe-to-fail.

Safe-to-fail provides a holistic assessment of the ability of a system of systems to meet essential requirements during failure or crisis. It can assure continued capacity when conditions have changed, such as occupancy, use and climate. It focuses on the capacity of the system (of systems) to adapt to failure rather than applied threats. However, to simulate a failure, we need to know how threats, hazards and global contextual change will affect the system. We need to build scenarios against which we can assess our system. We have established where our operational assets and dependencies are in time and space and the risks inherent to our location with the LRA. We can run automated assessment applications in our industrial control systems to see how a cyberattack or system failure will affect us and its consequences on our operations and broader systems. We need to understand better the behaviour of these threats and hazards and especially how we should prepare for them. This means that we must understand how quickly threats and hazards manifest and what that means for our reaction and response.

4.5. Hazard travel time

The hazard travel time (HTT) is the time taken for the threat or hazard to travel from the first point of detection to when it reaches the target. We know from our LRA where it can come from and its path to the target. The first step in analysing the hazard is to establish what we are dealing with. Recognise, of course, that the nature of the hazard can change with the trends in the risk context. For example, the warming associated with climate change may melt snow in the Canadian Rockies faster than historically recorded. When combined with a late thaw and rain, flooding in the Bow River can become more likely and more severe. This can significantly change the risk parameters for a major bridge rebuild in downtown Calgary, for example.

We need to start with an identification of hazards. The LRA will have exposed some, others will be identified from a scan of the historical records, and there may be others. At this stage, we are less concerned with drawing up a comprehensive list of possible hazards and more on the most likely and most severe. Remember that operational resilience is about the ability to respond, adapt and recover from shocks and stresses, not to defeat them. An in-depth analysis of the risk profiles and risk criteria will follow in Chapter 5.

We build our threat spectrum. It is a severity estimate of individual threats and hazards. The base of the threat spectrum is the statistical level of threat, known as the baseline threat. It is always possible that the actual threat falls below this level in severity. Still, we know that this is what has happened previously, and that is what we must prepare for as a minimum. More on this later. The top of the threat spectrum is defined by the lesser of how bad the threat can get, known as the maximum realisable threat capability (MRTC), and how much we are willing to deal with before we relocate elsewhere or cease to operate, known as the maximum acceptable risk (MAR).

The baseline threat is assigned a value of zero and the lesser of MRTC and MAR a value of one. All of the assessed threats are collected together and represented as spokes in a threat wheel (Figure 4.2). We will explore the threat spectrum and threat wheel further in Chapter 5. Still, it is important to note that everything in this process is based on evidence and not opinion. Therefore, rather than saying that the river could not possibly flood a metre above its dykes, look at how deep the floodwaters can physically get. Any consideration of likelihood needs to be left out of the analysis at this stage. The HTT for each spoke of the wheel, each threat spectrum, is now analysed.

No hazard exists in isolation. Some conditions give rise to a hazard, and these conditions have indicators. It is, therefore, possible to identify the presence of a hazard. As a hazard moves and affects its operating context, it will generate further indicators of its magnitude and direction. From these indicators, we can

Figure 4.2 Threat spectrum and threat wheel

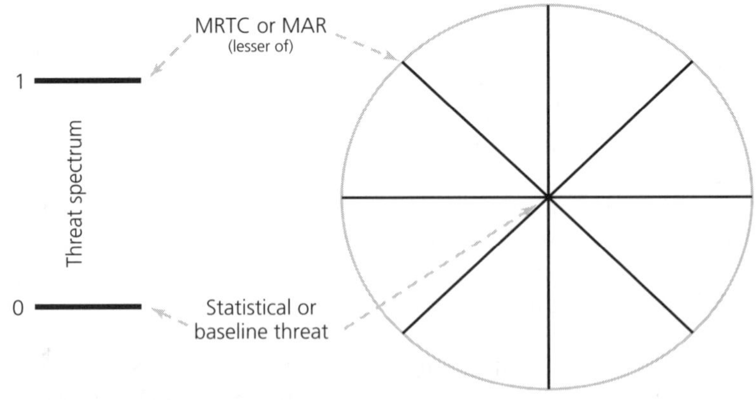

Figure 4.3 Hazard travel time (HTT) (from Hay (2016b))

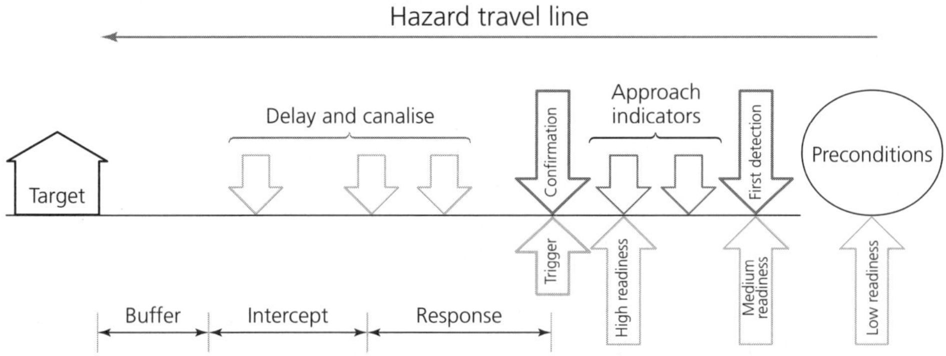

infer the type and scale of hazard that we face, the likelihood that it will affect us and how. From experience and our understanding of our operations and dependencies, we can say how our operation is affected and the impact that this will have on overall performance. Few hazards will impact the performance of well-planned services and infrastructure. Of those that do, we rarely have the luxury of time to analyse and defer any action until we have absolute certainty of it. We must use judgement, informed by likelihood and consequence. HTT analysis provides us with a relatively simple approach to informing that judgement.

Consider a hazard that threatens a specified target (Figure 4.3). The target could be one of our assets or an external service or infrastructure on which we depend. The hazard comes into being through a combination of precursors and occurrences, collectively termed preconditions. In our example, the hazard in question is the flooding of the Bow River, affecting our operations in downtown Calgary. The Bow River emerges from its catchment area in the Rockies. At the end of winter, the ground is frozen with a thick snow layer. The meltwater feeds the river. The catchment in the Rockies, the geography and the seasons' normal temperature cycle would be the precursors. In the absence of the precursors, there can be no hazard. If the thaw is delayed and it begins to rain, there is an increased likelihood that the snow will melt in the rain and run off the still-frozen ground into the river. These are occurrences that indicate a possible hazard. A late thaw would be an impetus to begin observing the HTT indicators closely, and we would initiate a low state of readiness or alert. In our example, we are assisted by GLORIA, the NASA satellite that measures ground temperature.

The rains remain light but continue. This is another indicator, and we may decide that it is our first detection of the flood hazard. We warn our agencies and move to a medium level of readiness, which would mean that we source the personnel, materials and equipment needed for a flood event. We also begin reducing the assets that would be threatened by such flooding. For example, we might move our archives out of the basement storage into a higher-storey storage vault, and we might test and repair flood protection seals and pumping equipment. Typically, this readiness level doesn't involve direct cost if we're already prepared for this. The Bow River is now in spate in the foothills, and there are reports of bank erosion and some property loss. It doesn't yet mean that we will flood, but this may be the indicator that prompts us to move to high readiness. At some point, the subsequent indicators will suggest that flooding is increasingly likely, and that will be our trigger. We won't have certainty, so what will be the critical indicator that triggers our response?

We need to calculate how much time we have for assessing the situation and making a decision (buffer), the time it takes us to get our resources to where the control measures will be implemented (intercept), and the time it takes to implement those measures (response). On the one hand, we wouldn't wish to be laying the last sandbag just as the levee breaches on the Bow River. Still, we would also wish to delay our response until we have sufficient certainty of an event before committing to the expense. That should be articulated in the risk criteria for the operation and organisation. In many situations, the time needed for a response exceeds the time available, and we must accept a degree of uncertainty that might not usually merit a commitment of expense. Ultimately, this calculation will depend on the value of the operation.

Canada is blessed with a comprehensive network of stream gauges and flood detectors provided by the federal and provincial governments and made publicly accessible online. That is not the case everywhere, and it is often worth establishing a simple remote monitoring station where you require an indicator. With smartphone technology, this option is becoming more accessible. Flooding is used in this example, but the practice of HTT analysis can be applied to any hazard, from natural to human-made. However, for this to be effective, we must know what the targets are. We need to understand how we fail and so what functions and assets can cause failure. We might run a cyber scan to see what assets are affected by a cyber intrusion and what that means for the operation. Irrespective, we need to understand our operation, its dependencies and how failure cascades through the systems. There are few instances where a service or asset function is binary, either on or off. Typically there is a graduation of performance with a threshold that constitutes failure, threatening our continued fulfilment of purpose.

4.6. Continuity of purpose

Our interest in resilience is our continuity of operations. More specifically, it is our continued fulfilment of purpose, both operational and strategic or unifying. It defines the value of the service provided and, therefore, the infrastructure. However, this means that the infrastructure is designed to enable a resilient operation rather than necessarily being resilient itself. Striving for resilience in everything can be expensive, and we need to know which functions and systems

Figure 4.4 Prioritisation of enabling operations by operational tolerance of interruption (from Hay (2016b))

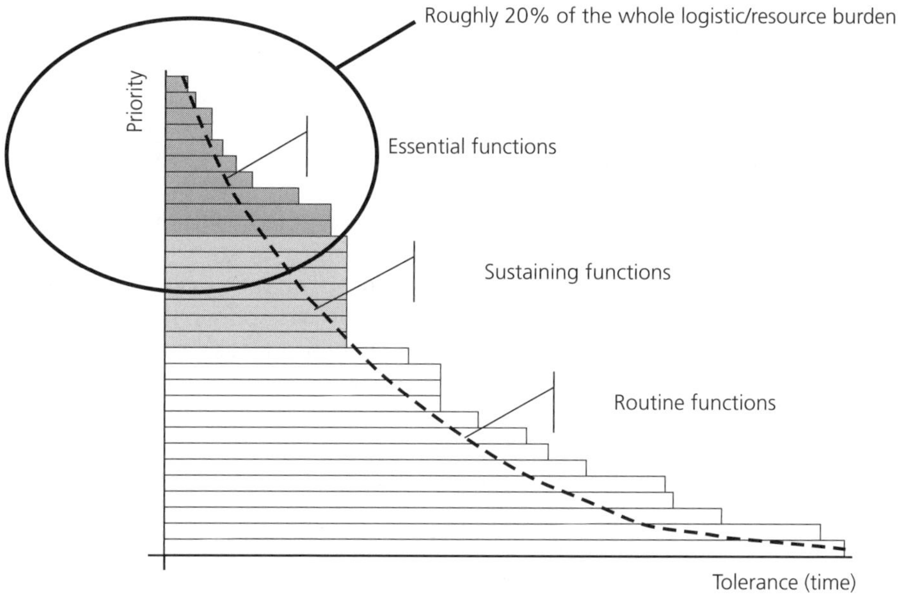

are vital. This can be challenging, as there remains no international consensus in the definition of vulnerability exposure to hazards in risk assessment (UNDRR, 2020). There is no codified practice, and we again need to follow an evidence trail and analysis that begins with the operational purpose. We therefore start by identifying every function that enables our operational purpose. These are the enabling functions of the operation and can be prioritised by operational tolerance of interruption (Figure 4.4).

We are focused on how long the function can be interrupted before it causes a failure elsewhere or otherwise impacts the system or, ultimately, the operation. For example, clients may only tolerate the loss of access to a data centre for 10 s, while the data centre may tolerate a loss of power supply for 10 min because of incorporated power storage systems. As long as the enabling function has value, that is, as long as it supports the purpose of the operation, its compromise will have an impact. The question is, how long.

Once prioritised by time tolerance, we can group the enabling functions by their importance in an incident or event that causes failure and an interruption in operating performance. Assigning the different enabling functions to the relevant period following an incident is an iterative process, which will be informed by the dependency model in the common reference. As a convenient rule of thumb, the first 20% of resource consumption is for the essential functions. These are the ones that define the operation. A significant part of the remaining ones will be sustaining functions that allow the operation to maintain stability and a net-zero or sustainable level of performance. The remaining functions are considered routine and are the ones that optimise operational value. These functional groupings refer to the performance levels of the operation and are represented in the incident sequence.

The incident sequence is shown in Figure 4.1. Let's briefly recap the essence of Section 4.3 and build on the idea of an incident sequence. The vertical axis is the percentage level of the operation's performance, ranging from zero to its peak performance. Peak performance can only be maintained for a maximum of one production cycle, typically one business day or shift. In some applications, we can use output, such as pairs of shoes produced or megawatts generated, or we might use resource consumption, such as megawatts drawn for an aluminium smelter. The horizontal axis represents time. The graph represents the idealised sequence of an incident. Tracing from left to right, the operation is at a routine level of performance. It abruptly falls to zero when an incident occurs.

There then follows an immediate reaction, irrespective of what caused the incident. This reaction restores the essential function up to the MOC. There is no operation below the MOC, and if we aren't operating, we aren't in business. The MOC is unsustainable, and before it is again lost, the response, a deliberate restoration of sustaining functions, must bring the operation to a stable level of performance, known as the MSC. When the operation is stable and at the MSC, it can theoretically continue indefinitely. As a business, it is not making money, though it isn't losing money either. Recovery to a normal level of performance is not possible if the operation is not already stable. The level of performance that the operation recovers will rarely be the same as before. Recovery is a predetermined sequence of functional restoration with assigned resources. The aim is to maintain operational stability through the recovery. However, it also has the effect of making some functions more efficient and exposing fragilities where resources were overeconomised.

Each phase of the incident sequence will have a predefined resource requirement and duration, which means that we can clearly articulate our business income loss exposures. Some organisations find this useful to demonstrate underwriting requirements. The resources for the reaction phase may be entirely different from the resources used in normal operations. For example, normal operations draw electricity from a grid supply, and there is a diesel generator farm for standby use. However, the reaction phase may have a gasoline generator and electrical storage to bring the operation up to MOC until the generator farm is brought online. Each resource is finite and will achieve an objective for a limited time. Incident management needs to maintain the momentum through the incident sequence, as normal operating dependencies are restored.

When we trace our operation across the idealised incident sequence, we will see where we need to focus our efforts. We need to maintain the stability of operations, minimise the event's negative impact and facilitate as rapid a restoration of functionality as possible while most efficiently using the resources available. This first tracing of our actual operation is a baseline profile. Each change made to incident planning can be traced and compared with the baseline profile. A standard comparison tool is the whole cost of risk (WCR), which includes the cost of the measures and the residual loss exposure. If the overall WCR goes down, the solution is considered workable.

When we have an optimum incident plan that meets our risk criteria and has a WCR substantially less than the baseline profile, we will know what we must be capable of doing where and when and under what conditions. It allows us to identify the resources and services necessary to restore operational performance. It tells us what the infrastructure must enable and what it must resist. These additional requirements on the infrastructure can be quite involved. A plan for a hurricane refuge in Central America for emergency response helicopters entailed developing a well-found camp for seasonal occupancy. Conversely, the plan may be as simple as an extension to a factory concrete slab and behind-the-meter feed-in panel for a standby generator and fuel store.

The critical features in each incident sequence trace are the MSC and the time available to restore MSC functionality ($t_2 - t_0$). This is the PP. The PP may be determined by contractual arrangements, such as a service-level agreement that obliges us to deliver a certain level of service within a maximum period. It may be determined by market tolerance of service interruption. Interestingly, the tolerance for business interruption following Hurricane Katrina, 2005, was around 2 weeks. The tolerance for service interruption following Hurricane Sandy, 2012, was down to a few days, even while many places were still flooded. Today, we generally plan on the start of the next business day. There will be some high-value and emergency response services with far shorter tolerances.

Often, the PP will drive the calculation; if we lose our market and customers or clients become accustomed to alternative service providers or are harmed through our delayed restoration of service, we will have lost the ability to recover. Recall that we must have stabilised our operations before we can recover. Then we follow a strict functional restoration sequence. Each step in that restoration of function needs to be associated with an increase in performance. If it doesn't, we will not realise the necessary revenue and will quickly become unsustainable. Our recent pandemic experience shows that it is possible to change subsidy levels to essential services quickly, but they are unsustainable. It is useful to recognise the effect of the subsidy on operations in crisis and during an incident, as they can mask true MSC and provide a false PP.

One way of establishing MSC is by establishing the level of performance that equates to net-zero cash flow. This will include the subsidy in the calculation. When the subsidy is an annual fixed sum, we can establish our MSC and PP as already described. However, when it is linked to performance, the subsidy tends to show an MSC that is higher than the operation can sustain. It also means that we get the false impression that we have more time available before we reach PP. Let's use a food aid programme to illustrate this point.

A region receives food aid to supplement nutrition and calories for a population of 100 000. Under stable conditions, this supplement represents some 20% of normal. An interruption to the local food supply system results in the available food dropping to little more than the food aid. This remains above the MOC, and so does not typically trigger an immediate response, though 'temporary hardship' is recognised. The tolerance of the population to a lack of food will depend on many factors. Still, there is a time tolerance before the food shortage leads to civil unrest, looting and migration. If 30% of the population leaves in search of food, the food aid to those remaining also goes down, further limiting the capacity to stabilise. Further, the food aid's controlled distribution will be to the advantage of a few who are connected to the distribution over the many who are to be the recipients. This is not unusual in protracted-conflict and postconflict areas and postdisaster, leading to a fragmentation of social capital and weak institutions.

We see a similar picture with an energy subsidy. The Gaza Strip receives its electricity from Israel under contract to the Palestinian Authority, in Ramallah in the West Bank. The supply of electricity changes with the political dynamics, and the back-up supply is from diesel generators outside every essential service facility. The diesel supply is a subsidy from Qatar, which is also subject to local political dynamics. When both electricity and diesel are flowing, the Gaza Strip hums along at its normal routine. When one is lost, the province scales back to a performance that is roughly the MSC. However, during those periods when both are interrupted, the province falls below the MOC and can quickly destabilise. The infrastructure relationship with energy is monolithic. When one supply fails, everything depends on the other. There is no diversification in supply or localisation of demand. One interruption will affect the whole province, disproportionately affecting the vulnerable. The infrastructure that we build could support a diversified supply and localised demand. It would also help locally contain the effects of periodic returns to violence.

Let's look at the same issue with transit ridership. A municipality subsidises subway ridership by 50%. A crisis that interrupts subway services' availability will encourage riders to find alternative means of travel, say bus or bicycle or their cars. When subway service resumes, it will need to attract the riders back to receive the subsidy. If the interruption has been too long, the former riders have settled into a new routine and will be slower to return to the subway. Without a return of riders, there will be insufficient revenue to operate and maintain the subway system. How long can the subway continue below a true MSC ridership? Suppose we add the reluctance of riders to return to transit because of a fear of infection, as we see with the recent pandemic. How long can the municipality afford an increased subsidy? Since the service defines the value of its enabling infrastructure, we must think carefully about what is involved in the restoration of service and how the infrastructure will support these transitions. We cannot plan and design infrastructure to meet every eventuality. Still, we must be able to describe the boundaries of its capacity and use. These are the residual risks. At what point does the infrastructure become a stranded asset? It isn't about predicting the combination of events and influences. It is about understanding the operating parameters of the infrastructure and articulating them to the service provider. Setting this example in a broader context, we can articulate the value of transit to the community's socioeconomic health as a whole. Such assessments have spurred a few municipalities to make transit a free public service. It then reverts to the same calculation as fire service coverage, for example.

This also brings us back to the question of service capacity and the infrastructure's carrying capacity. The infrastructure carrying capacity enables the service to meet demand. This demand will vary by time and location and is typically referred to as a demand density for a particular service, that is, a quantity per unit area. In planning our infrastructure, we need to establish how we can meet peak demand and what the MSC and the safe-to-fail or emergency capacity will be. Consider a water supply network. Electrical surcharge pumps pressurise the supply. The network can provide a peak flow for a limited period, though it retains this capacity to allow for sudden localised peak demands for firefighting. The serviceable capacity is below this level and represents normal capacity (Figure 4.5).

Below this level is the MSC, which is the threshold of water usage revenue, directly balancing the cost of operation and maintenance. Any demand above this level, up to and including the serviceable capacity, allows the water board to save for future infrastructure enhancements and upgrades. However, below

Figure 4.5 Relationship between infrastructure carrying capacity (CC) and service demand density (DD)

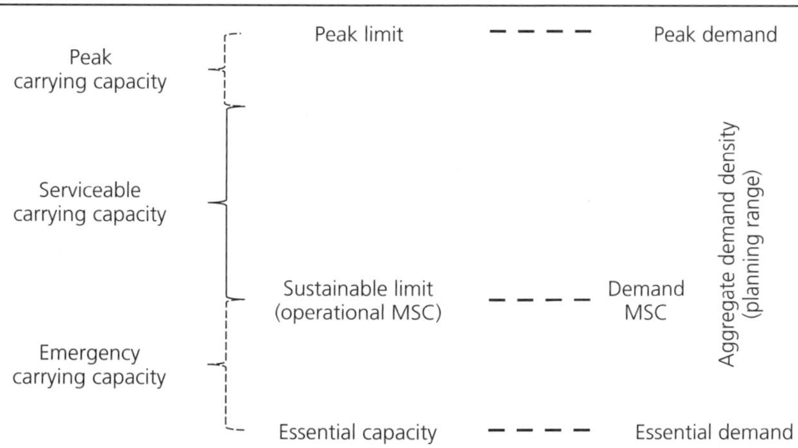

this level, there is an emergency capacity, necessary to meet the essential demands. In this case, we might say that the grid power supply is interrupted, owing to an ice storm that has also affected diesel supply. All available diesel is prioritised to the hospitals and emergency response. Can the water system still meet the emergency demand from the gravitational head alone? This may seem unlikely, but the consequences are significant, and it does happen.

4.7. Community and resilience

Any study or discussion of community resilience would require significantly more than one section or chapter in this book. We are looking specifically at the relationship of infrastructure with community and not community resilience itself. It is important to understand the role of infrastructure in community resilience. In general terms, operational resilience enables community resilience. An operationally resilient municipality does not necessarily have a resilient community. There are a number of influences on the resilience, or fragility, of a community. Chief among these is the community members' behaviour, which relates to lines of trusted communication around and through the community and how people interact and identify as a community. Aldrich's social capital (Aldrich, 2012) is a significant part of this. However, from an infrastructure perspective, we can identify three pillars that enable resilient communities. They are the municipal corporation, community housing and commercial real estate (Figure 4.6).

The municipal corporation delivers all the essential functions of a community, such as emergency response, governance, public health, civic engagement and

Figure 4.6 Community resilience is enabled by the operational resilience of the municipal corporation, community housing and commercial real estate

security, as well as the social well-being functions of learning, arts and recreation. Whether provided by the municipality, charities, faith groups or other non-governmental organisations, community housing provides shelter for the vulnerable. When the vulnerable can shelter in place during a crisis, the municipality can assign resources to the response and recovery rather than immediate (reaction) life support. The trend in several cities towards increased densification of residents has often compromised the ability to shelter in place. It may be because the building cannot maintain a reasonable environment during an energy interruption or that community amenities and sustenance, such as local grocery stores, have been lost to densification.

It can be surprising how many developed countries have extensive food deserts in their major cities. A food desert is where there is no access to groceries within 15 min walk, including the time from the apartment to the front door of the building. The (15 min) parameter of access will vary from country to country and region to region. Commercial real estate encompasses all the office space, retail space, catering and service industry space necessary for economic restoration and recovery. These three pillars are essential and must be resilient in their own right; they represent the community or city's operational resilience.

When these three pillars are functioning, there is confidence in the city, and confidence attracts the best, who attract high-value businesses and individuals. This generates revenue for the municipality. When the three pillars are operationally resilient, and the municipal administration is competent, crisis can be managed without drama, preventing depopulation (Figure 4.7). When there is a loss of

Figure 4.7 Role of resilience in the relationship between the carrot of sustainable economic development and the stick of depopulation

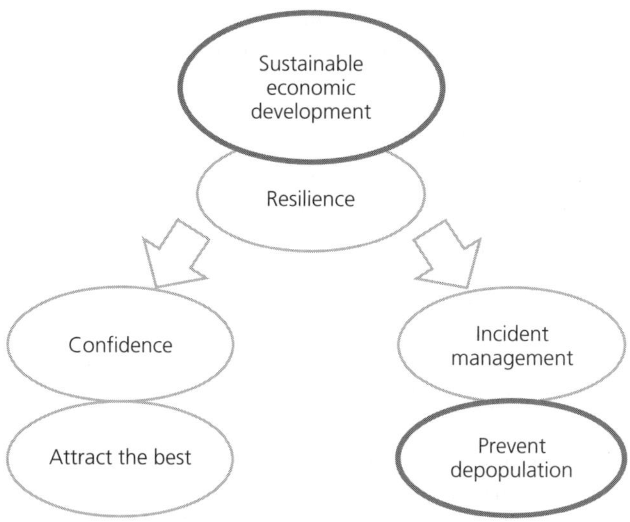

faith in the municipal competency and leadership, depopulation follows, with an associated loss in revenues to the municipality. This was summarised at CityAge (Philadelphia, Pennsylvania, USA) in 2013, and attributed to the Mayor of San Francisco, though I have been unable to verify it.

Nonetheless, it's a useful mantra that the promise of sustainable economic development gets you into office. Still, a loss of confidence in your ability to manage a crisis will kill any re-election for anything ever again. The effects of municipal fragility don't just rest with the political leadership. It is unlikely that New Orleans will fully recover from its experience of Hurricane Katrina or Detroit from its financial mismanagement. Externalities will always change. The things that a municipality can change and control are its planning, preparation, decision-making (risk criteria) and behaviours.

An early study by the Centre for Resilience of Critical Infrastructure was unable to determine correctly what causes municipalities to fail in a crisis. The focus switched to the characteristics common to those cities that proved to be resilient in a crisis (Hay, 2013). These characteristics are

- community identity
- community focus
- balanced infrastructure
- strategic framework
- confidence in leadership.

Community identity and focus go hand in hand. A community that identifies as a community will have implicit lines of trusted communication, not necessarily the official ones. Each community will have its opinion formers and influencers, who may not be elected officials and will often influence people's actions more than official direction from the municipality. There are many dynamics involved, which we do not explore here. However, we must recognise what 'truth' people in the community accept and inform it with the common reference. The community must also be self-aware of its situation and its members. Having a focal point where people interact, however briefly, in the normal routine of the day promotes that awareness and legitimises the lines of communication. These focal points are where people interact at a personal level, rather than merely driving past each other in a retail park parking lot. They form naturally at the accessible heart of a community, where each has access to meet routine needs, from cash to groceries to the post office to municipal services. A feature of successful arrival cities that most effectively transition immigrant populations to full citizens is the existence of these focal points in mixed-use (zoned) areas (Saunders, 2011).

Balanced infrastructure speaks to the balance of infrastructure carrying capacity to service demand density. If the demand is lacking, there will be insufficient revenue to maintain the infrastructure. Conversely, if there is too much demand,

Figure 4.8 Equilibrium

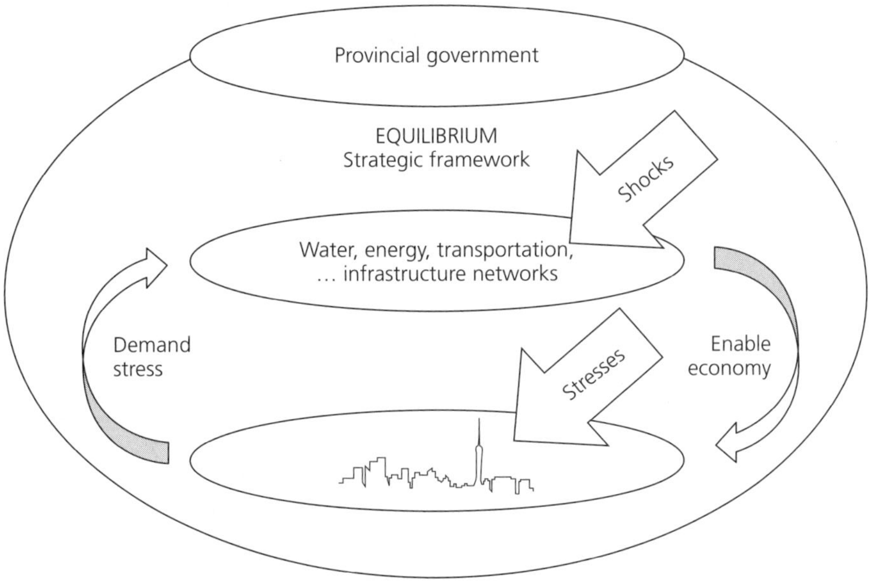

the infrastructure will be insufficient, and the service will falter. The strategic framework expands this idea to the municipal level. It looks at the relationship between municipalities and the higher authority in their use and control of common resources transported by shared infrastructure. This is the idea of equilibrium (Figure 4.8), arising from Ostrom's *Governing the Commons* (1990). The final aspect is more complicated.

Confidence in leadership is where the community believes that the leadership will look after the community's collective interests equitably and efficiently. Interestingly, this can exist in the total absence of actual effective leadership. This reflects studies by Boin and others into leadership dynamics in a crisis (Aldrich, 2012; Boin, 2005; Boin *et al.*, 2013). It will be interesting to see how this translates when we can look back objectively at the COVID-19 pandemic to see how different national leaders managed their response and the nature of their electoral support.

These five characteristics emerged from an initial study of roughly 30 cities, which gradually expanded to include large corporations and provinces. They are not conclusive but have proved remarkably consistent in each case study. They provide a useful guide and not a rule or principle.

4.8. Chain of consequence

Consequence can be a challenging concept beyond a cause-and-effect relationship. In Newtonian terms, any action will have an equal and opposite reaction.

In a system of systems, that reaction can be in parallel systems, affected by the operating context in which your active system exists. This will change the susceptibility of the whole and therefore the risk profile, or fragility, of the operation. In Chapter 2, we explored the idea that infrastructure changes the context in which it will function by its existence. We can see this in the new road that attracts more traffic rather than alleviating congestion, the proposed new build that attracts speculators or the new facility that attracts threats to the area that had not previously been an issue. We need to explore the consequences more carefully. Let us begin with its components.

Consequence can be broadly categorised into three components:

- operational or mission
- financial
- political or goodwill.

The operational consequence of an event is the one with which we are typically most comfortable. We can say that we can no longer use the fountain pen if the nib breaks. There is a functional cause-and-effect. Similarly, we can extend the example to say that ink will spill across the page when the nib breaks, which will ruin the elegant calligraphy in progress. We are associating our operational consequence with both loss of capability and loss of property or function. We capture this loss in the financial consequence, which is the directly attributable loss of that asset or function. Therefore, the financial consequence of the nib breaking will be the cost of the nib and spilt ink and the revenue loss of lost work until the nib is repaired. This is in addition to the operational impact of lost productivity and capability, potentially affecting deadlines. A different yet associated cost will be the loss of the work already done and the cost of the paper and ink that must now be discarded. They may arise from the same event, but the loss of nib and the loss of the work being done are two different entities. However, the political consequence may be a loss of confidence in the nib supplier or the calligrapher, possibly both. This may translate into customer loss of confidence in the business to deliver the artwork on time to the expected standard. Consequence in infrastructure systems is not dissimilar, in principle, to the calligraphy studio; it's many orders of magnitude more significant, though.

Our ability to understand the consequences of an incident in our infrastructure system and its effect on the service it enables affects our perception of how we manage the incident. Our successful management of any incident affecting the operational function of infrastructure builds on our understanding of the infrastructure systems and their enabled services, and the consequences of an incident. It doesn't matter if we are concerned about flooding, a gas explosion, tanker fire or train derailment. When infrastructure fails, the potential for harm is great, and it will attract significant attention. If we cannot be seen to understand the situation and have control of the response, others will unhelpfully fill in the information vacuum. A manageable incident can quickly become a crisis. In the example, Sir Richard Branson reports on the 2007 Virgin Trains derailment in *Canadian Business*.

> *On Feb. 23, 2007, at around 8:15 p.m., one of Virgin Train's new Pendolino tilting trains jumped over a set of points in Cumbria in the northwest of England, on a remote part of the West Coast Main Line. Margaret Masson, an elderly woman travelling to her home in Cardonald, was thrown around in the coach as the train slid along the railbed and then careered down a steep embankment.*
>
> *For 10 years, Virgin Trains had been safely carrying millions of passengers all over Britain. Virgin Atlantic, meanwhile, had flown millions of customers around the globe without injury. That night, life changed for all of us at Virgin. Margaret Masson was dead. Several other people were seriously hurt.*
>
> *When I arrived in Manchester that morning, the BBC was reporting that the train was intact, and that had helped to save many lives. That was heartening: all our new trains had been built like tanks for this very reason. A later report, which was confirmed, suggested that a track failure was responsible for the accident. Twenty-four people needed to be taken to hospital.*
>
> *I met Margaret Masson's family at the Royal Preston Hospital in Lancashire. They were clearly devastated, and I offered them my condolences. We found ourselves hugging each other.*
>
> *Soon I was facing TV cameras and journalists who wanted answers. At the time, I couldn't say much. I expressed my gratitude to the train operator, Iain Black, who stayed in his seat at the front of the train as it crashed, doing everything he could to save his passengers, and in the process sustained serious injuries. Our other employees on board had all behaved in an exemplary fashion, ignoring their own minor injuries in order to lead customers to safety.*
>
> *Why were we able to react so quickly? When Virgin Trains was putting its emergency procedures in place, we had analyzed a number of serious rail accidents, and had been appalled by the length of time that usually passed before anyone in charge started speaking to the press. Confusion and then blame set in quickly as anxious people waited to find out what happened and why.*
>
> *So our disaster planning had prepared us to accomplish three main goals: get to the scene fast; be efficient in dealing with the passengers, staff and*

> *media; and be honest about what was happening. We knew that those first steps would get communications established so that everyone – passengers, staff, the media – would be able to obtain the information they needed.*
>
> (Branson, 2011)
>
> On 29 February 2012, Network Rail indicated that it would plead guilty to the health and safety breaches that led to the derailment.

We need to understand the consequences to manage an incident efficiently. We also need to understand the consequences to reduce the risk of disaster. Informing that understanding is the role of the common reference and specifically the dependency model and the influence model. The dependency model is highly effective at capturing the operational and financial consequences of a change in the VSOS. When the influence model is georeferenced to the tableau and dependency model, we can trace the incident's political-social-governance implications. It is then up to the operator to interpret the common reference and devise a suitable crisis management strategy. As infrastructure engineers, however, we must feed that understanding by providing the necessary consequence information so that it can be effectively interpreted. As with any report, knowing how the information will be used and what interpretation will be required allows us to craft it most suitably.

So far, we have taken a systems-level view of consequence. However, when we get into the detail of operational consequences, we will need to know what to measure. It is useful to consider infrastructure in six dimensions, reflecting the domains. There are the three Cartesian dimensions that fix the infrastructure in space. There is a time dimension that defines its function in time. A human dimension describes how the infrastructure is actually used and perceived by operators and the public (related to the human domain), and there is the control dimension that defines how it is supposed to be used (related to the virtual domain).

Consider a level crossing. It cannot be a road and a railway at the same time. Though the road and rail infrastructure are collocated, their functions should not coincide. If they do, there will be an accident and probably serious injury. To deconflict their functions, we have control measures that prioritise rail over road, warn road users of an approaching train and advise them to wait until it has passed. However, since human behaviour is not always reliable, we may supplement our flashing lights and bells with barriers for both cars and pedestrians.

When we map consequences, we should always ask 'What if?' each time we introduce a control measure. Any measure can fail, and the safe and reliable operation of our infrastructure must be safe-to-fail. The level crossing example is relevant in both health and safety terms, for operators and the public, and service reliability terms. Our study of consequence is the analytical basis for our understanding of risk and fragility. What if the tsunami wave exceeds the height of the sea wall? The answer to this question may have led to a different outcome in 2011 at the Fukushima Daiichi Nuclear Power Plant. You will recall from Chapter 2 and 3 how our ability to withstand an unknown risk is defined by how our operation responds, rather than how we manage the hazard. We cannot know what hazard will manifest when, nor how bad it will be. However, we can build a sense of how bad it can get. We can determine how the service, and the infrastructure that enables it, will react, respond and recover from one or more failures in the subsystems on which it depends. We inform this level of planning with our analysis of consequence, and we measure the effectiveness of the whole through level 5 commissioning. So what does cause us to fail?

4.9. Black swans

When I have conducted operational audits, particularly after an incident, the effects of an incident are greatly amplified by the board or executive's blindness to the risk or a lack of understanding of the operation. The usual response to operational failure is that the event was a 'black swan' and [sic] unforeseeable. This reflects a misunderstanding of black swans and operations. It also reflects a preoccupation with regulatory and financial compliance and business performance over actual risk to the operation. There is no business without an operation. The infrastructure must enable that operation, and so is partly defined by the operation's resilience requirements.

The black swan is a native Australian bird, *Cygnus atratus*. It is also a metaphor attributed to Juvenal for something that is believed not to exist or to be impossible. The modern interpretation comes from Taleb's book *The Black Swan* (2010), and it is with this definition that we continue. Taleb describes black swans as causing hard-to-predict events beyond expectations informed by history or science, which cannot be calculated. He also says that they arise out of our blindness to uncertainty and describes how extremely rare events can shape the course of history. This idea of cognitive bias or prejudice is an important one and can be seen routinely in risk perspectives. We have explored the concept of a common reference and its role in informing our understanding of our operations and their fragilities. Taleb's discussion of black swan events expands this concept to encompass extreme outlier events. In effect, a black swan event is extremely rare, highly consequential and predictable in hindsight. These are not events that cause reasonably foreseeable consequences in operations, even if we purport to understand their occurrence after the event. Based on this description, the COVID-19 pandemic is not a black swan (Taleb, 2020).

Working with Yvonne Steiner of Zurich Canada, an insurer, I explored black swan events and their implications for the insurance industry. We presented this brief study to the Insurance Institute on 27 May 2020 as a webinar. One of our findings was that many of the structural fragilities in how we operate and manage risk arise from our reactions to the societal and political trends and pivotal outlying events. This layering of reactionary processes and administrative structures can conceal the inherent risks and influence our understanding of our operational fragility. One aspect of this drew us back to the essence of what is reasonably foreseeable and the development of a common reference. Writing in the January/February 2013 edition of *Engineering Dimensions*, the journal of Professional Engineers Ontario, Pat Koval, a senior partner at Torys LLP, a law firm, wrote:

> *For example, given knowledge of climate change effects in a geographic area as a result of the proliferation of climate-related information and projection models, if the 'standard practice' at the time of designing a specific type of infrastructure project is to ignore potential climate-change effects (despite widely available evidence), the standard practice itself may be negligent. Adhering to a deficient standard would be a breach of a design professional's standard of care to an injured person.*

The article is quite short and worth reading. While Canada-centric, it does place the emphasis squarely on the (infrastructure) engineer to understand and manage the risks, with the organisation carrying the liability. As we've discussed, we cannot be in business if we're not operating. We can understand and control how a subsystem's failure affects the operation, even if we cannot predict what will cause that failure. Codified practice reflects the experience of failure and provides a compliance standard only when the actual design standard will require something significantly higher. Technology and compliance will not solve our unimagined events and failures, but engineering can. As Steels (2011) so clearly puts it, risk management is the fundamental business of the civil engineer. We cannot safeguard against every eventuality. Instead, we must invest in understanding the situation and how our projected capability is susceptible to failure so that we can develop infrastructure that supports and enables safe-to-fail services and operations. This means looking beyond compliance and what is 'asked for' to recognise what is required and the difference in through-life WCR.

4.10. Chapter summary

Infrastructure is the foundation of communities. Resilient communities are enabled by resilient municipal services, resilient community housing and resilient commercial real estate. These three pillars must function in concert. Infrastructure enables each one. The infrastructure assets are not resilient, though they may be robust. However, the infrastructure systems can be resilient, and they enable resilient services and capabilities. The planning requirements for sustainable infrastructure necessarily include provision for resilience, which is the prerequisite of sustainability.

A resilient system is inherently safe-to-fail. Planning the infrastructure to support a safe-to-fail system means that we must understand the operation in its context, what it must be capable of and how the context is changing. Once we understand how the operation fails, we may understand what is required to manage that failure and the infrastructure required to support that risk treatment. A significant part of understanding is the ability to take a step back from familiar processes and received wisdom to see the operation as it is and will be.

Fragility in infrastructure systems, and in the services and operations they enable, is often due to a lack of objective understanding. Basing our knowledge on the common reference and interpreting what it means for the operation, and therefore the infrastructure, allows us to calibrate expertise and manage the unforeseen. The effects of a failure are foreseeable; by extension, so are the effects of unforeseen events that cause failure in subsystems and components on which we depend.

This exploration of (operational) resilience brings our discussion back to evidence and risk. We need to know what the situation is, both operationally and contextually. This allows us to communicate with stakeholders, not least our shareholders, lenders and underwriters. Our ability to interpret the common reference from our unique organisational or operational perspective means that we can state, with supporting evidence, where our inherent fragilities are and what effect different hazard scenarios will have on our business. This is, again, at the heart of our enterprise-wide risk management approach and of the development of a risk treatment strategy that focuses on how our operation adapts to changes and disruption, as opposed to the hazard likelihood. It is the basis of the TCFD reporting discussed in Chapter 3. We can articulate how different climate and other scenarios impact our operations and business development strategy with a supporting audit chain. We can justify what we are doing about it, measure success and ensure that the associated risk-based decision-making is appropriately informed.

When we create a resilient operation, we stabilise the immediate surrounding area. As we stabilise and make the essential services of a community resilient, we enable the development of a resilient community. Informing the community, and open dialogue with stakeholders that is unencumbered by conjecture and supposition, is possible through the common reference. This presents us with a choice. Either we persist with the familiar tools and measure the world around us in terms of what we know we can solve, or we build a common reference to identify the issues and select the tools most appropriate to address them. More succinctly, do we act on what is reasonably foreseeable or are we wilfully ignorant?

BIBLIOGRAPHY

Aldrich DP (2012) *Building Resilience: Social Capital in Post-disaster Recovery*. University of Chicago Press, Chicago, IL, USA.

Barros M, Salat N, Sarmant T and Nouvel J (2007) *Vauban l'intelligence du territoire*. N Chaudun, Paris, France.

Boin A (ed.) (2005) *The Politics of Crisis Management: Public Leadership under Pressure*. Cambridge University Press, Cambridge, UK.

Boin A, Overdijk W and Kuipers S (2013) Leadership in times of crisis: a framework for assessment. *International Review of Public Administration* **18(1)**: 79–91.

Branson R (2011) Branson: if disaster strikes, be fast, efficient and honest. *Canadian Business*, 5 Apr. https://www.canadianbusiness.com/lifestyle/branson-if-disaster-strikes-be-fast-efficient-and-honest/ (accessed 01/04/2021).

Butzer KW (1992) The Americas before and after 1492: an introduction to current geographical research. *Annals of the Association of American Geographers* **82(3)**: 543–565, 10.1111/j.1467-8306.1992.tb01964.x.

CRCI (University of Toronto Centre for Resilience of Critical Infrastructure) (2021) Frequently Asked Questions. https://crci.utoronto.ca/about/faqs (accessed 31/03/2021).

Flynn SE (2007) *The Edge of Disaster: Rebuilding a Resilient Nation*, 1st edn. Random House, New York, NY, USA.

Gunderson LH and Holling CS (eds) (2002) *Panarchy: Understanding Transformations in Human and Natural Systems*. Island Press, Washington, DC, USA.

Hay AH (2013) Surviving catastrophic events: stimulating community resilience. *Institution of Engineering and Technology: Transportation* **2013**: 41–46.

Hay AH (2016a) The incident sequence as resilience planning framework. *Infrastructure Asset Management* **3(2)**: 55–60.

Hay AH (2016b) *After the Flood: Exploring Operational Resilience*. Friesen Press, Victoria, BC, Canada.

Holling CS (1973) Resilience and stability of ecological systems. *Annual Review of Ecology and Systematics* **4**: 1–23.

Kahneman D (2013) *Thinking, Fast and Slow*. Anchor Canada, Toronto, ON, Canada.

Koval P (2013) Climate change risk: is liability lurking for professional engineers? *Engineering Dimensions*, Jan./Feb.: pp. 27–28.

National Research Council Canada (2020) Canadian National Master Construction Specification. https://nrc.canada.ca/en/certifications-evaluations-standards/canadian-national-master-construction-specification (accessed 31/03/2021).

Ostrom E (1990) *Governing the Commons: The Evolution of Institutions for Collective Action*. Cambridge University Press, Cambridge, UK.

Rodin J (2014) *The Resilience Dividend: Being Strong in a World Where Things Go Wrong*, 1st edn. PublicAffairs, New York, NY, USA.

Saunders D (2011) *Arrival City: The Final Migration and Our Next World*. Vintage Canada, Toronto, ON, Canada.

Steels HM (ed.) (2011) *Initial Professional Development for Civil Engineers*. ICE Publishing, London, UK.

Taleb NN (2010) *The Black Swan: The Impact of the Highly Improbable*, 2nd edn. Random House Trade Paperbacks, New York, NY, USA.

Taleb NN (2020) Corporate socialism: the government is bailing out investors & managers not you. *Incerto*, 25 Mar. https://medium.com/incerto/corporate-socialism-the-government-is-bailing-out-investors-managers-not-you-3b31a67bff4a (accessed 20/07/2020).

UNDRR (UN Office for Disaster Risk Reduction) (2020) *Hazard Definition and Classification Review*. UN, Geneva, Switzerland.

Xenophon (2000) *Xenophon: In Seven Volumes. 6: Cyropaedia; 2. Books V–VIII* (Miller W (trans.)). Harvard University Press, Cambridge, MA, USA. (Reprinted.)

FURTHER READING

I have found that the most illuminating reading on resilience is not explicitly about resilience. For example, reading the reports on the Fukushima Daiichi incident, 2011, I always ask myself what the plan for failure was. We can reduce the likelihood of a catastrophic event affecting us, but at some point the protection will be inadequate, or something will fail. Then what? Rereading case studies with that perspective changes the lessons that one draws from the report. Along the same lines, we see how a protective measure constructed to an acknowledged level of risk is then assumed by others to protect against greater threats. The impact of Hurricane Katrina, 2005, on New Orleans was greater because the limit of levee performance was rarely acknowledged. Asking what happens when something fails is difficult, yet this question would seem to feature in many disasters only in its absence.

The idea of an extremely low-likelihood and extremely high-consequence event has challenged us through history. It is not a simple calculus and is rightly given over to national governments to manage. Concerns over the rapid transmission of diseases through increased international travel and trade gave rise to the International Health Regulation (2005), which is difficult to match to some signatories' behaviours during the COVID-19 pandemic. There is an interesting TED talk by Bill Gates on global preparedness for a pandemic in 2015.

The most useful reading in resilience is not about how infrastructure in one place was successful and should be an example for other places. The most valuable reading is about understanding the resilient service and capability that the infrastructure is required to enable. It doesn't matter whether the issue is about local accessibility to amenities and the so-called 15-minute city (and what it means for the community) or the need to shelter in place for an extended period of time. When we look at infrastructure resilience, it means nothing if we don't understand what is needed of the service that we are enabling to be resilient. Purpose in context is everything.

Amano Y (2015) *The Fukushima Daiichi Accident: Report by the Director General.* International Atomic Energy Agency, Vienna, Austria. Report GC(59)/14.

Anon (2020) What's the worst that could happen? *The Economist*, 27 June: pp. 14–16. https://www.economist.com/briefing/2020/06/25/the-world-should-think-better-about-catastrophic-and-existential-risks (accessed 06/04/2021).

City of Toronto (2018) *Toronto Green Standard*, version 3. City of Toronto, Toronto, ON, Canada. https://www.toronto.ca/city-government/planning-development/official-plan-guidelines/toronto-green-standard/ (accessed 01/04/2021).

City of Toronto (2021) *City of Toronto Resilience Strategy*. City of Toronto, Toronto, ON, Canada. https://www.toronto.ca/services-payments/water-environment/environmentally-friendly-city-initiatives/resilientto/ (accessed 01/04/2021).

Gates B (2015) The next outbreak? We're not ready. *TED2015*, Mar. https://www.ted.com/talks/bill_gates_the_next_outbreak_we_re_not_ready?language=dz (accessed 01/04/2021).

US Congress (2006) *A Failure of Initiative: Final Report of the Select Bipartisan Committee to Investigate the Preparation for and Response to Hurricane Katrina*. US Government Printing Office, Washington, DC, USA. House Report 109-377.

WHO (World Health Organization) (2008) International Health Regulations (2005) 2nd edn. WHO, Geneva, Switzerland.

Yeung P (2021) How '15 minute cities' will change the way we socialise. *BBC Worklife*, 4 Jan. https://www.bbc.com/worklife/article/20201214-how-15-minute-cities-will-change-the-way-we-socialise (accessed 01/04/2021).

ice Publishing

Hay, Alexander H
ISBN 978-0-7277-6562-8
https://doi.org/10.1680/pris.65628.107

Chapter 5
Protecting value: ensuring continued use

With John Neily

As you will by now have surmised, infrastructure protection is about protecting the purpose of the infrastructure. We seek to protect the operation, and we plan our infrastructure to enable that. Protection is not the same as resilience. Protection is about preventing harm, while resilience is about adapting to failures and changes and recovering as rapidly as possible. There is a joint stem to both resilience and protection, and indeed sustainability as well. If we know what causes us to fail, we are in a position to allocate resources as efficiently as possible in our risk treatment strategy.

Often, the two terms are used to imply each other, potentially confusing the message. One might argue that in identifying the inherent vulnerabilities of a system and treating the attendant risks, the purpose is protected, and the system behaviour is capable of adapting to the associated changes. For example, putting the transformer on the third floor means that it is protected from floodwaters, and the associated service can continue through the flood event. This is a protection measure. Putting the standby generator on the third floor, above the floodwaters, will ensure that the electricity supply can be restored following an outage caused by the flood. This is a resilience measure. The difference can be as simple as the equipment's function in the system. So while it is true that one can imply the other in terms of output, the outcome of a protection strategy will be different from a resilience one. In practice, we recognise today that we need a balance between the two, but distinguishing the measures can be challenging. Arguably, this is as much about our mindset or perception of threats and goals as it is about risk treatment models.

When the US Department of Homeland Security (DHS) was established in response to the 2001 terrorist attack on the World Trade Centre in New York, known as 9/11, the approach was firmly one of protection. In many ways, this reflected an expedient-military approach to hardening sensitive facilities from attack. A purely protective approach is focused on the immediacy of a malicious threat and can compromise a facility's operation and maintenance over time, as discussed in Chapter 4. In 2009, the then US Secretary of Homeland Security, Janet Napolitano, pressed for an increased emphasis on resilience in critical infrastructure systems. This meant a subtle shift in hazard lists from primarily malicious actors to a more holistic view of all-hazards risks, and mitigation measures became more innovative and integrated. It is a question of balance.

On the one hand, we know that we cannot protect against everything. So we must ensure that we can recover from failures and interruptions. On the other hand, it is grossly inefficient to be adversely impacted by each stress and minor shock that describes our everyday risk context. In effect, we want protection to deal with the background level of stress and resilience for the more significant and less frequent events. This balance of resilience and protection should depend on the individual situation and, most importantly, the organisation's risk criteria.

In a study of the University of Toronto's St. George campus, Dr David Bristow and I investigated where the optimum balance would be between protection measures and resilience (Figure 5.1). We found that it was different for virtually every building. The optimum balance depends on the building use, the value of the operations conducted within, the associated service and resource dependencies, the levels of access that need to be maintained, and the stakeholders' perception of the risk. This aspect of perception is a critical determinant in protection planning, which is unsurprising given our risk biases and degrees of belief (Huber, 2009). Functionally, we can say that there is a simplified and intuitive relationship between resilience and protection for (infrastructure) investment purposes. We invest in protection to meet a background level of risk, which is the normal hazard level. We then switch investment to resilience measures with some continued protection investment to support resilience.

Figure 5.1 Generic balance of investment between protection and resilience

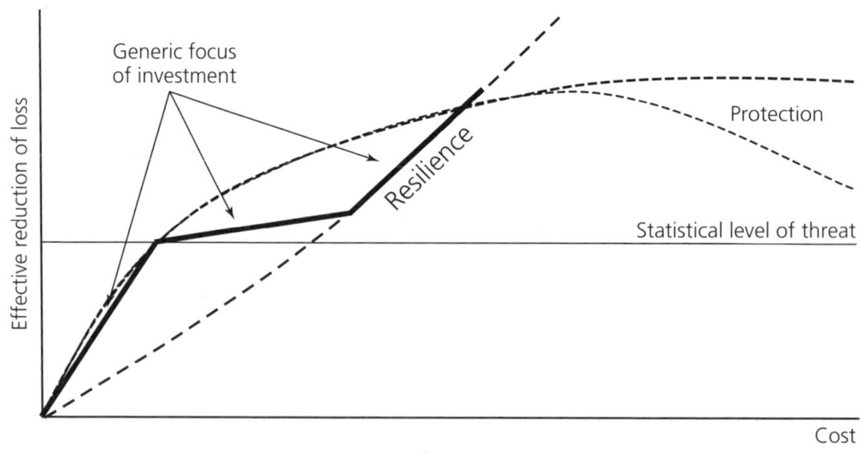

That doesn't mean that our protection measures aren't resilient or that our resilience measures aren't themselves protected.

The perception of protection is critical. The owner must perceive a need for protection, and the staff must see value in it. Furthermore, the local authority and the general public must acknowledge its need, and the aggressor must recognise its presence. At the same time, the protection approach and recovery plan must be secure and resilient. Confusingly, many jurisdictions wrap up the protection and resilience of critical infrastructure under a catch-all term, *security*, along with emergency management.

There is a fair bit to unpack here. This chapter explores the concept and application of protection in infrastructure systems and unravels some of the complexity around perception and terminology. Ultimately, we must know what we are protecting against, and we must know what level of risk we accept. The common reference and risk criteria will define efficient protection planning. We begin with a discussion of security and perception, focusing on the three components of security that link it to the VSOS. We explore the risk-based approach to security and the classification of hazards for investment and strategy development. With this contextual framework, we explore the principles of protection and the role of risk to discuss how we can protect through-life value. This brings us to measuring protection, representing the residual risks, and how we might manage protection in a dynamic risk context.

5.1. Security planning

Today, the term *security* is typically used to refer to malicious threats, and *protection* refers to accidental and natural hazards. This is a shift from the early days of the US DHS, where protection meant mitigating predominantly malicious threats. It is essential to make sure that we are clear on the definitions used in the current jurisdiction. In many jurisdictions, the collective term is *security* or *public safety*, encompassing protection and, increasingly, resilience and sustainability aspects. We will continue with this terminology; security as a collective term and protection as the prevention of harm to the operation's purpose.

Security comprises three components: physical, procedural and relational. The physical is everything that we build, fix and use in the world about us, across the natural and built domains of the VSOS. We may increase the percentage of reinforcing steel in a reinforced concrete frame to withstand the increased loads anticipated from a gas explosion, say. We may install screening equipment at a venue that we only use when there is a heightened threat. Similarly, we may create spillways and water meadows to absorb a flood's effects before it reaches the downtown core and causes more considerable damage.

Procedural security is from the virtual domain of the VSOS. It encompasses the decision-making and communication structures in the organisation, the protocols for reacting and responding to an incident, reporting routines, custodial and access routines, such as closing one door before opening the next in an 'airlock' arrangement, or how to transition to a higher state of readiness. We explore these things further in this chapter.

Relational security is, arguably, the foundation for the others and is entirely of the human domain. It is the relationship between human beings, their perceptions and behaviours. A sentry who greets every person entering the site each day forms a relationship with the staff. The sentry will recognise the normal pattern of life and the behaviours and demeanours of staff under various circumstances. When a person behaves uncharacteristically or abnormally, the sentry will notice. This awareness should trigger a further screening, perhaps merely a brief exchange of pleasantries or something more formal. In a secure facility, such as a prison or forensic hospital, this is the essential relationship between warder or carer and inmate or patient. This behavioural awareness can also be achieved without pre-established relationships by spotting patterns. For example, El Al, the Israeli national airline, employs ground staff to engage with passengers from the kerb-side, to interview and observe. This is highly effective but does not happen instead of physical and procedural measures. Boston Logan Airport, in Massachusetts, USA, adopted a similar approach after 9/11.

Relational security also refers to the attitudes of the staff. If the staff do not perceive the need for security or see security routines as an imposition on their work, they will often bypass or ignore the measures. This phenomenon is popularly known as the 'fire door principle'. It states that if you install a fire door between two busy offices, you will find it propped open by the nearest fire extinguisher. Perhaps a little tongue-in-cheek, but it does reflect the natural human tendency to take shortcuts when measures impose on familiar routine. We can see this where the main flow of pedestrian traffic cuts across the grass rather than following the path in a park. The same applies to the security personnel, who must both work on security and work securely. We can have detailed procedures and policies for security, but they are unlikely to be followed if they are unaligned with the usual routine.

Let's explore this idea of perception some more. We, as citizens, have a relationship with the police. We give up some freedom in return for security. The police will have a range of response capabilities available to them, up to and including the use of lethal force. We grant the police authority, based on our trust in them to act responsibly in our name. We grant the police a social licence to investigate, search, detain and use force in our collective interest. When the police are perceived to have overstepped the bounds of expected behaviour, inevitably defined in retrospect, we withdraw our social licence and lose trust. This means that, in many ways, the police are held to a higher account than the general public but have less freedom.

Where policing is imposed, that social licence can disappear and trust in the civil power is absent. However, when we are completely secure, we have surrendered our freedom and lose the drive to innovate. Some of the greatest works of art and inventions have emerged from crisis and human suffering; there is a natural balance between security and vibrancy. Juliette Kayyem speaks of the city's normal flow and how it is impeded by too much security (Genetec, 2017; Kayyem, 2016).

Conversely, an aggressor will perceive security and is either deterred by it or investigates how it might be defeated. The aggressor's perception and subsequent actions will come down to a question of intent and competency. A simple boundary, such as a garden fence, may be all it takes to keep an honest person honest. Since there is no restriction on idiocy, we might use more robust fencing, such as palisades, around dangerous sites, such as railways and electricity transformers, to stop people from injuring themselves. However, defeating a malicious intent raises the *levels of protection* according to its impact on the operation or purpose. The level of protection is relative to the hazard and its effect on the operation. Conversely, resilience is about how the operation behaves when something fails, irrespective of what causes the failure. Four aspects fall out of this, and they relate to how we manage risk.

5.2. Risk-based understanding

Security is part of the risk management process. When we look at the risks inherent to an operation in context and develop a risk treatment strategy (Figure 5.2) to address these risks, there will still be residual risks. We may go through one or more iterations of the risk treatment strategy but ultimately the residual risk will define the security requirements. That way, the security is always linked directly to the operation, rather than being imposed on it.

The second aspect is that we need to consider each hazard separately while addressing all-hazards risks. Once again, we can use simple protocols for this.

Figure 5.2 Planning sequence to determine security requirements that enable and protect the operational purpose of the infrastructure

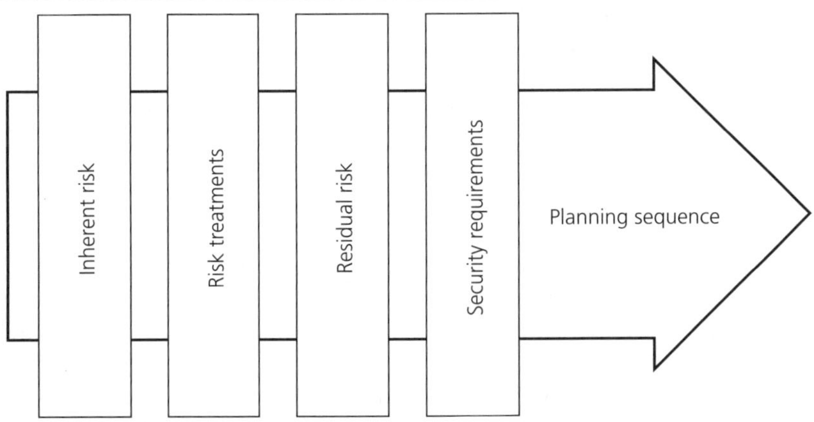

As discussed, all-hazards risks do not consider every possible hazard, but rather the analysis of a hazard in context to establish a hazard profile. Through the DTS (Chapter 1), we establish the primary hazards and then consider how they affect the operation. The appearance of one hazard may trigger another or make the operation more susceptible to yet another hazard that would otherwise not be relevant. The ice storm that caused the power outage also impeded access to the facilities and impaired wireless communication. We may not have a bomb threat, but the army recruiting office that opens next door does have a routine threat of targeted violence, and we are now in its area of collateral damage.

This leads to the third aspect of how we represent the hazard. We will have traced the HTT for each hazard and can say how the organisation or site can intercept the hazard and mitigate its effects. We represent this on a threat spectrum, using a scale from zero to one. Zero is the baseline threat or hazard level, or the statistical background level of threat. One is the lesser of the maximum realisable threat capability (MRTC) and the maximum acceptable risk (MAR). The MRTC is quite literally how bad the threat can realistically get. If, for example, the largest vehicle that can physically access the site is a sedan car and then only 35 m from the target, the vehicle-borne improvised explosive device (VBIED) MRTC is what a sedan car can carry at 35 m stand-off. If that sedan car is not physically prevented from getting closer than 35 m, the MRTC is for a sedan at the closest stand-off that the sedan can manage. The MAR is the level of risk that the organisation is willing to work through and manage before relocating or closing down. We assess what level of threat we can withstand (are protected against) and annotate this on the threat spectrum for each threat range. By doing this, we are showing what level or scale of hazard we can cope with, without making changes to our security posture and changing routines. Using a zero-to-one scale, we can compare a number of hazards in a single graphic, known as a threat wheel (Figure 5.3).

In line with the default investment relationship, protection to resilience, we would plan to design to the MRTC or MAR and construct, as a minimum, to the baseline. Of course, we would build to the compliance standards where they exceed the baseline threat. Designing to the higher threat level allows us to upgrade in the future, should it be necessary, without having to rebuild entirely. This approach reflects the priority of the operation or purpose for the protection. We may build increased protection, but if the disruption caused to the operation is as high as the threat would cause, if not higher, we have achieved nothing.

Here, we look at our investment relationship and the resilience thresholds of disruption taken from the incident sequence. Let's say that we are building a medium-rise commercial office block with a reinforced concrete frame. The baseline VBIED threat is 125 kg trinitrotoluene (TNT) eq. at 35 m. However, we have identified that, under certain circumstances, the threat could rise to 600 kg TNT eq. at 5 m. Our clients insist on the minimum protection level

Figure 5.3 Threat spectrum and threat wheel, showing the construction investment as an enabler of higher threat response capability; the threat wheel lines represent the levels of protection for the operation or purpose against the identified threats

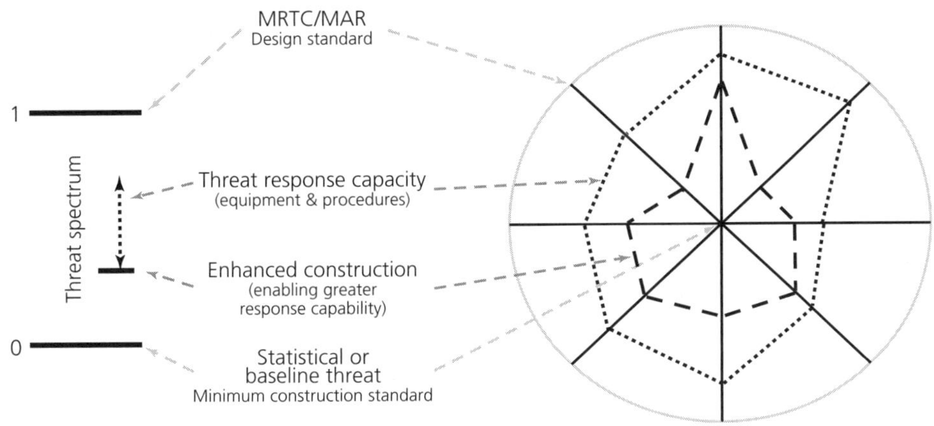

because they do not believe that the threat could ever increase. When we look at what would be involved in upgrading, the building would need to be rebuilt because the frame cannot support the increased loads. We may decide, therefore, to enhance the frame. We opt to keep the overall dimensions the same and just increase the percentage of reinforcing steel. We also put in bolt anchorages at 150 mm intervals along each external edge beam, top and bottom. The increase in steel costs is almost 60%, but it is negligible as a percentage of the whole project cost. This retrofit reinforcement is rear face strapping that anchors into the floor and ceiling. We have not enhanced the frame to the full VBIED MRTC or MAR, but we have achieved a significant improvement, to 225 kg TNT eq. at 15 m, say. We can also enhance the exterior panels with minimal disruption to operations in the building.

The fourth and final issue is that the security must be integrated. The definition of security integration is: 'No security measure may impede the effectiveness of another measure, or the efficiency of the (protected) operation.' There are some other variations on this, but we'll continue with this working definition here. It is not a liaison and communication matrix between different organisations working on the same operation's security. Security integration can be a challenge when security is imposed onto a design instead of being inherent to it.

I am sure that you will have noticed a wall that obscures part of a CCTV camera angle, or a CCTV camera that is blinded by an approaching car headlamp or the reflection of street lighting in the rain. However, more damaging is the hardening of an electrical substation against a perceived terror threat that prevents heavy plant access to swap-out transformers as part of routine maintenance. The result is that infrastructure failure becomes more likely from inadequate maintenance than from malicious activity. The diversion of infrastructure maintenance budgets to fund physical security measures compromises future operating value. One might argue that if the purpose of terrorism is to force a behaviour change that diminishes our way of life, the fear of an attack can be more effective than the attack itself.

5.3. Protection principles

As we explore this idea of protection, it is useful to look at the basic principles. There are three principles. They are: do no harm; no protection is absolute, and everything will change. The first, do no harm, is also known as the universal principle. Interestingly, it is also the one that appears to be overlooked most often. When we plan protection measures, we must ensure that we don't make things worse. Sometimes, the protection solution is worse than the risk and herein lies the issue. We discussed an example where an electrical substation was hardened to withstand a terrorist threat but in the process routine maintenance was made more difficult, with the net effect that there were more electricity supply interruptions. One would like to think that this is quite a blatant case of poor protection planning. What about when a blast wall is constructed and obscures a camera view of the avenues of approach? When applying the universal principle, many sum it up to say that no (security) measure may impede the efficiency of the operation (that we are protecting) or any other (security) measure. You will recognise this as the definition of security integration, which we return to later.

We also need to think of this principle in another way, specifically harm to third parties. We are building a new courthouse, police station or barracks in a high-threat environment, say. By our presence, we are drawing the threat of car bombs to an area that would otherwise not be attacked. That doesn't mean that we don't go ahead with the build. It means that we need to address the collateral effects and minimise the harm to third parties. For example, we open an army recruiting office next to a library. Our recruiting office has a series of standard protection measures but the library doesn't. The library will suffer disproportionately from any attack.

Alternatively, we are building bridge piers on a floodplain. The obstruction that the piers form in the primary (hydrologic) floodplain increases the likelihood that farms in the secondary (topographic) floodplain will be flooded more frequently than previously. This would not be the case if we hadn't obstructed the floodplain where we did. This is not just an issue of physical harm to property. It extends to the legal concept of nuisance, which is where our actions impede our neighbour's lawful enjoyment of their property. It might be related to the noise from our infrastructure, pollution or other disturbance. We might resort to a compulsory land purchase order, but imposed infrastructure does not lead to community adoption or social licence, as we've already discussed.

Ultimately, though, we come back to the purpose of the infrastructure. We have an operational purpose in mind, but if it impedes the unifying purpose of health, what have we achieved? You will recall that by health, we mean the physical, mental and social well-being of the population (WHO, 1948). Whether we go back to Dr John Snow's isolation of the cholera outbreak in 1854 Soho, London, UK, or look at present-day disease management through improved potable water supplies, that purpose is the same. Our protection measures cannot compromise the fundamental purpose of the infrastructure.

The second principle is that no protection is absolute. Once again, we instinctively understand this one, and yet we don't often demonstrate that understanding. We can, theoretically, keep investing in ever-higher levels of protection. We don't eliminate the risk; we only reduce the likelihood of a failure. The seawall protecting the Fukushima Daiichi Nuclear Power Plant was built to a defined tsunami height. That does not mean that a tsunami cannot exceed the seawall height, only that it would be highly unlikely. The tsunami of 20 March 2011 did exceed the seawall height. The protection afforded by the seawall was not absolute. Therefore, one might reasonably expect the planners to consider the possibility because the consequences are so extreme. This situation raises several issues that we need to consider carefully.

When we reduce the likelihood of a hazard occurring, it doesn't mean that it won't occur, and we still need to consider the consequence. If the consequence is manageable, we may decide that further investment is unnecessary based on our risk criteria. If the consequences remain severe, we should consider how best to manage the incident to reduce the consequence. Such questions are the essence of risk management around very-low-likelihood very-high-consequence risks. It is also up to the infrastructure planner to be as objective and evidence-based as possible. As Huber (2009) shows, our degree of belief in the possibility of something determines how we perceive the likelihood of an occurrence. We must inform the infrastructure owner and operator of the risks, free of bias and prejudice. This can be easier said than done, but it informs our design levels of protection, which we return to later.

The third principle is that everything will change. As we've discussed, the infrastructure's operation may change; the operating context, operating environment and threats may change. Our protection must be adaptable. Adaptability is not as difficult as it sounds. Still, it does require us to focus on the purpose of the infrastructure and plan our protection of that purpose. This idea of purpose is fundamental. I used the example of a garrison fortress built to project a capability; the fortifications are there to protect that capability rather than the asset itself. If we extend this concept to the protection measures themselves, we see that those measures must continue to protect the purpose during floods and incidents. We had already discussed the example of a flooded retail park where the security failed when the fuel for the standby power ran out. The purpose was compromised because the protection was not planned as a resilient operational system; it wasn't safe-to-fail. It was only designed for compliance.

We need to clarify a couple of things about compliance before continuing. When we talk of compliance, we are generally referring to external compliance requirements, such as industry norms, standards and contract conditions. We will also be subject to a range of organisational requirements from the owner and operator and perhaps our organisation. We will also have a significant selection of project-specific compliance requirements that have arisen from our risk evaluation and treatment process. The first two, external and organisational, are collectively grouped as ϕ_α (phi alpha); ϕ_α refers to the protection measures, including security, that must be applied or implemented, irrespective of their relevance to the situation. Conversely, the security requirements specific to the project are grouped as ϕ_β (phi beta). I do not know where these designations originated. Still, they are worth remembering, both as groupings and the designations, as they often crop up.

The cost of the protection is the cost of ϕ_β less the cost of ϕ_α. It is quite possible for the requirement ϕ_β to be less than ϕ_α, and this is not as unusual as one might imagine. However, the process of justifying a reduction in the compliance measures can be challenging. It is only worth pursuing when to proceed with the compliance measures would cause harm or where the cost difference is significant. Some large infrastructure owners have standardised their designs and security specifications to minimise site-specific adjustments. Such standardisation promotes operational conformity through the organisation and may be a way of addressing potential liabilities. For example, a major commercial real estate owner standardised a series of 'resilience' measures for all of their properties after their experiences in Hurricane Sandy. However, this can bias how we see the risk context and interpret our situation.

The critical thing to remember in applying the general principles to the purpose of the infrastructure and including the compliance measures is to ensure that the protection schema is organic to the operation. Refer to Figure 5.2. The security requirements are derived from the residual risks after primary risk treatment. In this way, we may ensure that the security requirements, and the protection measures, are an extension of the operation and not applied to it. This places a greater emphasis on security integration of the different systems, which we discuss next.

5.4. Through-life value

We explored the idea of the through-life value of infrastructure and how it changes over time with use. Protecting through-life value implies protecting its use, as much as its capability and capacity for use. It would be impractical to design infrastructure to adapt to a change in use. However, remember that infrastructure is the physical manifestation of systems that extend over the four domains of the VSOS. Our system can be responsive to changes in use. The infrastructure would, therefore, enable this responsiveness without necessarily being responsive itself. In effect, we plan the infrastructure to enable options for service response to changes. These options provide us with the means to respond to uncertainty in the future (Taleb, 2010).

Consider Figure 5.3. We see that what we build enables a range of equipment and procedural changes to security. It doesn't mean that the future security profile is implemented from the outset, only that it is enabled when needed. This idea of designing-in adaptability applies to any infrastructure system. We have two tools at our disposal. The first is capability-based planning, where we project into the future the (operational) capability we wish to have where and when, and assess how a changing risk context will affect our ability to deliver it. Through this future, or scenario, analysis, we identify the two most impactful trends and derive four alternative futures. We evaluate what the infrastructure requirements will be to enable the projected capability in each of these futures. We would then develop the infrastructure up to the point at which the requirements for the alternative futures diverge. This is known as the point of investment, which is discussed further in Chapter 6.

The second tool we have is the threat spectrum and our calculation of operational disruption from a change in infrastructure. We design to the (lower of the) MRTC or MAR and construct to the baseline threat level. The reason for designing to the higher threat level is to limit the need for extensive new works. However, the concept only works if we are adding to a system. What if we need to reconfigure or upgrade the existing structural aspects so that we can enhance or add other parts? When we look at the consequence of operational disruption after commissioning, we get a clear sense of the negative consequence of an upgrade or adaptation during the infrastructure's working life. When we design our future upgrade capability from the beginning, we can enable future infrastructure enhancements with minimal operational disruption. It is worth looking at a couple of examples.

Let's return to our example of the office building designed for a specific bomb threat. We recognise that this threat can increase and design incremental enhancements that will allow the building to withstand an increased threat. By upgrading the reinforced concrete frame build to the full design load and incorporating anchorages in the edge beams, we deliver a structure that can adapt to a change in threat with minimal disruption to routine operations. In this case, we can fix the rear panel reinforcement straps to the edge beam anchorages in little more time than it takes the cleaners to go through the building. In this way, disruption of operations is limited, responsiveness to an increase in threat is much improved and the initial development project cost is not significantly affected. This is a simple example, with a single threat to a single structure, albeit housing a complex high-value operation. Let's increase the scope.

Consider a local electricity distribution authority with a traditional monolithic grid infrastructure. It distributes the electricity above ground from a step-down transformer station at the end of the transmission line through a series of substations to industrial and commercial units and low voltage posts in residential neighbourhoods. The authority's market assessment and risk projections showed that there would be more shoulder days per year, owing to climate change. Shoulder days are when the ambient temperature fluctuates between 2°C and −2°C, increasing the likelihood of ice accretion and ice storms, with potential power outages. Furthermore, as part of the national policy to transition to a low carbon dioxide economy by 2035, there is a renewed emphasis on conservation and consumer demand management and localised alternative power generation and storage. The aim is to reduce the energy losses from long-distance transmission. The authority needs to upgrade its infrastructure to meet the effects of climate change and long periods of underinvestment. However, the future will not be the same as the past, and the authority is uncertain where to invest. To further complicate matters, the fiscal response to the pandemic's economic effects means that the government coffers are bare.

I've touched on clustering examples previously. Clustering, developed from a concept of economist Alfred Marshal (1890), sees groupings of like and compatible micro-generators and consumers. We touched on this previously. Within each cluster is a system of burden sharing through the two-way distribution of electricity as needed (Figure 5.4). This includes storage, both centrally and distributed around the cluster. When demand within the cluster exceeds its generation capacity, it draws on the grid. The use of surge protectors, digital switches, supply management, (public–private) co-owned storage and blockchain accounting of electricity transactions enables the cluster. It also reduces the demand and dependency on the main grid, deferring the investment in upgrade by one or two decades, possibly more. If the grid supply is interrupted by an ice storm, each cluster has sufficient capacity to meet at least the MOC. Burden sharing between clusters would ideally permit all to achieve the MSC for an extended period.

We can create a subset of the cluster, a panel, which might be a row of houses along a street. Each house has an electric vehicle charging capability that

Figure 5.4 Blockchain-enabled clustering arrangement with storage and smart energy management

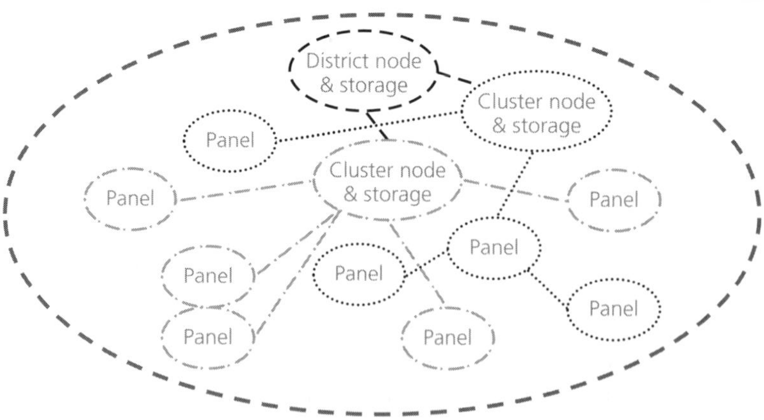

enhances storage as residents gradually convert to electric vehicles from gasoline or diesel. We can also group several clusters geographically as a district with substantial centralised electricity storage. There are many different ways to approach burden sharing, of which clustering is one. However, clustering is most illustrative of the concept. We can see something similar in newer retail and commercial developments. For example, the excess heat from the chillers in a community grocer, Longo's, heats the fitness centre swimming pool next door. Natural Resources Canada is exploring similar approaches on the theme of food security in communities. This brings us back to the fundamental question of what we require of the infrastructure. It can nuance our understanding of what we need to protect and how.

We've discussed the idea of community adoption of infrastructure and will explore this further in the next chapter. Fundamentally, adoption drives the adaptation of the infrastructure through the enabled service to the community's changing needs. The infrastructure needs to enable community stability, particularly during periods of stress and shock. The US Gulf and Atlantic Coasts military base commanders' experiences point clearly to a close working relationship with local communities. Their personnel are also part of the community; they contribute revenue and collectively provide a response and recovery capacity for the civilian population.

We see the same dynamic in non-permissive environments where the base's provision of municipal services in the surrounding community creates stability and fosters close cooperation and shared outcomes. My research into post-conflict (traumatised) communities suggests that these communities viewed infrastructure facilities with local caretakers and engineers as part of the community fabric, unlike those operated remotely (Hay *et al.*, 2019). When deciding whether to operate a single centrally operated supervisory control and data acquisition (SCADA) system or localised distributed control systems (DCS), this is something to consider (Hay, 2019). Can the local community be part of your infrastructure protection plan? We'll come back to this later.

You will have noticed that our approach to protection is necessarily flexible. It must be able to adapt to changes in threat and use. There are limits to this flexibility. Figure 5.1 describes a generic relationship between protection and resilience investment. As a rule of thumb, investing in protection to address the background or baseline threat makes eminent sense. The transition segment from protection to resilience investment covers the measures that enable change in use, discussed in this section. However, we can be more focused than that and find the transition points from our calculations of benefit–cost ratio (BCR) and return on investment (ROI).

As we discuss infrastructure, we must start from the purpose, the service that the infrastructure enables. This means that the BCR and ROI calculations are necessarily assessed environmentally or operationally, economically and socially. In reality, they are all related, and your organisation defines the system of metrics. Chapter 3 applies. Our emphasis so far has been on the operation that the infrastructure enables and controlling what we have control over. However, we do still need to understand the external causes of failure. Typically, we need to buy ourselves time to prepare and respond appropriately and efficiently.

5.5. Risk mapping

We are interested in how a hazard can generate and affect our operations, and we wish to know this in both time and space. Let us return to our Lego base plate, the tableau. This three-dimensional model shows us where our operations are in their spatial and risk context. Through the LRA, we have established where the inherent hazards are generated and how they approach the operation over what time. Using our HTT analyses, we can say what indicator we are looking for where. When we combine these in the same model, it is known as a surveillance trace. As long as we have clearly defined our AOO, AOI and area of interest on the tableau, we can develop a plan to collect the necessary data. The surveillance trace is an important document and should be part of the *common reference*, depending on what level of access there is to it. It is the basis of the security (systems) integration schema, data collection plans, the control measures for mutual assistance agreements and allocation of responsibilities, and the assessment of service access before, during and after an incident. Critically, it also allows us to build realistic hazard scenarios with correlated and coincident risks. This is all very much more straightforward with digitised records. However, even in more developed countries, there will be instances where you will need to revert to manual calculation and data management, necessitating strong engineering judgement.

We can group different indicators by location. Our primary concern with indicators is false returns. False positives can generate complacency when there are too many false alarms. In contrast, false negatives mean that we will miss the hazard altogether. We must address false returns and distinguish between different hazard types. The first step is to apply a detect–verify–confirm–validate protocol to our sensor arrays. When we detect a hazard indicator, we wish to verify that it is an indicator and confirm that there is a hazard. Once we have detected several indicators, we can validate those indicators against a specific hazard to determine its direction and magnitude.

For example, there is a controlled freshwater supply to a facility. We are concerned about contamination of the water supply and so have placed sensors on each access point. The detector, in this case, is a lift switch. When the access cover opens, the switch activates. Independently, the verification detector is a photosensitive switch that activates when light enters the access space. The combination of the two indicates that the access space is open. However, one detector without the other would still cue a confirmation. Our sensor analysis software would compare these alarms with scheduled maintenance and other authorised access. The most straightforward confirmation today is often a camera view of the space. Smartphone technology makes it possible to combine these sensors into a single unit for wireless or tethered communication to a data control node or central control room.

A confirmed indicator of unauthorised access can cue a response to the access space and the automated closure of the facility's water supply valve. We can apply this practice at any scale, for each hazard of concern. From our HTT analyses, we can have prepared our readiness levels, reaction capability, response protocols and resources, and incident management protocols. A remarkable amount of this can, and should, be automated. The weakest link in so many response systems is the human one. We cannot concentrate for extended periods and find it challenging to transition instantly from rest to being situationally aware. We will explore this some more in the next chapters. How quickly can a CCTV camera operator respond on seeing a possible marauding intruder on the premises or some illegal tipping into a reservoir? Even so, we are assuming that we have the right indicators and are interpreting them correctly.

What we do about the approaching hazards is the corollary question. We need to develop an efficient and pragmatic approach to delay, block, divert and deter hazards. We can change the ground around us to some degree, changing the surrounding land's going (terramechanical properties) to suit our needs or put up obstacles. However, we still need to know how effective these measures are and carefully design our response measures. It is useful to start by saying what effect we wish to have on the approaching hazard. By defining effects, we do not constrain ourselves to a specific measure or equipment, and we are better able to blend the often conflicting demands of different HTT responses. Once we have blended the effects by area and assigned the applicable hazards to them, we have the basis of the security integration trace, or schema. We can gradually develop this trace by introducing measures and comparing the security requirements we identified earlier.

Security integration is a particular skill, and it is worth bringing in an independent advisor to guide and facilitate the process at the master planning stage. This demands a degree of objectivity that can be difficult if we have run the planning analysis up to this point. We will all have our biases and degrees of belief. Similarly, not all security advisors are competent security integrators. When you look at security, specifically malicious hazards, few advisory sources are better than the UK's Centre for the Protection of the National Infrastructure (CPNI, 2021). They also hold a register of competent practitioners administered by the Institution of Civil Engineers, known as the Register of Security Engineers and Specialists (RSES, 2021). You will find a useful starting point for security considerations in your strategic planning of infrastructure in these two sources. Many more organisations will provide guidance and advice once you have a strategy.

The CPNI has produced two public documents to inform our thinking, *Integrated Security* (CPNI, 2014) and the *Guide to Producing Operational Requirements for Security Measures* (CPNI, 2010). Several professional associations' guidance notes are pertinent for different types of infrastructure and aspects of the planning process. From experience, I have found it useful to default to the Royal Institute of British Architects (RIBA) guidance documents and project timeline. While the detail may differ by jurisdiction, the essential structure and approach are commonly recognisable across most countries. The CPNI also conducts validation tests of a wide range of security products, which are sometimes useful to counteract marketing hyperbole. The Building Research Establishment's *LPCB Red Book* (BRE, 2020) is a similarly useful reference.

A final note on useful references is to acquaint yourself with what is locally referenced by the design profession. For example, Barbara Nadel's *Building Security* (2004) would appear to be the standard security reference among architects in northeast USA. The default reference simply reflects what was in circulation when security was topical. I have not found a single reference that applies across jurisdictions and can take the reader from strategic to detailed planning. Some of the concepts and details will not apply to your planning situation. Still, by understanding the local reference standard, you are better positioned to understand the local interpretations and definitions and inform your stakeholder management and perceptions.

We have touched on our systems of control at various points in our exploration of infrastructure planning. We need to protect our data, our communications and control systems. This is only possible if the systems are appropriate for the operation. Information and communications technology (ICT) is organic to your operations and the enabling infrastructure. It can be easy to lose that connection when ICT is considered a separate entity in the organisation and planning. We communicate, gather and process data, and store and use the data directly related to our infrastructure systems' operational risks. The EU's General Data Protection Regulation (GDPR) is rapidly becoming the de facto international standard for handling personal data, for example. It will be just as relevant to your operational liabilities and risk exposure as IT users' security protocols. Poor practices can compromise the security of an infrastructure system, as much as poorly arranged enterprise architecture. The challenge in infrastructure systems development is that the data systems are invisible, even though they now define operational routine and response effectiveness. There are two aspects to this. The first is the inherent fragility in standard systems misapplied to the operation. The second is human nature.

Supervisory control and data acquisition (SCADA) systems have evolved rapidly over the last 25 years. Modern software is frequently updated with generic capabilities that are rarely utilised. Often, it is just easier to use these standard SCADA systems. A remote system is not always applicable.

Sometimes, we benefit from not being connected to the World Wide Web. It can be useful to have an intelligent being familiar with a local sector of the infrastructure laydown, who can interpret and act on the early indicators that might not stimulate a response at head office. In such cases, we might consider a distributed control system (DCS), geographically defined and not connected to the Internet. Often, the complexity and rapid updating of modern SCADA software is such that it is rare for an organisation to have the in-house expertise to learn and understand the software and what its vulnerabilities are before the next version is installed. This can layer vulnerabilities, which needn't be software glitches but merely a misapplication of SCADA to infrastructure, system on system. Not so different from Koestler's warning in Chapter 2.

In our operational risk audits, it is remarkable how often human nature compromises effective engineering planning and design. An oil drilling rig in the Gulf of Mexico has an effective enterprise architecture, and all industrial control systems (ICS) are secure. The drilling manager wishes to monitor progress on his tablet and arranges a patch so that she can do that. Her tablet is also linked to the Internet, inadvertently providing an intruder access to drilling operations. A CEO wishes to monitor live pipeline performance data from his office rather than the collated dashboard feed so opens the ICS to external access. The point to remember is that the ICS and broader ICT need to be organic to the infrastructure planning process. They cannot be applied to planned infrastructure. When planned with the infrastructure, they become part of the infrastructure systems and not the operating context. To do this effectively, you must understand the interactions between ICS or ICT and the operating infrastructure to understand the consequences of compromise and where the risks reside. In our audit experience, my colleagues and I have found that many organisations focus on defending against the cyber threat without exploring what it means to their operations. The ICS are an integral part of the VSOS and must be considered as such.

5.6. Levels of protection

Each jurisdiction will have its unique interpretation of levels of protection (LoP). Even within a professional jurisdiction, that interpretation may differ. They will all be right, because ultimately the LoP reflects the risk criteria and appetite of the specifying authority or organisation. To understand the concept and the nuances in interpretation, we should start with the risk criteria. Risk criteria are 'reference standards, measures, or expectations used in judging the significance of a given risk in context with strategic goals' (Elliott, 2012). You will recall from Chapter 2 how the risk criteria influence the organisation's interpretation of the risk context and the common reference. They are how we interpret the relevance of the risk and what we should do about it. Implicit in this is the idea of risk appetite, which is 'the total exposed amount that an organisation wishes to undertake on the basis of risk-return trade-offs for one or more desired and expected outcomes' (RIMS, 2012). Both definitions are sadly cumbersome, but the nuances in these definitions are particularly relevant

Figure 5.5 Risk tolerance approach to treatment and the opportunity for innovation in infrastructure applications (after Philbin B *et al.* (2017))

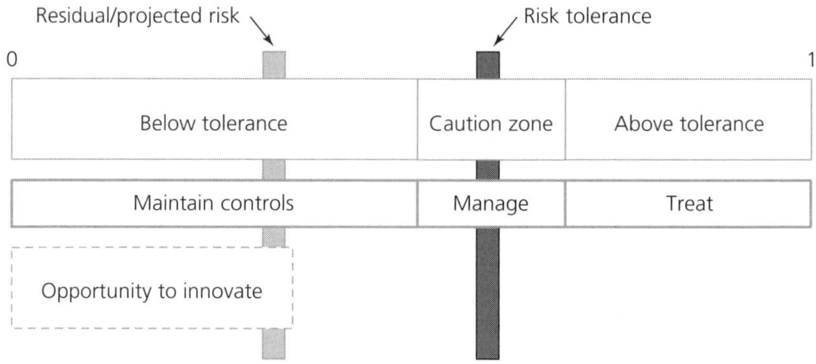

for infrastructure planning because of the significant impact that they can have on the community, the environment and the economy.

When we understand how risk affects us, we can make an informed judgement on whether the likely benefit outweighs the potential harm. We can decide how we will deal with the risk. This goes far beyond compliance and familiar practices and models. It is a fundamental approach dealing with risk, and probably why each jurisdiction will have its own interpretation. Recently, the Canadian Revenue Agency (CRA) devised a simple sliding scale to illustrate how it would approach intelligent non-financial risk management (Philbin *et al.*, 2017). When we apply this methodology to the service that our infrastructure enables, we can realise risk management efficiencies by innovating operational practice where the carried risk is significantly less than our tolerance (Figure 5.5). In effect, we are seeking an opportunity to benefit from our (evidence-based and quantified) carried risk.

Let's start with the hazard or threat. The typical threat and risk assessment (TRA) provides a snapshot of the situation at the time of assessment. Whether evidence- or opinion-based, TRAs are necessarily referenced by the past and provide an unreliable forecast of future threats. They should not be used as the basis of protection planning for an infrastructure development strategy. If we wish to forecast threats, we can control threat access and determine how large the threat to our operation can be. You will recall the example of limiting the size of vehicle that can approach a critical building, so limiting the maximum size of explosive charge and stand-off. Think again of our Lego base plate. We can define the threat access and capability spatially. Therefore, the question should be what access is needed for an efficient operation that delivers its purpose. It is useful to conduct a review of routine access requirements for the service or operation and begin the infrastructure layout. Any limitation in access for efficient operations becomes the benefit–loss trade-off.

Now that we have set the context for our level of protection (LoP), let's explore it more closely. You will recall that we are protecting the purpose, not necessarily the physical asset. It is important to be clear on what we are protecting. Let's say that we are protecting the national parliament. Are we protecting the buildings, the parliamentarians or the institution? It is easy to default to the protection of human life, which too often misses the point. No protection can be absolute; someone will die in an attack, and we must minimise the casualties in any attack. However, these individuals serve the purpose that we are protecting; they are only in harm's way because of the purpose. The purpose must remain our primary focus. When we do this, we plan a system that is safe-to-fail, and the purpose continues uncompromised. When we focus on dependencies and individual assets, we are unlikely to protect the purpose.

Consequently, the *operational* LoP is determined by the degree of (performance) loss that we can tolerate while protecting the purpose. Using the parliamentary example, if the purpose is the institution of parliament, say, we need to preserve a minimum decision-making capability and be able to relocate it with the necessary staff. The same can be said for the cabinet office or a ministerial office. How to protect personnel will be a derivative of this assessment. Incident sequencing is a useful tool for calculating the enabling function tolerances and recovery parameters once we know the overall tolerance that the purpose or operation has for interruption.

When we know what level of impact we can tolerate and still preserve purpose, we can know the minimum *structural* LoP. This means that any protection we can provide over this minimum structural LoP will reduce the overall loss exposure and impact of a threat. When used in conjunction with control of access for potential threats, we can manage the operation's risk profile through life. By planning and designing the infrastructure to support these parameters, we are also providing the security and response agencies the flexibility to directly adjust procedures, personnel and equipment to manage local changes in threat profile.

5.7. Chapter summary

Protection in infrastructure planning is about protecting the purpose or operation that the infrastructure enables. We therefore plan and design the infrastructure to enable the necessary protection approach and measures. The infrastructure is one part of protection, enabling the efficient and responsive allocation of personnel, procedures and equipment to address changes in threat. Protection is part of a broader concept of security, which encompasses public safety. Security has three components that must be harmonised in any effective security scheme. They are relational, procedural and physical. Though primarily associated with the physical component of security, protection contributes to all three.

There are three basic principles of security and protection. They are: do no harm; no protection is absolute, and everything will change. The first principle, also known as the universal principle, is adapted as the definition of security integration: no measure may adversely affect any other measure or the efficiency of the operation being protected. This requires a clear focus on the purpose of the protection, planning the infrastructure to enable that protection and its purpose.

When we look over the infrastructure's life and the operation that it enables, we cannot predict the hazards and threats that it will face. This means that we should not use retrospective assessments to project future risks, such as TRAs. Instead, we need to balance threat access with minimum LoP, defined by the preservation of purpose and a broader safe-to-fail approach to the system of systems. Effective LoP management builds on an understanding of the operational tolerance of the purpose to interruption. The structural LoP and infrastructure specification are necessarily derived from this operational LoP.

Once again, the common themes of evidence and risk define our understanding of the infrastructure protection requirement and strategy. When we standardise protection measures for facilities, we can project a bias on how we perceive the world around us – our understanding of the situation and the threats we face is defined by standard measures, blinding us to threats that exist and fall outside our compliance. Similarly, if we define the scale of threat by the compliance measure, we can fail to see the residual risk of the threat exceeding the compliance LoP. In hindsight, it would seem obvious that we should understand the situation before we look at protection measures. Once again, following a codified process is often more attractive than investing time and effort in understanding the situation. Protection and resilience are risk-based pursuits that rely on the common reference to be effective and efficient. Assumption rarely proves effective or efficient.

BIBLIOGRAPHY

BRE (Building Research Establishment) (2020) *LPCB Red Book*. BRE, Watford, UK.

CPNI (Centre for the Protection of the National Infrastructure) (2010) *Guide to Producing Operational Requirements for Security Measures*. CPNI, London, UK.

CPNI (2014) *Integrated Security: A Public Realm Design Guide for Hostile Vehicle Mitigation*, 2nd edn. CPNI, London, UK.

CPNI (2021) Centre for the Protection of the National Infrastructure. https://www.cpni.gov.uk/ (accessed 06/04/2021).

Elliott MW (ed.) (2012) *Risk Management Principles and Practices*, 1st edn. The Institutes, Malvern, PA, USA.

Genetec (2017) The educator. *Citywise* http://citywise.net/conversation/the-educator-juliette-kayyem (accessed 18/08/2020).

Hay AH (2019) Security force protection in the post-conflict arena. *The Royal Engineers Journal* **133(2)**: 69–72.

Hay AH, Karney B and Martyn N (2019) Reconstructing infrastructure for resilient essential services during and following protracted conflict: a conceptual framework. *International Review of the Red Cross* **101(912)**: 1001–1029, 10.1017/S1816383120000053.

Huber F (2009) Belief and degrees of belief. In *Degrees of Belief* (Huber F and Schmidt-Petri C (eds.)). Springer, Dordrecht, the Netherlands, pp. 1–33.

Kayyem J (2016) Terrorism only works on nations that aren't ready for it. *The Atlantic*, 12 Aug. https://www.belfercenter.org/publication/terrorism-only-works-nations-arent-ready-it (accessed 06/04/2021).

Marshall A (1890) *Principles of Economics*. MacMillan, London, UK. (Republished as 8th edn, 2014, Palgrave MacMillan, Basingstoke, UK.)

Nadel BA (ed.) (2004) *Building Security: Handbook for Architectural Planning and Design*. McGraw-Hill, New York, NY, USA.

Philbin B, Brown L and McKay L (2017) Intelligent risk-taking: a methodology to determine risk tolerance in a non-financial environment. *2017 Enterprise Risk Management Symposium, New Orleans, LA, USA*.

RIMS (Risk and Insurance Management Society) (2012) *Exploring Risk Appetite and Risk Tolerance*. RIMS, New York, NY, USA. RIMS Executive Report: The Risk Perspective. https://ermgovernance.com/Resources/RIMS_Exploring_Risk_Appetite_Risk_Tolerance_0412.pdf (accessed 13/08/2020).

RSES (Register of Security Engineers and Specialists) (2021) https://www.rses.org.uk/ (accessed 06/04/2021).

Taleb NN (2010) *The Black Swan: The Impact of the Highly Improbable*, 2nd edn. Random House Trade Paperbacks, New York, NY, USA.

WHO (World Health Organization) (1948) Constitution. http://www.who.int/about/mission/en/ (accessed 11/05/2018).

FURTHER READING

There is seemingly an abundance of literature on protection, particularly around ICT and structures. These would also seem to be the focus of many specialised security consultancies. There is also a growing body of work around the protection of personnel and human security. There is always something to learn in each book and paper. However, when we look at infrastructure protection in its entirety, further reading is limited. There are three commonly quoted references. The first two are Ted Lewis's (2006) *Critical Infrastructure Protection in Homeland Security: Defending a Networked Nation* and Radvanovsky and McDougall's (2010) *Critical Infrastructure: Homeland Security and Emergency Preparedness*. These are US-centric, though the essential ideas and applications translate well. The third is Tyson Macaulay's (2009) *Critical Infrastructure: Understanding its Component Parts, Vulnerabilities, Operating Risks, and Interdependencies*. This presents a more holistic exploration of infrastructure systems, their fragilities and what needs protecting to preserve the national economy and way of life. Each book is of its time, with a defined scope.

The guidance notes from CPNI (2021) are always worth exploring, not least because they focus on infrastructure protection, both as a whole and by industry sector, and they are kept current. Beyond this, further reading is available for those with the right security clearances. If we take a step back again and look at the VSOS holistically, we see that it is worth exploring more about the effects of risk, how our systems of systems are fragile and what we should protect. This contextual understanding is very much what this book endeavours to examine, and we find that we cannot separate the infrastructure from its purpose, the engineering from the society it enables. We are faced with questions about how to capture the meaning of these risks, going beyond the limitations of statistical analysis and risk management practice. This builds on our earlier reading of catastrophic risk.

CPNI (2021) Centre for the Protection of the National Infrastructure. https://www.cpni.gov.uk/ (accessed 06/04/2021).

Lewis TG (2006) *Critical Infrastructure Protection in Homeland Security: Defending a Networked Nation*. Wiley-Interscience, Hoboken, NJ, USA.

Macaulay T (2009) *Critical Infrastructure: Understanding its Component Parts, Vulnerabilities, Operating Risks, and Interdependencies*. CRC Press, Boca Raton, FL, USA.

Pate-Cornell E (2012) On 'black swans' and 'perfect storms': risk analysis and management when statistics are not enough. *Risk Analysis* **(32)11**: 1823–1833.

Radvanovsky R and McDougall A (2010) *Critical Infrastructure: Homeland Security and Emergency Preparedness*, 2nd edn. CRC Press, Boca Raton, FL, USA.

ICE Publishing

Hay, Alexander H
ISBN 978-0-7277-6562-8
https://doi.org/10.1680/pris.65628.129

Chapter 6
Infrastructure planning in theory: putting it all together

As we consider how to go about planning infrastructure, the complexity of what it is and how it fits into the world can be daunting. In a more technical sense, we have an extraordinary array of principles, concepts and constraints to consider and balance before adapting our strategy to political priorities. We know that we must do better than merely looking at our infrastructure project as an extension of a single system in isolation or an assembly of assets. Our strategy must draw together the infrastructure requirements, risks, financing, contracting and management aspects in an integrated whole. This is, in a genuine sense, a strategy from which we build the plan. We must, and can, know what to build where, when and how without causing harm, and we must be able to measure our success.

One of the challenges we face is that, in the abstract, we start to build a concept of how the world should be, based on a wealth of supporting research. In truth, we build from what is and enable what the community desires. The community desire may be articulated as government direction or board objectives, but they are unlikely to reflect the abstract that we construct. Our evidence-based understanding of the situation is critical to intelligently informing the decision-makers about the direction. The practicalities of this are explored in Chapter 7, when we discuss infrastructure planning in practice. However, this means that we are not planning perfect infrastructure development. It means that we are planning infrastructure development to achieve a stated requirement, and it is up to us to make it sustainable within the given constraints. We use evidence to understand the world as it is so that we may know what the directed development can mean and deliver an infrastructure development plan that is balanced, sustainable and efficient.

The strategy for developing infrastructure will ultimately define its success. There is no shortage of financing and delivery options available to us, and appropriately assembled these will lead to a successful project delivery. That doesn't mean that it will have a successful outcome, which is why the strategy is so important. The strategy aligns the directed end-state with the risk context and provides us with a sequence of objectives and conditions that allow us to transform the world as it is into the world that is demanded. The strategy identifies how we achieve a beneficial and sustainable outcome over the life of the infrastructure. Consequently, our discussion focuses on putting the strategy together. We do this by drawing together all of the principles and concepts discussed in Chapter 1 to 5.

This chapter explores the generic planning process, the infrastructure development plan, and process transparency and repeatability. This leads to discussions on what we know and understand, what we need to achieve and what role the infrastructure will play. There follows an extended exploration of a structured approach to strategy development before discussing outcomes, engagement, the common reference, measuring success and the community value of the proposed infrastructure development. The chapter concludes with a brief discussion on approaching the business case.

6.1. An overview of the planning process

We want our infrastructure strategy to be sustainable, just as the infrastructure must be sustainable. It also needs to fit within a national or regional development policy. ICE has developed 12 guiding principles for infrastructure planning (ICE, 2019). You'll have seen each echoed in the preceding chapters and addressed in the proper creation of an infrastructure development strategy. These guiding principles provide an invaluable check that you have done everything as you should; it is arguably one of the better guides available. However, such guides are typically written to address a perceived deficiency in current practice. They can, therefore, assume much of the background working and require intelligent application. The 12 ICE guiding principles are as follows.

1. Start by identifying your strategic objectives.
2. The UN SDGs provide a baseline for this task.
3. The best national strategic infrastructure planning systems embrace three stages: (i) they establish a vision, (ii) conduct a needs assessment and (iii) use that to build a national strategy.
4. The national vision needs to reflect a country's national characteristics, the challenges it has inherited and its aspirations for the future.
5. The purpose of a needs assessment is to support evidence-based decision-making.
6. An infrastructure strategy needs to cover all aspects of implementation.
7. Cost–benefit analysis (CBA) is vital for prioritising investments, but must embrace all of the environmental, social and governance (ESG) impacts of a proposal.
8. A measure of affordability can focus minds.
9. Prioritisation can help avoid the *affordability trap*.
10. Governments should identify where private-sector involvement will deliver benefits and be clear on how they will be engaged.
11. High-quality consultation and stakeholder engagement should be an integral part of the process and should not be an afterthought.
12. Governments need to focus on data quality and interoperability to unlock the benefits of digital transformation.

Table 6.1 Generic components of an infrastructure development plan

Part 1: Strategy	■ Capability projection (statement and narrative) ■ Summary of requirement (core and supplemental) ■ Residual risk profiles by risk horizon ■ Delivery model and sequencing ■ Stakeholder management ■ Metrics (key performance indicators and key risk indicators; indicators of anticipated outcome)	Calculation plan
Part 2: Finance	■ Contracting model (including risk allocation) ■ Programme financial strategy (including leverage, sources and instruments) ■ Risk transfers (financial and non-financial) ■ Risk criteria ■ Reporting (routine, standards and compliance)	
Part 3: Portfolio	Infrastructure projects listed by sequenced objective (project description, estimated cost time and variance, stakeholder actions, carried risks and allocation, communication plan, potential unintended consequences, tangible benefits, stakeholder engagement direction, risk profile, metrics, portfolio relationships to other projects and activities)	

The document that brings this together under a unifying structure is known as the infrastructure development plan (IDP). There are three generic parts to it (Table 6.1): strategy, finance and portfolio (of projects). This book seeks to inform your approach to developing the strategy part. The IDP strategy would also appear to be what several countries, including the UK, wish to improve. It provides clarity of purpose around an end-state with a narrative of how the infrastructure will realise it. The finance part focuses on managing finances through the whole infrastructure development plan to the outcome, including debt to equity ratios (leverage), contracting models, underwriting and financial risk management. The portfolio part comprises all of the individual project briefs in context, including, as a minimum, the summary requirements, pre-conditions, risk profiles by horizon, cost and time estimates, and metrics.

Building an IDP strategy is an iterative process, but where to start? Aside from taking a deep breath in an attempt to relax, it is useful to separate our initial analysis into three parts: (*a*) What do we know and understand? (*b*) What do we seek to achieve? (*c*) How will the infrastructure enable this outcome? Make sure that you record all data sources and detail your analysis at each stage. When something changes, we need to be able to trace back through the analysis of how it affects the IDP, and adjust accordingly. It also helps the jurisdiction's auditor general or the lenders satisfy themselves that the IDP builds on evidence and sound analysis. We use the calculation plan (Table 6.2) for this, though each organisation and jurisdiction will have its respective audit trail conventions.

Table 6.2 Typical calculation plan (CP) format: the CP provides an audit trail of data collection, analysis and findings – each organisation will have its particular requirements and format; it should allow for cross-referencing so that the reasoning in successive iterations is not lost and can be recovered if parameters change

Reference	Discussion	Outputs	Actions
Use a simple referencing system that distinguishes between IDP parts and iterations.	Make a clear statement of the information collected and identify the source. Note whether the source is authenticated. Record the analysis and any cross-referencing to reach a deduction or conclusion.	Record all outputs from the discussion with a serial number that can be used with the reference.	Record what is to be done with the output, and any further action needed from the discussion. In particular, include critical information requirements (items for further investigation) and requests for information from specific stakeholders.

6.2. What do we know and understand?

This question establishes the foundation of our planning. It is about building a detailed, evidence-based knowledge of the VSOS, as it is, and interpreting what that means for us. In effect, we are creating a common reference to know the current situation and discuss it with all stakeholders. We then interpret that common reference against our interests and operations to build a common operating picture (COP). The COP represents our understanding of the current situation so that we may know what is possible.

You will recall the common reference and how to build one. At the beginning of the planning process, it is improbable for this to be complete. We can certainly develop a comprehensive tableau, and we can map the dependency relationships for our operations. The influence model is more challenging at this stage. We start with the de jure governance model. The de facto influence model will remain somewhat opaque until we have progressed with stakeholder engagement and begun constructing our mental models. Nonetheless, we will have a perfectly adequate common reference to start the first iteration. We explore the common reference and its use next.

We must now look in detail at the risk context. To do this, we must have a clear idea of where our interest lies. I have found that a simple mission analysis is the most effective tool to do this. The basic concept is typically adapted to each jurisdiction and incorporated into a broader process. However, the simple method is robust and worth using anyway. It is just as valid in business, government and military applications to clarify purpose as the user or infrastructure planner. The four-step mission analysis presents four questions: What outcome does my organisation intend? What is my role in achieving this outcome? What are my constraints (what must I do) and limitations (what may I not do)? Has anything changed?

The fact that we are even looking at infrastructure planning, whether for reconstruction or development, means that our organisation has an outcome in mind. Typically, this would be about the projection of the desired capability to some point in the future. Therefore, we have a sense of what that future capability is. We'll come back to this.

As infrastructure planners, we can also understand what our infrastructure plan must achieve, much of which is implicit or which we deduce. It is rare for a corporate strategy to articulate the infrastructure requirement fully. Our analysis of constraints and limitations encompasses more than compliance. It needs to include audits and public, shareholder or beneficiary scrutiny. However, this analysis typically exposes items that we have to include in our infrastructure strategy to enable delivery but are not part of the core capability requirement.

For example, in a reconstruction project, my colleagues and I were required to exhaust local employment options before considering trades from outside the local area. This meant that we provided a secure clinic–school–childcare facility so that widowed households could work on the infrastructure, and the benefits of the employment would be local. We also identified the need to pay in cash weekly until local banking could stabilise, and formal markets restored over the informal markets that had expanded during the conflict. The question 'Has anything changed?' is a reminder to maintain a watching brief on the situation. We must periodically review and update our models. Once created, the common reference becomes a 'living document', reflecting the situation as it is. Of the models, the influence model is the one that will change the quickest, which is why starting with a de jure model is sufficient. The adjustments will become evident as we progress.

Mission analysis
What does the (organisation) wish to achieve?
What do we need to deliver this?
What must we do? What must we not do?
What is changing?

With this mission analysis done, we can conduct a risk evaluation. The risk evaluation is a summary approach to the risk context to get the process started. For practical reasons, we take an enterprise-wide risk management (ERM) approach, considering strategic, financial, operational and hazard risk *quadrants* one at a time (Elliott, 2012). You will recall from Chapter 2 that we conduct a DTS to identify what we need to know before establishing a need for infrastructure planning. It provides an excellent starting point for our analysis. Let's begin with the strategic and financial, as they are both external risks.

Identify the risks, reference them and cite all information sources that you are using in your analysis. Several of your citations will be published expert opinion, which will reflect the human domain. However, these still need to be set within an empirical context.

Strategic risks are the political, legal and cultural changes that affect our planning. For example, there is a geopolitical trend shifting global supply chains to national control. While this may support our intelligent resourcing criteria, it can lead to greater fragility in our strategy. It is generally better to diversify supply chains, as discussed in Chapter 4. However, the speed of change can mean that local supply chains cannot adapt quickly enough or become entirely dependent on a single localised point of failure. It may merely mean that we are limited in what we can design. For example, despite the abundance of sheet piling in Afghanistan, it was impossible to find a piling rig in 2007. The design called for a structure with a two-storey basement in silty–sandy soil in a city. Short of redeveloping an entire city block and beyond, the original design would not be possible while still maximising local employment.

Political instability, conflict and a tendency to issue sudden regulatory changes are typical considerations in some regions. Supplementary negotiation will be required before we can route our electricity transmission line or oil pipeline through a First Nations Treaty Area, for example. There is also the consideration of how the local population views the proposed capability, much less the infrastructure itself. NIMBYism (*not in my backyard*) is frequently an issue in developed regions and can hold up infrastructure projects for decades. It is also worth considering the public (and political) attitude to private versus public infrastructure investment.

Financial risks are about currency exchange and the cost of debt and underwriting. It is rare to operate in solely one currency when dealing with infrastructure. By its very nature, most infrastructure is international, if not in its costs, then in its value. Investors in infrastructure will be operating in their national currency, a trading currency (such as the US dollar, Russian rouble, Chinese yuan, pound sterling or euro) and the local currency. Exchange rates fluctuate, and these can directly affect cash flow and confidence.

Let's say that you are paying your local workforce in (Malaysian) ringgit. Your principal donor is the EU, paying in euros, and the international contracting currency is US dollars. You note that the ringgit-to-euro exchange rate has generally been stable. Still, there have been fluctuations as the markets reacted to shifts in the region's geopolitical rhetoric. To maintain confidence, you decide to keep minimum cash accounts in each of these currencies to reliably cover wages, expenses and other liabilities within a defined risk horizon. There is the (speculative) possibility of making some money on the foreign exchange rate (FXR). Still, it would be best to have confidence that an FXR fluctuation doesn't compromise your plan. Further, you may write a master insurance plan in your organisation's head office country and develop local subordinate plans for the infrastructure project. The cost of debt may be too high for the initial lending, and you adjust your leverage of equity to debt so that you have collateral that a lender can value.

While the strategic and financial risks typically affect the 'how' of implementation, you may find that they affect the 'what' as well. For example, local communities may agree to the disruption caused by the works in their area in return for some other form of development, like a new school, clinic or emergency response facility. These 'adjustments' to the infrastructure requirement will quickly build.

We can now turn our attention to the internal risks, hazard and operational risks. The hazard risks, also known as true risks, are the risks that are inherent to the region and rather than because you are there. They include the effects of climate change, extreme weather events and seismic events. These will directly affect the infrastructure, including its users, supply lines during construction and operation, and seasonality limitations of austere environments, such as projects in the High Arctic. You will recall the LRA from Chapter 4. It is the expression of those same risks during planning and construction, commissioning and operation, and final disposal.

Operational risks are the ones that exist because the operation exists. The operation delivers the outcome, and the infrastructure enables the operation. These risks range from workers and users' health and safety, third-party considerations and resource access to technological change during the works. The operation's conduct can control the hazard and operational risks and, by extension, the infrastructure requirements. These risk treatments build the core requirement into a portfolio of requirements that enable IDP delivery.

Through this process, we have established what is, as the common reference, and developed our understanding of the risk context and how it affects what we are trying to achieve. The net result is that we can build our (initial) COP. We interpret the common reference to understand what it means for our operation (services and enabling infrastructure) so that we can know what is possible.

6.3. What do we seek to achieve?

Building from our mission analysis and risk evaluation, we can now articulate what the intended outcome comprises. Goals and objectives will have been identified in the strategy to realise the intended outcome. We wish to be in a position to determine what infrastructure will be required for each objective. Note that this will be more than a technical requirement; it will be something much broader. With this understanding, we are also in a position to sequence the infrastructure for each objective. It is possible that this can disrupt the synchronisation between infrastructure and objective, but it is too early in the process to worry about that.

We will wish to identify what each stage of infrastructure delivery entails. There will be resource constraints and potential efficiencies, but I would caution against getting *into the weeds* at this stage. We must focus on risk sequencing the infrastructure delivery. You will recall how the risk profile can change during the works and how the cost of debt is affected by the collateral value available in the infrastructure. We must ensure that the infrastructure develops in a sequence that does not compromise the outcome through a sudden and unexpected loss.

I used the example of building bridge piers in a seasonal Omani wadi earlier. If the *Khareef* struck before the piers could withstand the flash floods, we could well lose the project altogether. The idea is just as valid at scale. We will wish to limit our exposure to loss at each stage of delivery, even if that means only partial completion of individual facilities in a particular phase. The VaR reflects our appetite for loss. What is the limit of what we can manage, and what must we transfer to underwriters if they are willing to accept the risk? In practice, these risks are better managed directly through risk sequencing.

The answer to the question 'What do we seek to achieve?' should, therefore, be straightforward. We know what capabilities we need for each stage objective, and we can sequence the delivery to avoid the risk of catastrophic loss in a crisis (Figure 6.1). We must also understand the infrastructure, community and organisational loss exposures and influences at each stage. It is useful to be as transparent as possible in our answer. Being clear about the corporate or organisational strategy outcome and what it comprises will define our core

Figure 6.1 Delivery of capability objectives do not necessarily align with risk sequenced infrastructure delivery: all the supplemental requirements for objectives 1, 2 and 3 had to be delivered in risk horizon 1, even though only capability objective 1 would be delivered in that period; the infrastructure that enables a capability does not have to coincide with the capability

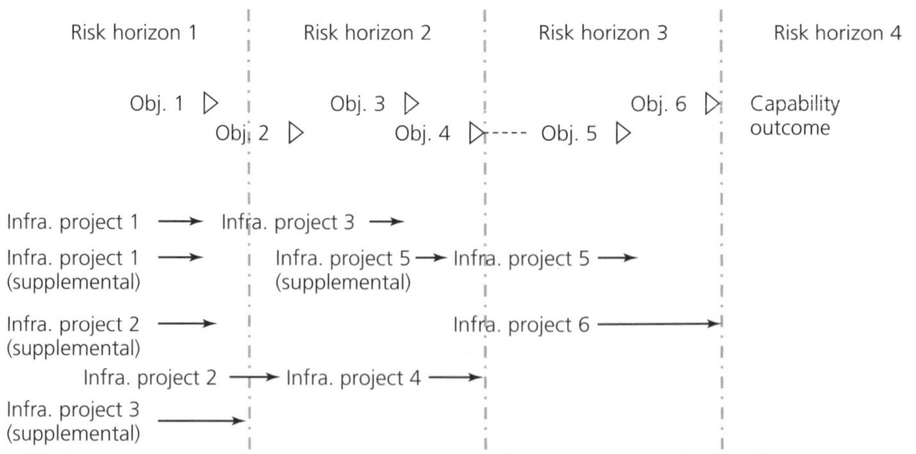

requirements. The process of achieving it will add many additional requirements and influence the sequencing, finances and much else. Importantly, it must stand up to scrutiny by local and higher authorities, as well as shareholders. It is rare for any form of infrastructure to have no political dimension.

6.4. How will the infrastructure enable this outcome?

To be clear, we are discussing how the infrastructure will enable the corporate or organisational strategic outcome. We also have a broader unifying purpose of complete physical, mental and social well-being and not merely the absence of disease or infirmity. These are not incompatible. The corporate outcome is and will remain the core requirement. Public health informs how the infrastructure will be developed and delivered, leading to a broad range of secondary or enabling requirements. We have done the hard work. We must now determine how the IDP will provide the desired outcome. This is the substance of part one of the IDP, strategy, and the essence of this book.

We want to deliver infrastructure that delivers a corporate outcome, but that also maintains its value over its life, is sustainable, and enables a resilient operation. It must represent value for money for owners while also being valued by the staff, operators and local community.

6.5. Approach

There is a generic approach to IDP strategy development. We've discussed how we set about framing the question. Now we do something with it. The process is necessarily iterative because each adjustment to requirement or conduct will change the risk profile. We only arrive at a strategy when there is a natural balance between all of the factors, each iteration no longer resulting in substantive changes.

We can summarise the generic approach as a series of steps.

(*a*) *Risk evaluation*

We would use the DTS and its risk horizons for our first iteration, but this will evolve into the common reference. Using an enterprise-wide framework, we evaluate the risks in each quadrant associated with delivering the requirement. It is useful to distinguish between the core or technical requirement, which directly enables the projected capability or service, and the supplementary requirements that allow effective infrastructure delivery. The ERM quadrants are strategic, financial, hazard and operational. Remember that the first two are external and reflect the operating context. We need to systematically pick through these risks, assess each and devise treatments. We are less concerned with the likelihood of these risks occurring than whether they are possible. Remember that it is virtually impossible to predict which risk will manifest and when over the infrastructure's decades-long life. Look carefully at the hazard risks, which are predominantly the naturally occurring hazards that can affect your physical locations. Once again, extract the appropriate risk treatments. Only once the other risks have been evaluated should you finally begin on the operational risks. The external and hazard risks often give rise to changes in the infrastructure's operation and the delivery of the service that it enables. We want to sweep these adjustments up in our assessment. Operational risks exist through performing our operation in that location and under those circumstances. It is too easy to become paralysed by detail. Consider the key risks in the first iteration, such as accessibility and reliability of the supply chain and resources. Remember that we are looking over the infrastructure's life and must include the planning, construction, operating life and disposal in our assessments. The risk evaluation becomes more detailed with each successive iteration. Your calculation plan will show a comprehensive audit trail from source reference to actions after each iteration, recording your analysis by quadrant and risk horizon. It should also show the risk treatments and their associated residual risks and effect on the core requirements. You will produce a summary of requirements, a residual risk profile and an infrastructure strategy narrative. Rudyard Kipling's (1902) honest service men remain a useful starting point for this narrative: What, where, when, who, why, and how?

(*b*) *Delivery structure*
Considering the client or (ultimate) owner risk criteria, this is where we explore how we might deliver on that strategy narrative. We will start with the allocation of risk and any constraints on operation and finance. Don't assume that the answer is a public–private-partnership. Remember that the core maxim of any contract development is that the risk is allocated to the party best equipped to deal with it. Start with that. Siemiatycki produced a useful explanation of the contracting model by risk allocation, as shown in Figure 6.2.
It can be tempting to predetermine the delivery method before adequately considering the evidence. It happens a lot. It remains unclear whether this results from poor contract management, financing difficulties or stakeholder miscommunication. Still, there appears to be a definite correlation between predetermining the contracting method with difficult

Figure 6.2 Carried risk by public and private partners under different delivery models for transportation infrastructure (after Siemiatycki and van Koeverden (2021))

infrastructure delivery. I suspect that in setting the delivery method as part of the policy agenda, the only evidence fully explored is that supporting the policy or individual stakeholder interests. There is undoubtedly a doctoral thesis in exploring the actual cost and benefit efficiencies of such an approach. However, we will have a more balanced and less complicated delivery if we can devise a delivery method based on the optimum allocation of risks. Armed with the delivery method, we can now explore possible delivery structures. The delivery method is the concept of how the infrastructure will be delivered. The delivery structure describes what the organisation will look like and which stakeholders take on which roles. There will be two or three possible structures in each iteration, but the core roles, responsibilities and risk allocations become consistent over successive iterations.

(*c*) *Financing*

Once we know what our delivery model can be, we can begin thinking about finance. There are several questions to consider, including leverage, the amount of debt against equity to fund the delivery and sourcing. Generally speaking, debt is money that we borrow from a financial institution at a cost, and co-owners or shareholders invest equity in the service that the infrastructure enables. The attraction of investing is that the potential profits can be significant, but these pay over the longer term. Loans or debts are serviced from the moment that the loan is taken and at a defined cost.

The priority for allocating revenue is to service the loan. Therefore, lenders are paid before investors. Lenders have a reasonable expectation of getting their money back with a defined profit, the interest on the loan. Investors take higher risks because they anticipate getting their money back and potentially all additional earnings after the loans are paid off. However, if the project fails, they can lose everything. Therefore, the whole financing structure hinges on confidence in the delivered service's value and revenue. Let's deal with leverage first.

You will recall how value changes over the life of the infrastructure. There is a speculative value during the initial public discussions and planning. Still, operational value or revenue-generating value only begins when the infrastructure is commissioned, and the enabled service can commence. When we take out a loan, we need to have some form of collateral. We need to be able to compensate the lenders if everything goes awry. Similarly, the lenders need to have confidence in the infrastructure project. This confidence will also inform the interest that they charge – generally, the higher the confidence of recovering the debt, the lower the interest on the debt.

To create collateral and confidence, we need to have something tangible for the lender to value. Therefore, it is usual for the initial stages of the infrastructure planning and design, and often the preliminary groundworks, to be funded directly from equity. Equity is capital held by the infrastructure owner, used to 'launch' the infrastructure delivery.

Figure 6.3 Reducing risk and cost of debt as the project is delivered: each reduction in the cost of debt will be determined by a number of factors particular to the risk horizon, and is not automatic over time

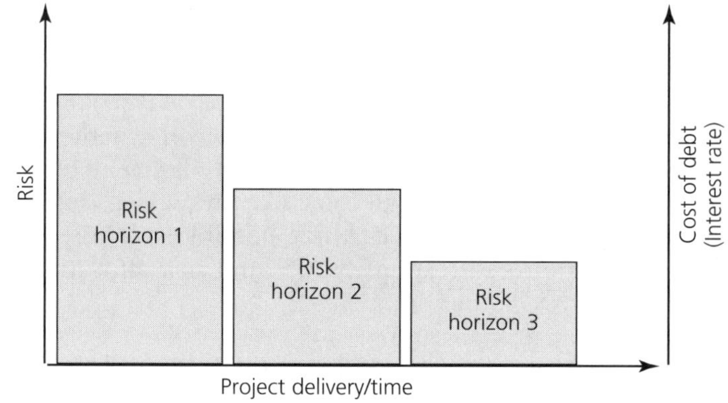

Once these initial stages are delivered, prospective lenders can see the value and are more willing to lend money. As more is delivered, the higher the collateral value and confidence in the outcome, so, generally, the better the cost of debt. We can restructure our debt during an infrastructure project by taking loans at different stages of delivery. The first loan has relatively little collateral, and so has a high cost, or interest rate. As this money is used to build collateral, we take out a further debt that can service the first debt and build more collateral, but at a lower cost. We may repeat the process a few times (Figure 6.3). The collateral value of the infrastructure is growing through the delivery process, but remember that it is not real value until it enables a service. The amount of capital that we need to deliver this infrastructure will be the minimum amount of equity. When we calculate all of the debts, and their service costs, we can estimate the leverage. At this stage, it is little more than an estimate that informs the rest of the planning process and prospective equity investors. Remember that our initial operation and maintenance costs will also need to be covered by loans until the enabled service delivers revenue to cover these. This is where the sustainability policy is critical because it dictates what the revenue is to cover and what supplemental income is needed to provide the service. For example, the service provider may receive a monthly service fee from the municipality in addition to revenue collected from service users. We see this particularly in public transport systems, where the ridership fees are kept deliberately below the actual cost of service to attract ridership.

The question of confidence is not something that can be assumed. Each major infrastructure project will attract a credit rating, typically assigned to the service delivery organisation responsible for the infrastructure. The calculation of the credit rating will depend in large part on the quantitative risk evaluation and value projections through life.

The more this is based on evidence within an integrated VSOS scheme, the more reliable the analysis. Anticipated revenue may be slow during the early days of a new public transport system. This would influence lender confidence in the service provider's ability to service its loans reliably. One possibility is credit enhancement, where one lender or investor underwrites the repayment risk to another lender. In effect, it is about risk spreading.

We see the same with the equity. We may sell shares in our project company, known as a special purpose vehicle (SPV), to raise the capital necessary to begin the project delivery. This means that, rather than one or two investors carrying all the risk, a portion of the equity is shared across a number of smaller investors. This brings us on to the second point, the source of funds.

When the cost of an infrastructure project is much greater than the value of the service provided, the consequence of any mishap in infrastructure delivery or adoption could bankrupt the service provider. Therefore, major infrastructure project delivery is typically through SPVs. The SPV exists for a specified function and time, usually the complete delivery of the infrastructure and all debts paid. It can extend for a fixed period to generate supplementary benefit for the equity holders, depending on the delivery model used. However, this also means that the money raised for the infrastructure delivery will be used as project finance. It is different from corporate finance, where the corporation, as a whole, is responsible for paying off any debts. Project finance is ring-fenced, which means that the liability to pay off the debts stops with the SPV and cannot transfer to the equity owners or the service corporation. This is known as non-recourse; it means that lenders do not have recourse through a chain of ownership to recover their costs. Everything stops with the SPV. It also means that the risk of non-recovery of debt is higher than with corporate debt. Still, the interest rates and potential profits are also higher.

Each source of funding will carry an associated risk with attendant advantages and disadvantages. One of the most common arguments centres on whether a municipality or the SPV should carry the debt. As a government entity, the municipality can raise taxes and so should always be able to raise the necessary funds to service a loan. Should is the operative word. Detroit imploded because of its debt burden and had to decommission infrastructure and clear neighbourhoods to re-establish stable cash flow (Saunders, 2018). Several developing countries have low credit ratings. It is not unusual to see regional multilateral development banks and well-planned infrastructure projects with better credit ratings than their equity holders. A good example is CAF (2021), the development bank of Latin America, which has a far better credit rating than its contributing nations in the region. Interestingly, it also pursues a social impact development criterion in infrastructure investment. We need to know that we will get the loan instalments as planned.

That confidence goes both ways. We need to know that we will get our funds as scheduled, and the lenders need to know that their loans will be serviced. With each iteration of the risk evaluation, we can narrow down the possibilities for financing, and more importantly, identify those carrying too much risk. This discussion provides no more than a sense of the infrastructure financing considerations during the IDP strategy's initial iterations. It is wise to work with a primary lender for such planning. There are regional multilateral development banks for international development work, national infrastructure development banks and sovereign development funds for humanitarian and reconstruction projects. It is also worth noting that sovereign investors do not generally require strict collateral.

(*d*) *Stakeholder impact*

We know our core requirement and, through our risk evaluation, we have a sense of some supplemental requirements to facilitate delivery. Our narrowing delivery model options, with associated delivery structures and financing options, bring us a further set of supplementary requirements and constraints. However, more importantly, we are now able to generate a stakeholder map. We need to include owners, operators and local authorities and beneficiaries through to all those with interest in the delivery of infrastructure and enabled service. Some may be activists with an agenda and no direct stake in the project, such as the Sierra Club representatives at the Turkey Point Nuclear Generating Station's licence renewal, or the Ministry of Finance auditor seeking to assure value for the public purse.

Our stakeholder mapping exercise includes three tasks. The first is to identify who the stakeholders are. By this, we mean organisations and points of contact and their relationships to each other. For example, are several stakeholders members of an association with a particular point of view or agenda? The resulting map of stakeholders and their inter-relationships forms our stakeholder context. The second is to understand their interest in the infrastructure and the enabled service. An important aspect of this is to identify their expectations. The third is to categorise the stakeholders in an influence matrix. This is a useful initial graph that shows us how to view and deal with each stakeholder (Figure 6.4).

As we go through our iterations, it is particularly useful to include mental modelling in our stakeholder impact assessment. As developed by Morgan *et al.* (2001), this process reviews the stakeholder identification to build the stakeholder map. It is the basis for an 'expert' mental model describing how stakeholder interest and decisions should influence the infrastructure and service delivery. It connects with the influence models that we build as part of the common reference. More on this later.

An accurate mental model of stakeholder decision-making emerges through a series of stakeholder engagement exercises. From it, we can know how stakeholder decisions are informed, relevant to our strategy.

Figure 6.4 Power–interest grid (after Eden and Ackermann (1998))

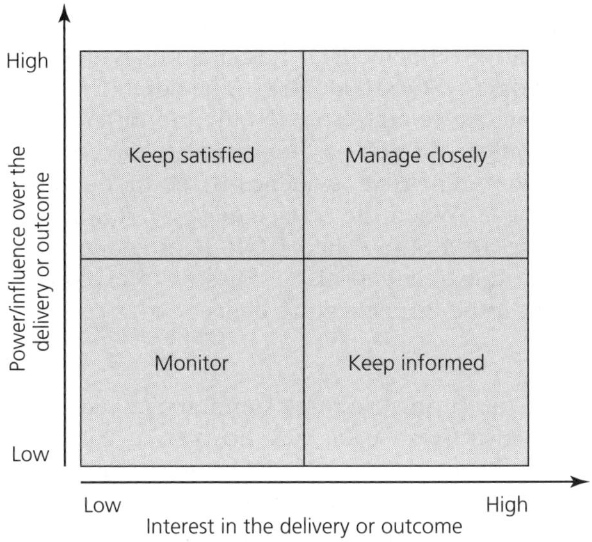

This was the process used in the Turkey Point example. It is highly effective and makes genuine community engagement viable.

(*e*) *Summary of requirement*

Each step in this process has added new (infrastructure) requirements and qualified existing ones. We need to capture all of these requirements and assess how they affect delivery sequencing, sustainability and resilience, and through-life value. This is best articulated by the service delivery phase, in the form of a design brief. We can now conduct a rough estimate of delivery cost, core and supplemental requirements, and review how we have addressed the risks evaluated at the beginning of the process.

(*f*) *Residual risk*

By associating the summary of requirements with the risk treatments identified in the risk evaluation, we can calculate the residual risk. In the first couple of iterations, this is necessarily quite generalised and high-level. However, once we have built the common reference, we will have a method of risk-profiling the infrastructure and service delivery. This means that we will have risk priorities to address in each iteration until all the risks are within acceptable, or at least manageable, ranges. Furthermore, we can build greater confidence in the financial estimates of fixed and variable costs for each strategy option with each iteration. These estimates allow us to describe the loss exposure associated with each option, and hence the VaR during each risk horizon in the delivery programme. This is only possible if our planning approach is strictly evidence-based and uses the common reference.

(*g*) *Repeat*

The consolidated summary of requirements and residual risks provides us with the starting point for the next risk evaluation, and the process repeats. This iterative refinement of risk in strategy development is typical of ERM frameworks (ISO 31000:2018). The core of a strategy crystallises with each iteration, as we add more detail, and different options are explored and adopted or rejected. Importantly, the common reference develops into a comprehensive, evidence-based model that informs stakeholder dialogue. When the service delivery organisation interprets the common reference, it becomes their COP. It provides reliable risk profiles for each strategy adjustment. It also allows us to explore the effects of various hazards on the infrastructure delivery over each risk horizon (Figure 6.5).

It is useful to check the (infrastructure) summary of requirements against the projected demand density over each risk horizon at each iteration. You will recall that infrastructure enables a service. The infrastructure, therefore, has the carrying capacity to meet the demand for the service. There are three points of reference: peak, sustainable and emergency. As we plan and build the infrastructure, we are already influencing the speculative value and hence the demand for services.

Similarly, the process of infrastructure delivery will also create a demand on the existing infrastructure. It is possible to destroy the existing infrastructure's financial sustainability, and potentially the economy, if our demands during the delivery exceed its carrying capacity. Similarly, the delivered infrastructure can imbalance the existing infrastructure, and the combined whole becomes unsustainable. Let's use an example.

Tourism represents approximately 70% of the economy of a Caribbean nation. It has one international airport and one regional airport. The new generation of air carriers will be using the latest wide-bodied aircraft, which exceeds the international airport's existing capacity. This airport is also in need of flood protection rehabilitation and other upgrade works. The summary of the international airport's redevelopment requirements extends to enhancing local utilities and new water treatment facilities.

The summary of requirements was risk profiled against each risk horizon. It was unclear whether the international tourist trade would return after being diverted to a neighbouring island for the two and a half years of construction. Without the upgrade works, the increased load on the existing utilities would significantly exceed their carrying capacity. Any unreliable utility supply would prompt the resorts to offgrid. If the utilities lost the resorts, 60% of their customer demand, they would become financially unsustainable. This meant developing a cruise ship homeport close to the international airport, which generated the sustainable demand for local utilities enhancement. This, in turn, supported the airport

Figure 6.5 The common reference composition and its interpretation: each iteration of strategy development enhances its completeness and improves confidence in interpretation; subsequent delivery of objectives and changes to the risk context will affect each component differently, and, ultimately, the impact on the purpose of the IDP and the intended capability

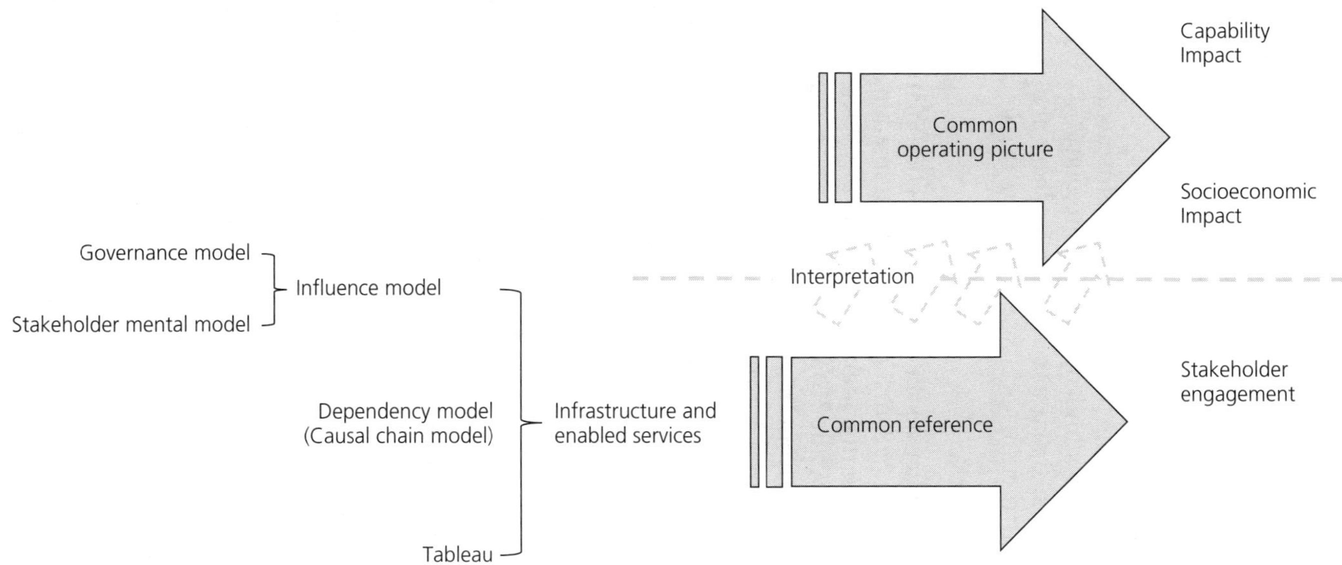

development without compromising reliable supply to the resorts. Furthermore, the risk of the temporary relocation of international flights to the neighbouring island becoming permanent was reduced because the homeport facility would naturally restore the international flight connection. By phasing the development works through each risk horizon, the total VaR was kept manageable, and the risk of collapsing the island economy during the development was significantly reduced.

6.6. Beneficial capability

How do you know that the delivered infrastructure will positively affect the intended beneficiaries and the local community? It is an interesting question, and there can be no guarantee. However, there are two parts to this question. Does the infrastructure meet a need? Can the intended beneficiaries benefit from it?

This seems to be entering the realm of feel-good platitudes, but these questions can be profoundly challenging in practice. Something that makes good politics, say, doesn't necessarily make a good reality. The 2018 proposal by Jared Kushner, then US White House senior advisor, to build factories in Sinai across the Rafah Crossing from the Gaza Strip, offered the prospect of employment to Gaza residents (Bar'el, 2018). When we look at the practicalities, it isn't easy to see how Gazans might benefit from such a facility. They would need to commute through the Gaza Strip, queue for several hours to cross the border, travel to the factories, work and reverse the process on the way home. Judging from the mean travel and crossing time measurements, it would require 8 h of commute for 8 h of work each day. How practicable and sustainable can that be? As it was, the Egyptian Government did not agree to the proposal.

During my research into postconflict infrastructure rehabilitation, the question of the benefit came up repeatedly and was almost always associated with post-conflict poverty (Hay *et al.*, 2020). Following a period of prolonged violence, households are mentally and physically affected. The community's social fabric is damaged, as it struggles with the reintegration of former combatants and reconciling neighbours and family's actions. Across the community, many households are actually or effectively widowed. When the primary income earner has died, it is almost easier to identify the vulnerable. When the conflict physically or mentally disables the primary income earner, that person's care consumes more scarce household resources. A person's capacity to secure income reduces further when there are also infants and other dependents in the household (Brück and Schindler, 2012).

The immediate needs of the family members push out work and reinforce a dependency on aid. This extends to the care and development of the next generation. When the aid stops, the need to generate income to buy food pushes out the option of vaccinations, education and nutrition for young children (Banerjee and Duflo, 2011). In both situations, we see the creation of poverty.

When accompanied by trauma, such as a conflict, it can have a profound intergenerational effect (Perry, 1997), including a genetic effect (Sokolowski *et al.*, 2013). How we deliver infrastructure in such situations will directly influence the outcome. When these vulnerable people can directly benefit from the infrastructure delivery and enabled service, we can achieve a beneficial outcome without compromising the next generation. The means to do this entails the accessibility of both infrastructure and service delivery. It's a simple concept, known as beneficial capability.

Beneficial capability has three components: facility, access and capacity. There needs to be a facility that provides a benefit, typically through employment or a service. The facility must be accessible to the intended beneficiary. The intended beneficiary must have the capacity to benefit.

The idea of a facility ties closely to intelligent resourcing. Infrastructure designed to maximise local supply chains and labour allows the community to benefit directly during its delivery and maintenance and the subsequent service provision. Building a facility that depends on external expertise, trades and labour, has next to no benefit during its delivery and limited benefit subsequently. We discuss the necessity of local ownership as part of *community ownership*. The Great Ditch in Libya will support agriculture and industry but remains wholly dependent on international contractors to develop and maintain. Building an external dependency into an infrastructure scheme creates a fragility in service reliability when it is no longer economically viable to retain the foreign contractors and procure resources. The Caribbean water treatment plant example is a case in point.

Access to the facility is more than just physical. If I have no physical access to the well, I cannot draw water. Do I have indirect access to the well so that I can still get water? This can be a challenging issue for various reasons, not least because we all have differing abilities to move around. It may be a function of age or infirmity, or simply that we have to struggle with an infant in a pushchair. I posed a question to my students a few years ago. An elderly, infirm woman lives alone on the 24th floor in community housing. How does she feed herself during a prolonged winter power outage? Bear in mind that we were discussing a central Canadian winter of potentially −40°C. When we explored this question in class, it exposed how many community housing areas are in food deserts, and the by-laws only require 2 hours of standby power.

The elder, losing heat quickly, owing to the building's poor insulation, has to walk down many flights of stairs and then back up with bags of groceries because the elevators aren't working in a power failure. It is also unlikely that she will have a reliable water supply because the pumps that lift water supply in the building are also off. The municipal answer is typically to use school buses for heated shelter until the power is restored. However, access remains the core issue. After Hurricane Sandy wreaked havoc in New York City, boy scouts and neighbours brought water, groceries and prescriptions to the elderly isolated by stairs. The Sinai factory proposal can provide only limited benefits because it is only accessible by a few. This brings us to the concept of equity of access. Quite simply, everyone should be capable of accessing the facility for there to be an inclusive community benefit.

The capacity to benefit is about the individual beneficiary and the beneficiary's situation. It is the capacity to benefit from the facility through professional and trade skills directly, the supply of feedstock resources or some ancillary service. Some are unable to benefit directly, through age or infirmity or because they are carers. This is more prevalent in traumatised communities. It means that we need to look at how those who might otherwise be able to benefit can be freed of their time constraints. Facilitating community early-years schooling is incredibly successful in reconstruction contexts, with the added advantage that it is associated with reversing the intergenerational transfer of trauma (Black *et al.*, 2017). This includes full vaccination and nutrition for infants and preschool children and a community role for elders and those unable to work in the facility.

These illustrations of responses in postdisaster, postconflict or other traumatised communities remain relevant to infrastructure development in stable and developed regions. We can incorporate community college programme affiliations in our IDP strategy. This promotes local skills and stimulates supply chain development, diversification of dependencies and, perhaps, even stimulate a circular economy. When our delivery strategy has a beneficial outcome, both locally and for equity holders, we align with the UN SDGs and meet the UN PRI. It's about improving the physical, mental and social well-being of the community.

6.7. Community engagement

If we are to preserve the infrastructure's through-life value, we need to enable development in secondary value. For that, the local community needs a sense of ownership. This goes beyond adopting the infrastructure as part of the area's identity and vernacular; it includes adapting the infrastructure to the community's changing needs. That requires dialogue – we often need participatory learning to understand fully the balance of local needs over time (Chambers, 1997). That entails a prolonged and immersive engagement with the local community to distinguish between needs, wants and expectations. This is not always practicable, though there are ways to accelerate the process (Plush, 2013). When there is a greater local familiarity with infrastructure and an expectation of its benefits, we can decide our community engagement according to our available time, resources and desired outcome. You will recall Arnstein's (1969) *ladder of citizen participation* from Chapter 2 and 3, which shows partnership with the local community as the third highest level of community engagement; it is the basic level of citizen empowerment and underlines local ownership viability. Realistically, if we are to be compliant with the UN SDGs and PRI, local partnership should be the desired minimum standard; anything less is a compromise.

Stakeholder engagement is a discipline in its own right and not something that can be dealt with comprehensively here. However, it is essential to identify what we require of stakeholder engagement to inform a successful infrastructure development strategy. In other words, how do we use stakeholder engagement to build a strategy that is implementable and infrastructure that is relevant and sustainable? To answer this, we need to understand the stakeholder influences on the service or capability and its enabling infrastructure. We considered mental modelling in the iterative process of strategy development; it gives us insight into the context for our infrastructure delivery and operation and local ownership. We seek to inform stakeholder decision-making, bringing it from an opinion-based decision to a judgement-based decision. That means that users need to have trust in the information, and they have to appreciate, if not always to understand fully, its relevance. An opinion-based decision is either uninformed or founded on selected information or bias and prejudice. It can be influenced by the general political dialogue, polarised as that can be. In extreme cases, this can lead to an outright rejection of scientific evidence in favour of a fixed world view.

Interviewed in the May 2016 edition of *Texas Monthly*, Dr Katharine Hayhoe, an atmospheric scientist at Texas Tech University, reported how some reject climate science and evidence because it contradicts a fixed political narrative (Smith, 2016). Climate change is as polarising an issue in the USA as guns. So what? The City of Austin Office of Sustainability presented a summary of her findings, as lower and higher projections. It leaves developers and planners with a problem. While few accept the potential liability of ignoring the projections altogether, some will choose the lower scenario, which describes the current situation. Others will opt for the higher projection. Austin is not an isolated example.

The disparity in demand densities creates an imbalance in infrastructure use and reduced efficiency (revenue by cost of infrastructure capacity). If the utility aims for the higher scenario, it cannot secure the revenue necessary to maintain the infrastructure. When development policy is consistent, the supporting infrastructure can develop sustainably. We cannot know the likelihood of how quickly the climate will change or how often we will experience peak temperatures above the ability of a skyscraper's design to cope. If the infrastructure is economically sustainable, it can be upgraded as the situation dictates. We can know what it means when the design cannot cope, and we can allow for that. Sometimes, 'What if?' is more compelling than rhetoric.

Building a comprehensive mental model that contextualises the expert model allows us to understand what is important to the decision-making stakeholder and what sources of information they will trust. It isn't the same as marketing, where one might present a vision of a better experience. Nor is it like information warfare, where one uses evidence to elicit a desired response. It is about creating ownership of the decision by moving stakeholder decision-making to a deliberate and objective consideration of the facts. It is about moving the stakeholder to judgement-based decision-making.

This is an important distinction because we want local adoption of the infrastructure and enabled service. As such, it will incorporate an understanding of the influence of swings in political opinion. When the political mood changes, a new report may be commissioned to challenge the requirement for an infrastructure delivery and facts collected to support one view or another. We need to have created an environment of understanding that is above agenda and affords a holistic perspective. If that means that the infrastructure requirement changes after 10 years of deliberation, it will be based on a balanced assessment, transparent to all stakeholders. Remember that the operating authority and government agencies are also stakeholders and need to have this sense of ownership.

The influence model integrates the stakeholder mental models and the governance model. It allows us to interpret, de facto, what the jurisdiction, physical sciences and engineering tell us, de jure, about the infrastructure in context. It represents the human domain in the common reference.

6.8. Common reference

Chapter 2 discussed the three constituent models of common reference: tableau, causal chain model and influence model. The three connect by function and georeferencing. The common reference expands through the IDP development and delivery. However, from the beginning, it provides all stakeholders with a shared knowledge of what exists, how it works and the consequence of an event. Bear in mind that even when people agree with the evidence, it can be interpreted differently according to each person's perspective and interests. Therefore, while it is good to inform stakeholder dialogue, it is also important to identify a shared outcome.

The common reference is a living model. It is 'living' because we continually update and refresh it as our understanding and authenticated data availability improve. It is a model because it aids understanding of how the infrastructure systems function and relate to the whole VSOS. It shows us how a failure in one part or a change in another propagates through the VSOS and affects the whole socioeconomic fabric. It is not a simulation, which would provide a prediction of how an event unfolds. A model offers insight and aids understanding (Louie, 2010). It brings us back, once more, to the need for a shared outcome, also known as the unifying purpose. The unifying purpose (*in my view*) of the VSOS is public health, that is, physical, mental and social well-being, and not merely the absence of disease and infirmity. You must decide on your unifying purpose. Articulate it clearly in the IDP strategy because every IDP resource prioritisation and decision will ultimately have this final consideration and eventual outcome. The IDP also declares its interpretation of the common reference and how it understands the model.

The question of interpreting the common reference is a different matter and, as explained, will be unique to the organisation using it. An expansion of the electricity transmission line through northern Ontario will be viewed differently by the different stakeholders, according to the impact that it will have. For example, how does it affect the local air freight service, electricity supply reliability in remote communities, accessibility to healthcare and food security? Depending on each stakeholder's situation, their interpretation of impact will be different. As the IDP author and owner, it is in our interest to have a unifying purpose that most stakeholders can see themselves within. It accepts and in no way discounts their interpretation of the operational or functional purpose and the associated impact of changes to individual services and enabling infrastructure delivery.

When the IDP recognises that the extended electricity transmission line makes air freight services more expensive per flight, affecting food prices and food security, it demonstrates relevance. It can show that one of the secondary requirements of the infrastructure delivery will include measures that address these adverse consequences so that the outcome is positive for the local beneficiaries. Our example might include the provision of an expanded community food store with a transcritical refrigeration system to minimise sensitivity to power interruptions. Each situation will be different, but we cannot discuss it with the stakeholders without the common reference. Without the IDP's unifying purpose of a shared outcome, we cannot demonstrate the net benefit for all affected by it. This also leads us to the question of metrics.

6.9. Measuring outcome

When an infrastructure project is underway, it is usual to use output metrics of progress to demonstrate success or otherwise. The problem with this approach is that the project can become isolated from the VSOS of which it is part. We explored this issue in Chapter 2 and 3, as the *tyranny of metrics*. There will be other changes in the VSOS that will affect the impact that our project has and vice versa. The most explicit demonstration of this is that one can have a successful project with no value because it cannot be commissioned into use. The success of infrastructure asset delivery, within budget and on time, does not imply IDP success. Think of the wastewater treatment plant delivered on time and to budget that isn't operating, or the water treatment plants that cannot be maintained. These issues should have been captured during the contextual assessment of the requirements and the iterative process of developing an IDP strategy. However, we must know if we remain on track or if an IDP strategy adjustment is required.

The challenge of an outcome-based metric is that it is typically retrospective. We may only know our project's outcome, and whether it meets our IDP strategy, after it has been delivered. It is already difficult to say to the stakeholders that the recently delivered project will not have the intended outcome, especially when it was successful. It is much more difficult to explain why the project has a negative outcome, actually harming the intended beneficiaries. We need to plan and measure projects by outcome rather than output. Once more, we must fall back on our common reference and its evidence chain. As a model, the common reference allows us to understand how changes affect the VSOS. When aligned with a unifying purpose, we can say how a particular change affects the desired outcome. Two things arise from this.

The first is that if there is a negative impact on the desired outcome, we can know the issue and determine the necessary adjustments and interventions. In effect, this is an extension of the scenarios that we ran through our models in determining the core requirement. As a living model, the common reference becomes a useful risk management tool through the delivery. It also allows us to test how proposed changes in the delivery and requirement will affect the desired outcome.

The second is that it allows us to extract the indicators of anticipated outcome (IAOs) (Hay and Kilburn, 2018). In modelling the IDP delivery and each incremental change in the VSOS as the delivery progresses, we can identify the IAOs that tell us we are moving towards the desired outcome. The IAOs on their own are of relatively little value because they are explanatory and not predictive. However, when the IAOs converge, our confidence in achieving the desired outcome increases (Figure 6.6). Diverging IAOs indicate that there is an issue that merits further investigation. In our example of the power transmission line

Figure 6.6 Metrics that are aligned to the objectives and outcome, derived from the common operating picture (COP), which is a living model that allows the planner to interpret the possible consequences of contextual changes, both arising from and unrelated to the development works underway: key performance indicators (KPIs) record progress to-date against an objective while key risk indicators (KRIs) identify the risks to attaining the objective so that the planner understands how to allocate resources and sequence work to treat the KRIs; understanding the possible consequences of each action indicates the possible outcomes and a convergence of indicators of anticipated outcome (IAOs) provides confidence that the project is on track

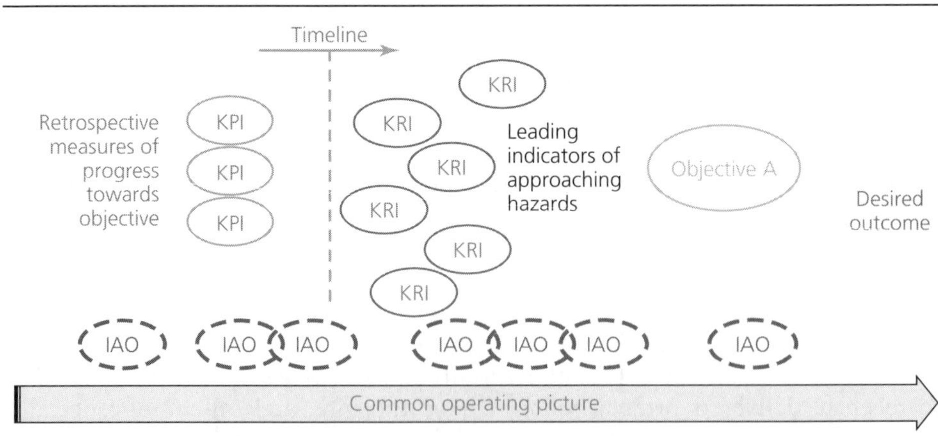

extension, an IAO might be non-fuel air freight. A drop can suggest a reduction in food delivery and, therefore, a decrease in food access, nutrition and, ultimately, health. On its own, this IAO does not mean that we will not achieve the desired outcome. It may merely mean that a proportion of the working-age population in the first communities to be connected is part of the IDP delivery. So the demand for food has reduced temporarily. However, when combined with no change in demand distribution across the communities, it would warn that something may be amiss before it becomes a problem.

The IAOs can be a powerful tool in measuring any IDP delivery. However, it is useless if it isn't based on a robust evidence-based (VSOS) common reference and a unifying purpose (or shared outcome). It is scalable to any size of VSOS, urban or rural, regional or provincial.

6.10. Community value

The community value of the IDP is the confluence of all the concepts and practices discussed in this book. It is not just whether the community has an improved water supply or continuous access to electricity supplies. Nor can it be calculated in monetary terms by the community benefiting from the local employment and supply chains' infrastructure delivery processes. Nor can it be assessed in terms of the changes in the environmental impact. It is more than the three parts of a sustainable system: people, economy and environment. It goes beyond the tangible to how the community perceives the infrastructure and adopts it in their community identity. The vehicle for this is psychological and not explored in this discussion. Still, the characteristics are well-documented in engineering and planning publications.

Joseph Aicher (1998), a general (medical) practitioner, described the essence of a healthy community in how it develops, functions and communicates. This is a prescription for community health by the WHO definition. There are strong echoes of Jane Jacobs and other sociologists in his work. In *The Death and Life of Great American Cities* (1961), Jacobs discusses the interaction of community behaviour with the built and natural environment, advocating integrated, inclusive and mixed-use neighbourhoods. Her work was compelling as a counter to (New York City Planning Commissioner) Robert Moses's redevelopment plans for New York City. Her ideas have been adopted and developed by different practitioners over time. We see her influence in Anholt's (2011) sense of place or 'place branding'.

Two other trends in thinking have converged with Jacob's concepts. The first centres on community security by design. Oscar Newman (1973) developed an architectural approach to (1950s Chicago Housing Authority Executive Director) Elizabeth David's pioneering theories and work. It subsequently became Crime Prevention Through Environmental Design (CPTED), codified by the SPARTA Consulting Corporation. Judith Rodin's (2014) call for resilience expanded the definition of community security to include external and catastrophic threats. Juliette Kayyem's call for balance between the vibrant flow of a community and its security (Genetec, 2016) tempers the trend in total security. The second trend concerned the professionalisation of community roles (McKnight, 1996; McKnight and Block, 2012) and the associated fragmentation of the community fabric. This fragmentation affects community cohesion, known as social capital, which, as Aldrich (2012) demonstrated, is the foundation of community resilience. Rodin's Rockefeller 100 Resilient Cities initiative drew broad attention to urban resilience. As we discussed in Chapter 4, the resilient city's three enablers are the municipal corporation, community housing and commercial real estate (BOMA Toronto, 2019; City of Toronto, 2021).

The municipal corporation is the glue that enables a city, providing the services that enable it to function. Community housing that provides shelter for vulnerable people means that critical municipal resources are available to respond to and recover from a crisis rather than merely reacting to it. Commercial real estate provides the facilities for recovery and economic regeneration. The three are indivisible, and infrastructure enables each aspect. Each service, interaction and perception is influenced by what we build and how we have built it. How we deliver infrastructure is as important as what we deliver in defining the community value of our IDP.

So what? Back to that driver of successful infrastructure delivery, the idea of community sense of ownership. As discussed, this is not a financial or equity share in the real property value of service provision but adoption by the community. This adoption drives secondary value in the infrastructure, whether it is repurposing the Camden railway arches for a market in London, UK, or the redevelopment of the Torpedo Factory as an art centre in Alexandria, Virginia, USA. When there is no sense of ownership, there is no adoption and inclusion in the community function; the Ghanaian community water wells, or the Caribbean membrane water treatment plants, for example. When there is community value in the IDP, there is a beneficial health outcome for the community, and it is sustainable. This relationship runs through the SDGs. Community value is part of the health outcome of the IDP. It is also the basis for preserving through-life value and can be used to inform the business case.

6.11. Informing the business case

It would be senseless to describe an IDP business case approach that would be relevant to all jurisdictions. So much will come down to who the infrastructure owner is, whether public money is involved and the sponsors' investment criteria. It would be irrelevant to speak of the socioeconomic and environmental impact when the investment decision is based solely on the value at the point of investment. However, there are some useful tools and considerations when articulating beneficial value in a business case.

A common argument in infrastructure business cases is cost avoidance, more widely termed protection against loss. In this approach, we identify the direct financial costs of not having an essential service, compared with its presence. The avoided cost over time is compared with the cost of the infrastructure and service delivery. For example, we can use epidemiological data to compare healthcare costs associated with water-borne diseases and the cost of improved wastewater management. Mortality and infirmity statistical models can further provide estimates of the associated loss of productive working life.

When we look at this from a positive impact, the calculation becomes more subjective. Using a financial metric of social impact is never a clean calculation. However, the appeal in providing a monetary estimate of the social impacts of a proposal is that it could give stakeholders an independently verifiable and auditable analysis across the capital supply chain. It would allow comparisons between projects and an aggregation of sorts for the whole of the IDP. The aggregation is qualified because, with each stage delivery, the context for the subsequent delivery changes, as does the risk profile. Therefore, any aggregation can at best only be an estimate at the point of investment. Nonetheless, capturing social impact in a financial metric has real value and has been pursued by governments and various development agencies for many years. It is more broadly known as impact monetisation.

The challenge is that impact management and financial management are typically conducted in isolation with different specialist teams, each with its own language and data collection criteria and processes. Efforts to integrate them are rarely effective. With each investment group tackling this differently, reflecting their shareholder or beneficiary interests and agreed policies, there will be little in common between them. However, each investor will qualitatively filter out the harmful social impact projects and consciously filter in the positive ones, before starting the investment calculation. We must inform that filtering process. The calculation will be different for each financing organisation, depending on their approach to asset-class-specific financial valuation. For example, NESsT (Nonprofit Enterprise and Self-sustainability Team) invests in social enterprises that generate jobs for those in greatest need and use net present value. Some institutional and private equity firms use an internal rate of return or a risk-adjusted return on capital. We'll return to this in a moment.

The Impact Frontiers collaboration is a group of capital investors, led by Prudential Financial, interested in social impact projects. They proposed a four-step process to help investors integrate impact and financial analysis in decision-making. The approach is flexible enough to accommodate the different decision-making criteria of each investor. It affords each the ability to compare the proposed investment social impact against their existing social impact portfolio and measured financial performance. In this way, it generates a model relevant to the particular (portfolio) investor. This means that we are not informing an absolute measure for the business case but comparing portfolios and investment policies.

The cost of loss argument often supports an IDP for the improvement or enhancement of existing infrastructure. You may recall the dairy example in Chapter 3, where a change in refrigerant addressed an existential fragility. It is rare to have such stark comparisons. However, it is important to note that, when comparing the cost of loss, we assume that a failure event's likelihood is constant. The most prevalent version of this is the whole cost of risk (WCR) comparison, which we discussed previously. It should include a risk management strategy for dealing with the residual risks. Without this, there is little confidence that the risk is manageable.

Chapter 4 discussed how individual and organisational behaviour would determine whether the risk treatment is implementable. The IDP must be compatible with stakeholder behaviours. We have seen this acutely during the 2020 COVID-19 pandemic. Most businesses wrote contingency plans after the 2008 SARS epidemic. Many plans proved ineffective during the pandemic because they focused on SARS' effect on the business instead of how business operations responded to disruption and failure. The latter produces a more generic contingency plan for operational continuity but carries greater confidence of success against a broad range of threats.

Considering the impact and cost of loss argument, we may use a benefit–cost ratio (BCR). The only real question here is what to include in the benefits category. Any BCR analysis will probably need to be tuned to the principal investor audience, using their investment criteria. Interestingly, the increased emphasis on carbon footprint provides an independently verifiable and objective measure to compare existing and proposed options using life-cycle analysis (LCA), which is an evidence-driven approach that builds on an agreed inventory (LCI) of what to include. It is flexible enough to consider only scope 1 (direct emissions from owned or controlled sources) and scope 2 (indirect emissions from the generation of purchased energy) of the Greenhouse Gas Protocol (WRI, 2021), or to include scope 3 (all other indirect emissions not included in scope 2). This categorisation broadly resembles the UNEP static, mobile and process-related emissions. Note that all emissions in these calculations are standardised to carbon dioxide equivalence.

Under a scope 1 and 2 LCA carbon dioxide equivalence calculation, we may find a compelling reason not to invest in the IDP proposal that would transition an oil and gas company to renewables, say. When we consider the social impact of not investing, we see that we risk diminishing the local community's physical, mental and social well-being, particularly where it is heavily engaged in and around company operations. Under the UN PRI, we can present the argument that by participating in the IDP to facilitate transition, the investor can actively reduce the LCA emissions overall and maintain the local population's well-being. We briefly touched on this example already.

These approaches rely on selection criteria that increasingly reflect internationally recognised standards of sustainable and responsible development.

The outcomes are a general and focused improvement in the local population's physical, mental and social well-being, overall social and economic resilience and adherence to the SDGs, improvements in social equity and justice, and improved collaboration communication towards common benefit. This last one entails a degree of transparency in risk reporting, specifically around the risks associated with the effects of climate change on business operations (TCFD), but more broadly in terms of environmental impact.

By way of an after note on business cases, it is useful to associate the key performance indicators (KPIs) for each deliverable in the IDP with the key risk indicators (KRIs). It affords the user clarity in interpreting what constitutes progress and how it can be protected. The other point is that demands for return on investment (ROI) calculations are better suited to individual real property assets rather than infrastructure. Calculating an ROI on a system whose value is vicariously defined by the demand for a service necessitates the inclusion of boundary conditions and assumptions that cannot be verified. It is better to calculate the total investment in the delivered service, including its enabling infrastructure, against the revenue generated. When we build a business case, we must avoid an asset-based valuation of cost against financial return wherever possible. It invariably leads to a different outcome than the one intended.

6.12. Chapter summary

This chapter draws all of the theory and heuristic practice strands together to generate an IDP strategy. It is the foundation part of any IDP and provides purpose and structure to each infrastructure project's delivery. Throughout, we need to ensure that we maintain a fully referenced audit trail while recognising that circumstances and risks will change. The strategy builds on understanding how the infrastructure systems interrelate to enable the services that support our community's socioeconomic fabric.

We start with a mission analysis and a desktop study to orient our process direction. Each iteration of strategy development begins with a risk evaluation through the four quadrants of an enterprise-wide approach. Each identified risk treatment will adjust the core requirement. The risk treatments are collected to inform the IDP delivery, first defining the delivery structure, financing constraints and options, and stakeholder impacts. Each analysis identifies further changes to the requirement, which are collected and presented as a summary of requirements. This summary comprises the core requirements for the capability to be developed plus supplemental requirements that will enable its delivery. The residual risks for each requirement and delivery are reassessed, and the process starts again with a full risk evaluation. These iterations continue until there is no substantive change in the requirements definition and an implementable strategy has formed.

With each iteration, we assess the developing strategy for its alignment with the desired outcome. We evaluate its beneficial capability and community engagement because we need it to have value in thc community. We need the community to own the delivered infrastructure and services. However, the need to understand the changing VSOS drives our continual development of the common reference. Without a current common reference, there is no continuing informed dialogue with stakeholders. Nor is there an understanding of how planned and unexpected changes influence the risk profile and anticipated outcome or relevant measurement of progress against the anticipated outcome. We concluded with a brief discussion of how we can inform the business case to maintain an audit trail of evidence, transparency and relevance for the investing institution.

The essence of IDP strategy development is engaging with the future to define how it affects our capability goals, rather than being defined by it. We must use evidence in a comprehensive VSOS model, the common reference, to identify the issues in delivering the IDP and select the right tools to deal with them. Using familiar tools to define IDP delivery problems assumes that the future will reflect the past and wilfully ignores contextual influences and risks.

BIBLIOGRAPHY

Aicher J (1998) *Designing Healthy Cities: Prescriptions, Principles and Practice*. Krieger Publishing, Malabar, FL, USA.

Ainger C and Fenner R (2014) *Sustainable Infrastructure: Principles into Practice*. ICE Publishing, London, UK.

Aldrich DP (2012) *Building Resilience: Social Capital in Post-disaster Recovery*. University of Chicago Press, Chicago, IL, USA.

Anholt S (2011) Beyond the nation brand: the role of image and identity in international relations. *Exchange: The Journal of Public Diplomacy* **(2)1**: 1.

Arnstein SR (1969) A ladder of citizen participation. *Journal of the American Planning Association* **35(4)**: 216–224.

Banerjee AV and Duflo E (2011) *Poor Economics: A Radical Rethinking of the Way to Fight Global Poverty*. Public Affairs, New York, NY, USA.

Bar'el Z (2018) Deal of the century might be up to Cairo. *Haaretz* (Tel Aviv) 24 June; **30149(99)**: 1.

Black MM, Walker SP, Fernald LCH *et al.* (2017) Early childhood development coming of age: science through the life course. *The Lancet* **(389)10064**: 77–90, 10.1016/S0140-6736(16)31389-7.

BOMA (Building Owners and Managers Association) Toronto (2019) *Resilience in the Commercial Real Estate Industry: Designing for a Graceful & Survivable Future*. BOMA, Toronto, ON, Canada, Technical Guidance Note.

Brück T and Schindler K (2012) The impact of violent conflicts on households: what do we know and what should we know about war widows? *Measuring Vulnerability in Developing Countries: New Analytical Approaches* (Naudé W, Santos-Paulino AU and McGillivray M (eds)). Routledge, Abingdon, UK, pp. 107–128.

CAF (Corporacion Andina de Fomento) (2021) www.caf.com/en (accessed 07/04/2021).

Chambers R (1997) *Whose Reality Counts? Putting the First Last*. Intermediate Technology Publications, London, UK.

City of Toronto (2021) *City of Toronto Resilience Strategy*. City of Toronto, Toronto, ON, Canada. https://www.toronto.ca/services-payments/water-environment/environmentally-friendly-city-initiatives/resilientto/ (accessed 01/04/2021).

Eden C and Ackermann F (1998) *Making Strategy: The Journey of Strategic Management*. Sage Publications, London, UK.

Elliott MW (ed.) (2012) *Risk Management and Treatment*, 1st edn. The Institutes, Malvern, PA, USA.

Fischhoff B, Brewer N and Downs JS (eds) (2011) *Communicating Risks and Benefits: An Evidence-based User's Guide*. Food and Drug Administration, Washington, DC, USA.

Genetec (2017) The educator. *Citywise* http://citywise.net/conversation/the-educator-juliette-kayyem (accessed 18/08/2020).

Hay AH and Kilburn RG (2018) Measuring success in post-conflict infrastructure development. *Proceedings of the Institution of Civil Engineers – Municipal Engineer* **173(2)**: 78–86, 10.1680/jmuen.17.00040.

Hay AH, Karney B and Martyn N (2019) Reconstructing infrastructure for resilient essential services during and following protracted conflict: a conceptual framework. *International Review of the Red Cross* **101(912)**: 1001–1029, 10.1017/S1816383120000053.

ICE (Institution of Civil Engineers) (2019) *Enabling Better Infrastructure: 12 Guiding Principles for Prioritising and Planning Infrastructure*. ICE, London, UK. https://www.ice.org.uk/ICEDevelopmentWebPortal/media/Documents/Media/ice-enabling-better-infrastructure-report.pdf (accessed 07/04/2021). See https://www.ice.org.uk/news-and-insight/enabling-better-infrastructure for further details (accessed 07/04/2021).

ISO (International Standards Organization) (2018) 31000 Risk management. ISO, Geneva, Switzerland.

Jacobs J (1961) *The Death and Life of Great American Cities*. Random House Canada, Toronto, ON, Canada. (Republished 1993.)

Kipling R (1902) *Just So Stories For Little Children*. Macmillan, London, UK.

Louie, A. (2010) Robert Rosen's anticipatory systems. *Foresight* **12**: 18–29. https://www.researchgate.net/publication/228091658_Robert_Rosen's_anticipatory_systems (accessed 11/02/2020).

McKnight J (1996) *The Careless Society: Community and its Counterfeits*. Basic Books, New York, NY, USA.

McKnight J and Block P (2012) *The Abundant Community: Awakening the Power of Families and Neighborhoods*. Berrett-Koehler Publishers, San Francisco, CA, USA.

Morgan MG, Fischhoff B, Bostrom A and Atman CJ (2001) *Risk Communication – A Mental Models Approach*. Cambridge University Press, New York, NY, USA.

Newman O (1973) *Defensible Space: People and Design in the Violent City*. Architectural Press, New York, NY, USA.

Perry BD (1997) Incubated in terror: neurodevelopmental factors in the 'cycle of violence'. *Children, Youth and Violence: Searching for Solutions* (Osofsky JD (ed.)) Guilford Press, New York, NY, USA, pp. 124–148.

Plush T (2013) Challenges for participatory development in contemporary development practice. *Development Bulletin* **75**: 55–58. The Development Studies Network, Australian National University, Canberra, Australia. https://crawford.anu.edu.au/rmap/devnet/devnet/db-75.pdf (accessed 08/04/2021).

Rodin J (2014) *The Resilience Dividend: Being Strong in a World Where Things Go Wrong*, 1st edn. PublicAffairs, New York, NY, USA.

Saunders P (2018) Detroit, five years after bankruptcy. *Forbes*, 19 July. https://www.forbes.com/sites/petesaunders1/2018/07/19/detroit-five-years-after-bankruptcy/?sh=59801f6fcfeb (accessed 29/03/2021).

Siemiatycki M and van Koeverden A (2021) Visualizing Trends in Transportation Infrastructure Public–Private Partnerships: Introduction. http://individual.utoronto.ca/siemiatycki/PPP%20Introduction.html (accessed 07/04/2021).

Smith S (2016) Unfriendly climate. *Texas Monthly*, May. https://www.texasmonthly.com/articles/katharine-hayhoe-lubbock-climate-change-evangelist/ (accessed 07/04/2021).

Sokolowski MB, Boyce WT and McEwen BS (2013) Scarred for life? *New Scientist*, 26 Jan.: pp: 28–30.
WRI (World Resources Institute) (2021) GHGProtocol.org (accessed 08/04/2021).

FURTHER READING

The CBA has strengths and weaknesses, which we need to understand. It is a simple tool to evaluate decisions free of bias or opinion, yet it is only as good as the factors and understanding that inform it in the first place. As we layer on complexity, specifically around the intangibles of a decision, we are necessarily introducing subjectivity to a calculation that doesn't readily accommodate it. There is an *engineering* view by Snell (2010) that is worth reading. The Independent Evaluation Group of the World Bank published a report on its use (Independent Evaluation Group, 2010), which also provides a useful perspective. The challenge, as ever, centres on measuring the social value in such calculations, which provokes diverse positions. The recent insight paper by the Royal Institution of Chartered Surveyors, *Measuring social value in infrastructure projects*, offers a timely addition to the discussion (RICS, 2020).

When we conduct our risk evaluation, much of what we perceive and how we analyse it will reflect our socioeconomic culture and frame of reference. The *Risk Analysis and Management for Projects (RAMP)* guidance (ICE and Institute and Faculty of Actuaries, 2014) is an established, practical and widely used framework and is worth studying. Nevertheless, it does not assure universal success, and as with all such guides, we must always consider whether the underlying assumptions carry to our current situation.

This book has, I hope, demonstrated that there is surprisingly little that is revolutionary or particularly new in planning and delivering resilient and sustainable infrastructure based on an evidence-based understanding of requirements and impacts. In many ways, we come full circle. While there are many valuable guides and new initiatives that promote one aspect or another in response to a current weakness, real or perceived, the fundamentals have not changed. You might consider rereading the Armitt Review, Sir John Armitt's independent review of long-term infrastructure planning, commissioned for Labour's Policy Review in 2013.

Armitt J (2013) *The Armitt Review: An Independent Review of Long Term Infrastructure Planning Commissioned for Labour's Policy Review*. The Labour Party, London, UK. https://www.policyforum.labour.org.uk/uploads/editor/files/The_Armitt_Review_Final_Report.pdf (accessed 08/04/2021).
ICE (Institution of Civil Engineers) and Institute and Faculty of Actuaries (2014) *Risk Analysis and Management for Projects: A Strategic Framework for Managing Project Risk and its Financial Implications*, 3rd edn. ICE Publishing, London, UK.
Independent Evaluation Group (2010) *Cost–Benefit Analysis in World Bank Projects*. World Bank, Washington, DC, USA. See https://openknowledge.worldbank.org/handle/10986/2561 (accessed 08/04/2021).

RICS (Royal Institution of Chartered Surveyors) (2020) *Measuring Social Value in Infrastructure Projects: Insights from the Public Sector*. RICS, London, UK. https://www.rics.org/globalassets/rics-website/media/knowledge/research/insights/measuring-social-value_1st-edition.pdf (accessed 08/04/2021).

Snell M (2010). *Cost–Benefit Analysis: A Practical Guide*, 2nd edn. ICE Publishing, London, UK.

ICE Publishing

Hay, Alexander H
ISBN 978-0-7277-6562-8
https://doi.org/10.1680/pris.65628.163

Chapter 7
Infrastructure planning in practice: a perspective on application

In the preceding chapters, we discussed the risks and influences to our infrastructure plans, ensuring that it meets the strategic requirements and remains in harmony with its context through life. It can, therefore, be a little frustrating to see practice diverge from what we intend. After all, we have allowed for changes in the risk context. Sometimes, this divergence is caused by a policy shift to suit a domestic agenda unrelated to our project. Other times, stakeholders, unwilling to accept a solution that they're not familiar with, can limit our plans. It may merely be that interests and priorities elsewhere have changed, fundamentally affecting the project. We should also recognise that perhaps we haven't been as thorough as we ought to have been, whether limited by time, money or simple institutional inertia.

Do not underestimate all people's ability to resist change, irrespective of how compelling the argument to change might be. However, sometimes, indeed, quite often, it is because we have not communicated effectively to all stakeholders. Consider Aristotle's artistic proofs that form the basis of a compelling argument and persuasion in *Rhetoric* (Aristotle, 2006). They are *logos*, *ethos* and *pathos*. *Logos* is the logical argument, using facts, statistics, reason and a structured arrangement of the supporting information. *Ethos* is the credibility of the speaker and the trust that the audience has in them. *Pathos* is the emotional appeal of the argument. Arguably, *Pathos* is the most important when presenting change. When people can share an emotional attachment to your vision and positively see themselves in it, they are more receptive to your argument's logic and supporting evidence. You will recall the Turkey Point Nuclear Generating Station's licence renewal example.

Nowhere are these diverse influences more exaggerated and convergent than in protracted-conflict and postconflict areas. In the aftermath of a conflict, there remains the risk of a return to violence. With time, the likelihood should recede, but reconciliation and former combatants' reintegration is never straightforward. Vocational education for common benefit can provide an excellent vehicle (Dennis and Fentiman, 2007), with major infrastructure projects as a key enabler. Except for the two World Wars, most master tradespeople and skilled professionals tend to flee the conflict area because they have transferable skills and means. This local loss of skills reduces the technical leadership and planning capacity of the broader community, which often reduces the ability to communicate what is required, despite an understanding of their needs. It creates the perfect conditions for misunderstanding and assumption and is vulnerable to malicious misinformation. The combination of these factors further undermines trust within and by the community (Hooghe *et al.*, 2012).

There is no codified perfect approach to infrastructure planning. By its very nature, infrastructure is intimately bound with the human domain and affected by human frailties and interests. It is never as simple as communicating correctly to the audience, basing the strategy on evidence and community benefit, or doing what is right. As discussed at various points in this book, successful infrastructure is as much about how it is delivered as what is delivered. At its core, it carries all of the complexities inherent in systems of systems. Little wonder that a persistence with siloed planning practice and simplified models based on assumptions that are fast becoming invalid is leading to consistent overruns in time and cost (Crudgington and Kitching, 2020). As the scale of the infrastructure development challenge increases, so does the waste. We can do better, and there are various initiatives by academia, government, industry and the professions to address this. We have these recurring themes of evidence and understanding, multidisciplinary or integrated planning and design, risk-based planning, and systems of systems approach. Still, we have rarely diverged from familiar practice.

We do know that an infrastructure strategy based on evidence and risk-based planning will deliver a sustainable and effective solution. However, we need to build on this and navigate towards a situation with which all stakeholders can identify. This journey is beset by misinformation, obfuscation, prejudice and self-interest, all essentially human traits. This chapter discusses the realities of the journey and what we need to be aware of and consider in developing an effective infrastructure strategy, from our approach to the particulars of different community types and the influence of technology.

7.1. Articulating need

When infrastructure engineers arrive from the international community, they will ask what is needed and too often project their interpretation of a deficiency on what they see and hear. This is human. We are each a prisoner of our own experiences, yet it would not typically be considered professional practice. Ordinarily, we would expect professional humility to listen to the local beneficiaries and fully understand their needs. This is undoubtedly the basis for effective international development work (Chambers, 1997). The listening process can accelerate through video applications (Plush, 2013). When we remove the time and resources needed to understand the local situation while pressing an imperative to be seen to be doing something, it ceases to be a question of delivering what is needed and shifts to delivering what is internationally perceived to be deficient. We may enhance the infrastructure engineers' situational awareness significantly through stand-off recognition and the rapid development of a *common reference* in the time available. However, we still face the realities of geopolitics and the need to justify international actions to domestic audiences. That is, assuming no strategic or resource rent interest in the area (Girod, 2015).

The situation is not hopeless by any means. It needs clear and straightforward communication with local stakeholders and international donors and agencies. The infrastructure engineer sits at the centre of this maelstrom and must interpret and communicate local needs, free from bias. It takes professional humility and an acceptance that the solution may be less than perfect from an international (best-practice) perspective. The solution must work for the local beneficiaries if they are to benefit as individuals and as communities. That also means that we do not create a dependency on us if it is to be locally adopted. To quote Lawrence, who was describing the structure of the Arab nations following the defeat of Turkey in 1918, 'our successor and solution must be local' (Lawrence, 2008).

Since he wrote that, we have learned much more about what it takes to foster local ownership, and Lawrence's words remain true. One might even say that they are an extension of the Pareto principle, or Voltaire's 'The best is the enemy of the good,' or Aristotle's golden mean. It is a historically consistent conclusion. Rarely is the perfect (de jure) solution the right (de facto) solution, whether for traumatised communities or to stimulate economic growth. We return to this. When we do not communicate our understanding to all stakeholders, the default will tend to be a build-back *antebellum* reconstruction policy. Development policies that reflect infrastructure systems seen in stable advanced countries are rarely suited to local circumstances.

This question of local circumstances includes how the infrastructure systems will be used, maintained and adapted to changing local needs. We discussed intelligent resourcing issues, but the question of how the resourcing will be adapted is more challenging. It is instructive to look at states that face a threat of violence, even if they have stable economies. Several buildings will have additional roles, suited to both routine and emergency functions. For example, a school gymnasium in Qiryat Shemona, northern Israel, has an enhanced air conditioning plant to serve as a temporary disaster victim identification facility during an emergency. Ninewells Hospital, outside Dundee, UK, was designed during the Cold War with corridors that could become wards because of the threat of a nuclear strike on Rosyth Dockyard, with associated mass casualties. The incorporation of secondary functions in design is not unique to the threat of violence.

Queensland, Australia, has incorporated secondary functionality into its development policy. Known as 'asset sweating', the idea is that adaptation of existing infrastructure must be explored before considering new construction. The same jurisdiction requires the revenue from service users to cover the cost of infrastructure replacement. These policy changes, brought in by Darren Crombie, as Deputy Director-General for Infrastructure Policy and Planning (2015–2018), brought infrastructure development into a more sustainable framework through effective demand management. The policy prioritises: (*a*) reforming the requirement; (*b*) better use of existing infrastructure; (*c*) enhancement of existing infrastructure, and lastly, (*d*) building new infrastructure (Queensland Government, 2016). This resonates well with the *reduce–reuse–recycle, and only then buy new* mantra that many of us will be familiar with. However, it also brings a new dimension to infrastructure planning that adapts the existing infrastructure rather than adding to existing infrastructure. In both cases, we must retain balance. Still, we must also be acutely aware of the increased risk of fragility in the VSOS.

Using school classrooms to teach adults in the evenings and running community courses and events during the holidays gets more use out of school properties than if they were only used for child education. However, when we run a number of operations at a facility, we need to understand how they function during an emergency. A crisis may affect one operation, but not another. There is a potential conflict in time and space, or, of more significant concern, a spike in demand density that falls outwith the (emergency) carrying capacity of the infrastructure. For example, a community centre that provides shelter and feeding for homeless people during extreme weather is also the community response coordination node during an emergency. A winter ice storm that causes such an emergency shouldn't mean that the homeless are ejected when they need shelter the most; this is a local and straightforward example, but easily overlooked. This applies at any scale of infrastructure. This concern should be a matter for careful coordination of operations over risk horizons, for a range of scenarios, to ensure that we do not create the conditions for an infrastructure failure (of purpose) at a time when we depend on it most. In the postconflict setting, 'asset sweating' is a basic necessity for existence. Still, we cannot ignore this potential fragility.

In the (UK) Armitt Review (2013), the point is made that successive governments had failed to set strategic priorities for infrastructure based on clear projections of future needs. The LSE book *Investing in Prosperity* (Aghion *et al.*, 2013) made similar comments. Both reports concluded, in effect, that politics needs to be taken out of infrastructure planning and delivery if we are to build for the future. The UK's National Infrastructure Commission is the result, establishing itself as a *catalyst* for a different approach to infrastructure strategy. The UK is making significant progress in this area. Still, difficulties will always remain, no matter how administratively distinct and evidence-based infrastructure planning becomes in practice.

When infrastructure has such a profound influence on all aspects of human health and is inherently emotive from any stakeholder perspective, it is difficult to remove politics from infrastructure. It doesn't matter whether we are operating in the UK, North America, Africa, Asia or elsewhere. Politics will always have a part to play. In a more benign sense, this can result in a tendency not to make decisions, as we can see with the historic delays in many major infrastructure projects in the UK, from the expansion of Heathrow Airport to high-speed rail links. We see this problem across the globe. In some cases, this can lead to paralysis in development or the authorisation of low-value projects, such as isolated airports that are barely used.

The issue returns to the perception of infrastructure and its value. A leader in *The Economist* (Anon, 2020a) discusses the grey vote and the impediment it represents to economic growth in the UK. The resistance to change when one's situation seems secure is common. Juliette Kayyem touched on the same sentiment concerning the balance of security and the flow of communities. The perception of security is present rather than a forecast. In the UK example, the pensioners who feel secure and resist the proposed development of new infrastructure that will stimulate economic growth lose sight of the need for that economic growth to generate jobs and revenue that will pay their pensions in the future. The public perception of infrastructure and change doesn't need to make sense. Often, it doesn't.

The Victorian sewer works in London were agreed on by Parliament, but not because they sought to prevent further outbreaks of typhoid and cholera and improve public health. The vote followed an awful smell of sewage coming from the Thames, known as the *Great Stink*. Little has changed in the intervening years. We could change our approach to housebuilding to remove any carbon footprint without diminishing comfort or increased cost, yet we don't. The unifying purpose of infrastructure and its perception rarely align, affecting how and where we invest.

Recognising that the impetus to invest in infrastructure is not necessarily the same as the need for it, we must understand the current situation and how it is changing the actual service needs. Real understanding is founded on evidence and the willingness to listen to what is needed and associated concerns. We need to find that pragmatic definition of requirement that will satisfy the real needs, enable local community adoption and be politically acceptable. It is imperfect, a compromise that may not be an ideal of efficiency. However, out of this, we can articulate the need, both what is needed and how it should be delivered.

7.2. A vision of the future

Depending on the jurisdiction, a policy is either agenda- or issue-based. An agenda-based policy will draw on research evidence that supports the policy position or agenda. It might even be curated. An issue-based policy draws on an objective and holistic understanding of the situation. One is not better than the other, and both have merit. Agenda-based policies force change. Issue-based policies improve existing systems. However, it can be challenging to present an evidence-based argument that may counter an agenda-based policy.

For example, let's say that a significant infrastructure development lender adopts a policy of portfolio decarbonisation. The lender has been a long-term investor in petrochemicals and now wishes to divest. Our infrastructure strategy provides a path to greater efficiency across scope 1 and 2 criteria, while maintaining the socioeconomic fabric developed around a particular company. The policy alone would prevent further investment in this proposal. However, if set within the UN's PRI, the lender can continue direct engagement in the company's transition to reduce its carbon footprint while preserving local livelihoods and social fabric. It becomes a question of timescale. Depending on the policy and its interpretation, no amount of justification for direct engagement with the petrochemical company to reduce their carbon footprint will shift an agenda to cut petrochemicals from the portfolio. In this case, the irony is that the means to reduce life-cycle carbon dioxide emissions is not delivered, resulting in no carbon reduction despite continuing demand for the product. It doesn't have to make sense.

Logos and *ethos* cannot justify the continued release of funding, but *pathos* can. Being able to explain in simple language what a particular infrastructure investment means and the attendant risks is vital. So, how do we overcome the situation described in the example? We change the narrative or frame of reference. Don't challenge a policy 'head-on' with evidence; work with the policies to change the administrative routine of inspection and decision-making. Change will happen; it just won't be immediate or accompanied by fanfares.

It is worth briefly turning our attention to fast-developing regions because we will face a different set of impediments to our IDP implementation. Typically, we have all the political support we can bear. Still, we are challenged by the capacity of the developing economy to support the development. In a fast-developing region, the infrastructure is necessarily just ahead of the economic development, akin to a *Red Queen* effect, rather than lagging behind the lead, as is the case in more stable development areas. The more stable development region is pushing infrastructure development and can enable it. Briefly, the Red Queen hypothesis (named for the Red Queen in Lewis Carroll's (1872) *Through the Looking Glass*, who had to run very fast just to stay in the same place) says that a species must continually adapt and proliferate to survive in competition with evolving opposing species. We can apply this to the system's adapting to rapid changes in technology and what it means for infrastructure. We will return to this idea.

When investigating the impediments to infrastructure development in fast-developing regions of China, Nie and Ye (2017) identified five issues: (*a*) difficulties in surveying and designing during the construction process; (*b*) weak support from the economy; (*c*) insufficient funding; (*d*) harsh regional climate, and (*e*) cost overruns. Allowing for the real capacity issues of a fast-developing economy, the list of impediments doesn't look different from the challenges faced in stable economies.

Unsurprisingly, we are better at costing projects of a familiar type. Flyvbjerg (2006) found that cost estimates improved with the number of projects in each category. For example, 20% of road projects were inaccurate, compared with

Figure 7.1 Internal and external risks applied to the conceptual refinement of a cost estimate (after Ashley *et al.*, 2006)

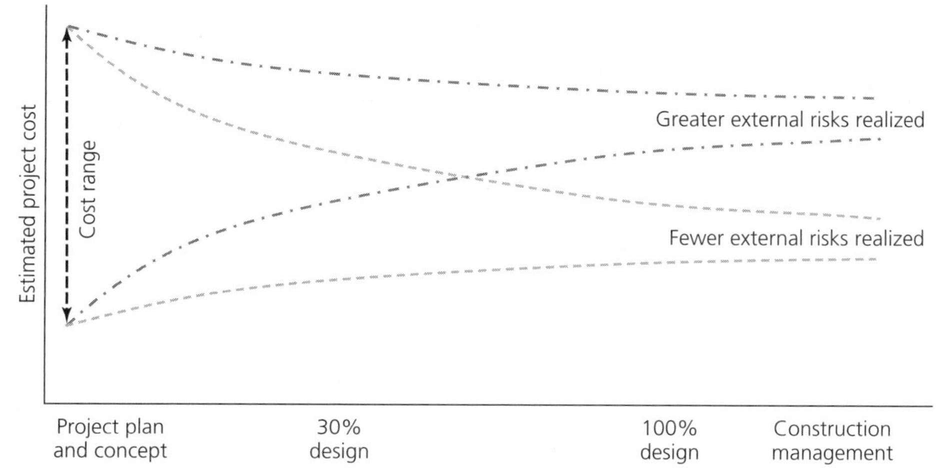

34% of bridge and tunnel projects and 45% of rail projects. The same year, the US Department of Transportation published its *Guide to Risk Assessment and Allocation for Highway Construction Management* (Ashley *et al.*, 2006), which presented a simple concept that shows the refinement of cost over a project's development (Figure 7.1). One might say that it looks like a funnel, graphically. However, the centre line of that funnel is determined by the risks experienced. When we take an evidence-based approach to our risks within an ERM framework, we might interpret this same concept as the funnel's centre line, reflecting the project's external risks. In contrast, we are progressively managing the internal risks as the project progresses.

The problem that we will always face is our optimism bias. To exaggerate the benefits and minimise the risks is human nature. Over the years, cost estimators and quantity surveyors have experimented with uplifts to cost estimates, though this tended to create a structural overuse of contingency funds and contract inflation. However, when we inform our estimating with evidence-based risk analysis, we have a more reliable result. The (UK's) Infrastructure Risk Group (2013) concluded that it is better to use reference class forecasting in conjunction with risk analysis. As we have discussed, that risk analysis is less effective when opinion-based, no matter how expert. It needs an evidence basis and should be fully auditable. This call for greater use of evidence in infrastructure planning and delivery brings us back to the Armitt Review (2013). However, it also brings us back to the issue of language.

7.3. A shared understanding of the vision

When we talk about the infrastructure gap, we have an intuitive impression of a lack of infrastructure to meet our needs. More typically, the infrastructure gap is the financial shortfall in necessary infrastructure investment. In the public debate, this may be semantic. Still, the term also reflects the disparities between jurisdictions across which the infrastructure is built, and how suited it is to future needs. You will recall the example of different jurisdictions negotiating flood mitigation measures along a shared river and who pays for what. When we look at the practicalities of how two municipalities will have evolved, we see a patchwork of regulatory requirements, jurisdiction disparities and differing priorities. Our project will mean something different for each community and jurisdiction it crosses. It will also carry a different risk profile, and this can change its portfolio of requirements. You will recall that the requirements definition process is typically iterative. We must maintain synergy through these iterations while recognising the unique value in each jurisdiction. One size does not fit all.

With these larger projects, it is quite usual to have several teams working on risk valuations. It is normal to have inconsistencies, and we must ensure that we establish a method of calibration for all planning teams. It is not enough to standardise. Consider, for example, a standardised failure modes, effects and criticality analysis (FMECA) model, such as the CARVER matrix (criticality, accessibility, recuperability, vulnerability, effect and recognisability). When the (US) Department of Homeland Security (DHS) was established following 9/11, teams were trained to use FMEA or FMECA tools and survey the critical national infrastructure. Each team will have a subtly different interpretation of the classifications and scale for each criterion. With experience of conducting these surveys, the teams become more consistent. Still, their later surveys do not resemble their earlier ones. When all of the results are collected and compared, how can we prioritise resources between the different sites against an inconsistent survey assessment? Interpretation and estimation during the data collection phase builds inconsistency into these surveys and their subsequent evaluation. We can address this issue by building a common reference but that takes organisational discipline and involves resisting the urge to interpret data and information during collection. Easier said than done.

An objective view of evidence applies as much to world trends as to the system dynamics in question. Technological disruption can be one of the more profound impediments to our infrastructure strategy. Think about the smartphone's mass introduction and how public payphones became a rarity in a couple of years. So much in our lives, in every respect, has been changed by ICT. It is precipitating such a profound change that the German Government referred to it as 'Industry 4.0'. This fourth industrial revolution is altering our service demand, which will have knock-on effects for its enabling infrastructure.

Otto make autonomous electric vehicles. Their vehicles are replacing rolling production lines and warehouse operators. Each vehicle is programmed for a specific product configuration or order and then independently moves in sequence to whichever task is required. Once the programme is complete, the product is delivered, and the vehicle returns to its charging station until tasked again. This automation process realises considerable efficiencies in production and warehousing that are attractive to the business owner and operator. However, it also means that the electricity demand is lower and maintains a flatter profile. This change in demand profile affects the electricity tariff structure. It can also mean that the principal customer no longer justifies the transmission and transformer infrastructure enhancement planned for a particular development site in the area. When one considers that the conversion of a production line or warehouse can happen in days and weeks, rather than months, the change in sustained demand profile is comparatively sudden.

The question of technological change affecting how we work is also a reflection of the choices we make. When we seek increasing automation of work, we displace jobs. Technology can also make us more productive. As Acemoglu and Robinson (2019) argue, we need to balance displacement and productivity to avoid popular dissent. In many countries, we have chosen capital over labour, particularly with the application of taxes. Once again, as infrastructure planners, we do not take a position on the political direction of the countries in which we work. However, we must be pragmatists. We should recognise that local adoption is more challenging when significant new infrastructure projects contribute to job losses with no (apparent) compensating community benefit. A lack of local adoption impedes the long-term sustainability and resilience of the infrastructure. The government can make policy decisions to encourage particular directions for technology development, as many have with clean energy. We need to focus on protecting the value of the infrastructure we plan, which is difficult when its introduction adversely affects local communities, however briefly. In both cases, artificial intelligence (AI) promises to amplify our actions' effects and the government's, for better or worse.

For the most part, AI today is machine learning. The system of satellite-based stand-off recognition of infrastructure laydown and condition is essentially the detection and association of anomalies and the likely meaning inferred. This is set to change. Thermal cameras installed in nursing homes can detect patients' skin temperature and indicate an increased likelihood of cardiac distress. It is not widely employed because people do not like to be watched or rather feel that they are being watched.

Nevertheless, mass public surveillance is becoming more common, both in the physical world and our data communications. Similarly, online meetings and learning have advanced significantly, thanks largely to the enforced isolation during the COVID-19 pandemic. As we become more dependent on advanced ICT and comfortable with its presence in all aspects of our lives, it becomes a tool that we can use.

We can leverage the economic stimulus that broadband access provides by including its laydown in our other communication infrastructure, such as roads, railways and pipelines. We can develop a more detailed common reference more quickly and draw in crowd-sourced data to populate the influence models. We can incorporate 4D BIM into our planning so that stakeholders can rehearse emergencies. Property managers can detect the indicators of system faults before they cause actual loss and operational disruption, as well as the promise of more efficient project delivery. We can use ICT and advances in AI to facilitate communities' transition to alternative economic and social structures and growth. This can offer communities greater ownership of their lives and environs and opportunities for their children's future.

7.4. Changing the vision

The oil and gas industry worldwide has always been able to offer well-paying jobs to school leavers. In oil town communities, there was little incentive to gain postsecondary education. Innovation in the industry was piecemeal, defined by specific issue projects at universities and colleges. The lack of advanced learning in the labour force means that innovation was unlikely to come from within the industry. As the industry falls on hard economic times, it seeks transition in the economy, and in-house innovation is absent. The situation is made worse by more institutions divesting in carbon. We are witnessing this today in Alberta, as we did with the Newfoundland fishing industry in the 1980s. Providing an interactive learning structure to the infrastructure development is one approach that can help us protect infrastructure value in these communities.

In some northern Alberta community development planning in 2014, my colleagues and I explored the collocation of wastewater and combined heat and power plants and a community college workshop in the same facility. The idea was that the community college would provide training in trades and local work on community infrastructure through the facility workshop. The interactively enhanced learning environment would include simulated problem identification and crisis response scenario planning, along with more typical trades development programmes. The local apprentices would be working on their community infrastructure and learning a broader trade and knowledge base. As importantly, this would be seen by the community and facilitate adoption within broader resilient community initiatives. While this example was about transitioning satellite communities to a more resilient essential services configuration, it can also apply to economic shifts. It isn't about replacing lost jobs. It is about protecting infrastructure value and promoting community ownership. There is no standard answer, and each situation will demand our intelligent imagination to find the unique solution that works for the infrastructure in its context.

We see similar shifts in demand profile from consumer adoption of smart energy management systems, storage and independent generation. The increased possibility of sudden change in demand profile can profoundly influence investor confidence and the infrastructure owner's fear of stranded assets. However, a lot of this comes down to whether one looks at the service and its enabling infrastructure system in isolation, a network of assets, or takes a more holistic view. When we can realise the secondary value of the infrastructure or extend the life of existing infrastructure for a lower demand, we focus more on where and how we invest our resources. When we take a system-of-systems view, the answer can be found in how the infrastructure is used.

Nevertheless, such sudden changes in demand profile do cause investor hesitation. They can indefinitely pause or curtail projects that still have significant secondary value. Once again, so much can come down to our interpretation of meaning and our use of language.

We discussed earlier the tendency for many infrastructure investors to use asset models to inform investment decisions. Aside from the fact that infrastructure value is not asset-based, we can see a contradiction in how a project fits within the strategy. For example, an asset management strategy sets a long-term desired position and associated service-level goals. These goals inform a tactical plan that assigns priorities for development into operational plans. These are short-term plans of up to 3 years. This process's effectiveness and efficiency will come down to the quality of the asset management system that the organisation is running. When we look at infrastructure, the value is not in the asset but in the service it enables. Individual assets within an infrastructure system will have a cost of replacement and the land they occupy, but not a direct real property value.

The translation of an infrastructure development strategy into programmes and then a portfolio of projects may follow a similar hierarchy of reduction from strategy to actions. Still, it operates in parallel and at a more holistic scale. The infrastructure development programme sets the conditions for the asset management strategy, and the conditional goals for stage delivery set the priorities for asset enhancement and investment or waste-out. At some point, an effective asset management information system is sensitive to IDP priorities and automatically adjusts resource allocation priorities. Instead, we see schools refurbishment in the same year that they are demolished and similar actions.

Part of the issue would appear to link to the interpretation of 'through life' and 'whole life'. It is useful to think of through-life and life-cycle costs as directly attributable to the system or asset. This would include the cost of construction, operation and maintenance, occupancy and final disposal. Whole-life costs will include the through-life and non-construction costs, income and external demands (ISO, 2017; Kreye *et al.*, 2009). Often, the terms 'whole-life' and 'through-life' are used interchangeably yet have entirely different meanings. We've discussed how basic risk definitions can be different according to discipline and jurisdiction. These structural confusions can result in an entirely different interpretation of meaning.

When we draw these various strands together, we see an inconsistent use of language, confused investment and resource allocation priorities, and a lack of evidence in planning and decision-making. These impediments underpinned *Finweek*'s assessment of infrastructure investing in South Africa (Rangongo, 2020), for example. They cited poor maintenance and neglect, undermining the resilience of the existing infrastructure, which induced fragility in the whole. Furthermore, there was inadequate data collection, evidence to support decision-making and management. Overall, *Finweek* cited a general shortage of skilled professionals. To that last point, I am inclined to qualify it by suggesting that there was a shortage of skilled professionals with a systems perspective.

It would be a mistake to think that these are localised problems or limited to particular continents. These problems exist everywhere, to one degree or another. There is a finite number of skilled professionals. When there is more work than they can handle, their skills are diluted. When time imperatives prevent full consideration of the issues and policy direction changes with the political flavour, there will be noise, and the best-conceived plan will be imperfect. This is a reality that we must recognise. As we discussed, it is necessary to focus on the operation and the impact of change on it, not the likelihood of hazards causing that change. A railway may be rerouted to suit a constituency interest, such as influencing a swing vote in the next election. Does the reason and the nature of the change impact the operational or unifying purpose? If not, work with it and present the cost of such decisions impartially. We'll leave this discussion here before straying into political ethics and the challenge of corruption.

7.5. Noise and liminality

The COVID-19 pandemic has exposed both the good and bad in our society. Of course, our respective interests influence our interpretation of what is good and bad. The polarisation of capital and labour, the greater government involvement in day-to-day society or the fact that governments can no longer afford the capital investment in many infrastructure schemes will impact people differently. Irrespective, as of February 2021, we are all in a liminal state. Liminality means crossing a threshold into a new role. It is something that society has traditionally ritualised, with a master of ceremonies guiding supplicants through the process. As a society, we are in such a liminal state. We do not yet know what the post-pandemic world will look like, and we are unclear about our place in it. Even those seemingly unaffected by the pandemic economic impacts so far can have no greater knowledge of the future than those facing eviction and foodbank charity. There is no master of ceremonies or shortage of opinions. Some of it is informed and considered, and some of it is motivated by individual interests. Clarity of vision and the articulation of what world we would wish to live in remains scarce, though it is traditionally the preserve of those we elect to represent and lead us. There is a significant housing shortage across much of the Western world, yet there remains widespread opposition to it and new communities' development.

The lack of a commonly shared vision or process makes established and familiar procedures and bureaucracy the default. The background noise distracts and makes our planning today more challenging than it needs to be. It will continue to do so for the foreseeable future. This instinctive grasping of familiar procedures, irrespective of their validity in the situation, is a recurring issue. As we have discussed, it is human nature. Still, we need to think carefully about how we might manage it.

To reiterate, infrastructure planning is complex but needn't be complicated. When we gather the evidence and consider the situation and requirements holistically, the issues emerge, and we can address them in a time-proven process. Like so many inherently complex things, people will seek to provide simplistic solutions, policies and procedures. Some of this is driven by a constant demand for 280-character descriptions of solutions and political positions. Sometimes it is driven by the need to be seen to do something or, more often, the desire to be seen to know what is happening and be in control. Reality and collective benefit is not part of the argument, and we see this, particularly around new community development. We return to this. We cannot lay this at the feet of any particular group or profession. Academics will keenly enthuse their perspectives and agendas to students, as politicians will reflect on the electorate opinions most likely to get them elected. The problem this creates is that these oversimplifications of issues make what is already highly complex far more complicated. The centralisation of wastewater treatment in a postconflict community that still faces the threat of violence can create worse health outcomes for the population than doing nothing. Building a power transmission line to an isolated community that makes airlift uneconomic can compromise that community's overall health and viability.

This presents us with two real challenges. The first is how we can plan inherently resilient infrastructure. The risk context and demand profiles change as they always have, but now we are unclear about how we wish to live, work and play. We face a more fundamental shift in social fabric than the end of World War II, which heralded an extraordinary 40 years of unparalleled prosperity. That period of whole-of-society liminality had the vision of the 1942 Beveridge Report to provide a roadmap to social equity and the considered concerns of Young's (2008) meritocracy to caution overenthusiasm. The challenge, ultimately, is to identify what the outcomes must be. We can stick to the unifying or strategic outcome being physical, mental and social well-being. But the operational outcome cannot be based on the assumption of our current working patterns, income distribution and household expenditure. Infrastructure planning is in greater demand today and for the foreseeable future than, arguably, at any time in the last century. It is also the most challenging of environments to practice, and we must avoid complicating what is already complex. It requires a solid foundation of evidence and reason, the intelligent imagination to incorporate innovative solutions, and a significant improvement in communication. Have we attracted the right talent into this discipline?

The second challenge is how we will pay for it, or, more to the point, how we prioritise conflicting socioeconomic imperatives. That will be a matter of risk-based decision-making against a holistic understanding of what we seek to achieve. The point is that an asset-based assessment of cost and benefit does not expose the investment in its entirety and the impact on the health of the population, the economy and broader society. It means that professionals working to define the infrastructure's operational purpose and its coordination with other development initiatives must abandon much of their familiar practice and bias. We explored the issues around social equity and its role in the adoption and, therefore, long-term sustainability of infrastructure and its value. The greatest challenge would appear to be the attraction of best practice.

Best practice, I suggest, does not exist. Each situation is fundamentally different. Each site, requirement and context is a unique combination. While the technology and design approach may be similar, the practice and outcome are different. For example, a stormwater management scheme for Frederiksberg, which is surrounded by Copenhagen in Denmark, will not be suited to a plain city in North America. Frederiksberg is on a hill. While the technology may be transferable, its application is not. Too often, best practice is the replication of what has worked elsewhere. Curiously, we never hear of a successful use of best practice that defines best practice for others. We need to be more critical of what best practice is and what aspects are transferable. In our audit work, the most successful projects have been based on an in-depth understanding of the situation and the formulation of solutions using tools suited to the situation.

I should qualify my suggestion that best practice does not exist by saying that best practice is not practised. The approach and intelligent application of the technology is what distinguishes best practice from mediocrity and failure. When we understand why a practice was successful, we understand how it may be relevant to our situation. We see the same in the use of case studies. Case studies can provide valuable insights into how and why, but are too often interpreted in terms of what happened. Perhaps, as Kahneman (2013) suggests, we are naturally inclined to look for a familiar decision-making pattern rather than spend the intellectual effort determining the problem. This becomes all the more apparent in a world experiencing an accelerating rate of change. Our decisions are always judged with the benefit of hindsight. That judgement is ever more vocal and influences social and commercial behaviour. Infrastructure is often the most tangible intersection between these two spheres. As infrastructure planners, we must inform the understanding of impact and how it will change the context, and how a changing context will influence it.

Gartner, an international business research and advisory firm, identified the top ten emerging risks in the second quarter of 2020. They were: the second wave of the COVID-19 pandemic; the new working model; strategic corrections due to changing macroeconomic dynamics; the 2020 US presidential election; US–China trade relations; misguided cost-cutting efforts that prioritised a short-term response to the pandemic over the ability to recover and resume strategic direction; cyber-physical convergence in the increasing connectivity of things previously unconnected and the shifting vulnerabilities that this entails; profound social instability; work–life convergence; and extreme weather events. It is interesting to note that these are all liminal risks and in stark contrast to the top risks identified before the pandemic. Fears of liminality didn't change with the US presidential election and a third pandemic wave of infections. The World Economic Forum's *Global Risks Report 2021* is consistent (WEF, 2021).

The pandemic has had the effect of accelerating and converging many issues that we knew were coming over the next generation. Assumptions around the influence and impact of an infrastructure scheme cannot hold. We need to look holistically at the role of infrastructure in a changing world. In effect, we need to get back to a first-principles approach to an IDP strategy. Gartner concluded their summary of emerging risks with a comment on risk velocity, namely those risks likely to manifest first and to greatest impact, with corporate social negligence at the top of the list, closely followed by the new working model and the second wave of the pandemic. The WEF (2021) focuses more on societal risk and the fragmentation of the social fabric, including and perhaps amplified by digital inequality. The relationship between society and infrastructure would suggest that this emerging risk context will amplify the benefits and unintended consequences of infrastructure projects.

The discussion raises the question of whether planning resilient (sustainable) infrastructure can be effective amid such liminality. The short answer is *yes*. These changes are part of the risk context, and less can be assumed. Infrastructure can provide a way out of the situation, but it can stall economic development if poorly conceived. We can take a more holistic and fundamental evidence-based approach to infrastructure planning if we choose to. We can build zero- and negative-carbon residential buildings if we choose to. We have had the technologies at our disposal for several years to do things differently. If we had chosen such a path, perhaps our situation today would be less uncertain. It has rarely been a financial question, more typically, one of familiarity. I think that we, as infrastructure planners, can make that change more tenable and less intimidating with the right evidence and language. One might even say that we can affect change with a blend of *pathos*, *logos* and *ethos*.

7.6. New communities

There are many approaches to new community design and development. However, from an infrastructure development perspective, sustainable infrastructure development constraints can limit some of the options. We have already discussed carrying capacity and its relationship with demand density. We have discussed the need to develop the infrastructure in pace with the sustainable demand so that the revenue generated meets the infrastructure's operational costs and the service it enables. We also explored the idea of stability and community adoption of the infrastructure and services, including basic planning concepts of intelligent resourcing and beneficial capability. These are operational aspects, tools that allow us to plan and deliver the right infrastructure for the task. The problem is one of vision.

At what point is there a clear description of the world we wish our children to inherit? It is that step beyond the current functionality of the community under development. It is increasingly common for resource rent conditions to include a community development, capable of self-sustaining, on a mining operations' successful conclusion. This goes beyond the increased onus on mining companies not to cause harm. In August 2020, the UN Environment Programme published the *Global Industry Standard on Tailings Management*, a voluntary industry standard produced in response to a series of high profile tailings pond failures, most notably at Vale's Brumadinho iron mine in Brazil. On 25 January 2019, the tailings dam failed catastrophically, causing 259 recorded deaths, with a further 11 people unaccounted for. Throughout the standard, common themes include using evidence and care for the environment and communities affected and potentially affected by the mining operations. It should not be that surprising, given the general trend in SDGs and the UN PRI. However, it is shining a corporate social responsibility light on an industry that has largely been out of sight and out of mind, and the communities it creates.

Communities establish for many reasons, but they do establish for a purpose and carry a range of inherent risks and fragilities. As we've discussed, each location has a unique hazard profile that defines the community's inherent risks and the industry or other economic interest that causes it to exist. We have an opportunity to configure the community to address many inherent fragilities. This was something our forebears understood somewhat better than we do today. The frontier towns with concentric rings of diminishing value as one blended into the wilderness provided a configuration that would survive the threat of wildfire, flood and storm. We could layer on area administration and protection against malicious threats and similarly protect these operations from loss under these threats and hazards. The common feature through these developments was the coincidence of spaces to live, work and play. When we look at the organic development of these (young) communities, they resemble ecological systems. Single-function zoning fractured that dynamic and separated our connection with the environment and any appreciation of the inherent risks.

We see this separation between an organic development and the spatial projection of functions in Armbruster's interview of Hiram and his father in *The Nature of Economies* (Jacobs, 2000). We also see it in how communities perform under the stress of a disaster. Those with electoral districts that resemble organic communication structures are more cohesive and more inclined to trust and act on the authorities' information. Conversely, drawing a straight line through a community to define an electoral boundary fragments the very communication structures we depend on in an emergency. Sometimes, it is better to exert less control than more. It is a question of where we exert that control and to what end. It affects how the community behaves. When we see the essential services of the community (and the enabling infrastructure) as enabling community function and benefit over individual benefit, we see greater social engagement during periods of stress.

It has not been possible to find textbook examples, since anything community-based is a complex dynamic of influences. However, returning to Copenhagen, the pandemic stimulated a sense of *samfundssind*, community-mindedness. In Toronto, my colleagues and I saw similar behaviour in the more integrated mixed-use areas, known locally as *villages*, and not so much in the dormitory communities and unserviced suburbs. At a broader scale and under Hurricane Katrina's weight, Aldrich (2015) observed much the same. How we choose to develop our built environment does influence our attitudes and behaviours.

Interestingly, as Cutter *et al.* (2008) have proposed, we can also measure the community's resulting resilience. Therefore, we can plan resilience into our infrastructure development and subsequently measure the effect on the community. We need to recognise that value is ascribed to what is tangible in the market perception: *marble countertops sell a property, its structural integrity does not.* Conversely, we can ensure that a new housing subdivision includes some basic community amenities, isn't located in a high flood hazard area or other inherent risk exposure, and can serve changing demographics. New development residents will grow older, have families and change jobs, require access to different community services at each life stage, and interact between the generations and households. We need less homogeneity and more through-life heterogeneity in our development plans.

7.7. Post-trauma communities

There is increasing reference to post-trauma communities. Historically, these were communities that had been physically destroyed by war or natural disaster. This postconflict and postdisaster categorisation gradually extended to include communities in protracted conflicts, internally displaced persons and refugee camps. More recently, it includes aboriginal treaty lands and reservation communities and those affected by postcolonial intergenerational trauma. It is a broad catch-all term that appears to take on whatever meaning and nuance the user wishes. However, I suggest that post-trauma communities' common characteristics are that (*a*) they remain under a continuing external threat of harm and (*b*) there is no trust in the higher authority or administration. There is also a distinction between what might be termed a traumatised community and a post-trauma community. The traumatised community is one where the population is mentally and socially traumatised by a catastrophe or policy. The post-trauma community has experienced a catastrophe that has damaged the community's natural and built fabric and may well have traumatised the community. One might categorise regionally marginalised communities that have lost major industrial employers in the same way. Some former coalmining communities' sense of abandonment remains palpable 40 years after the pits closed, on both sides of the Atlantic.

Successful infrastructure development in post-trauma communities will depend primarily on the community's social capital. It is the essential enabler, and we need to be sure to protect that as we evaluate the requirements and attendant risks. In the preceding chapters, we discussed the consequence of a return to violence or aftershock in our assessment of the infrastructure network scale. A centralised wastewater treatment facility will impact a larger population if it is damaged than will dispersed smaller neighbourhood facilities. The smaller variant is also more suited to alternative energy sources. It can generally operate independently of central supply or administration. However, the need for adoption by the community means that we must also consider such programmes as former combatant reintegration and community reconciliation as part of our beneficial capability and intelligent resourcing constraints. Ultimately, this is about the individual and collective benefit to the end user. It demands a degree of sensitivity and humility that typical time constraints rarely permit. However, this is not limited to communities that have suffered conflict, hurricanes, floods and earthquakes.

When there is social capital, we can generally work with the community towards a beneficial outcome. When social capital is absent, it forces us to communicate differently. We need to appeal to the individual and enable cohesion through shared opportunities to benefit. This can mean that one ward will be planned for and communicated with in a different way from another ward in the same municipality. Aldrich (2012) and Boin (2008) made similar observations in their examinations of catastrophes. This means that infrastructure planning would ideally begin with the local beneficiary, which makes sense. That is not the way we typically respond to crises and postdisaster rehabilitation. The international response to the Haiti earthquake is a case in point (Haver, 2011; Kirsch *et al.*, 2012). There is a delicate balancing act that we must perform as infrastructure planners, ensuring that the strategic delivery is adequately informed and coordinated and that the infrastructure components of that strategy are adequately integrated with other components.

Social capital can exist in the absence of community trust in the higher authority. The identity and self-concept of the people of Sarajevo during the siege (1992–1996) meant that they worked together to position trams as sight-shields to frustrate sniper fire, hold local art exhibitions in the bombed-out post office and keep the *Osloboenje* newspaper running. This was as much a statement to the world that they felt had abandoned them as it was maintaining social cohesion. The same can also turn against outside assistance. A fully equipped fire station and clinic were built in Janvier, an aboriginal community in Alberta, Canada, but soon looted. It was not because the facilities were not needed or suited to the locale, but a lack of trust in the authority that delivered them. Similar examples can be seen in postcolonial aboriginal communities in Canada,

Africa, Australia and elsewhere. We see similar results in communities where there is a cultural misalignment with the higher authority. In such cases, the infrastructure planning consideration is not so much what to build, which we tend to be somewhat better at, than how it should be delivered.

My experience is mixed, and I do not have a simple answer. When we read case studies, they are too often focused on the project conduct and outputs and do not relate conduct with outcome. We must rely on our professional judgement. We must be culturally sensitive, have an evidence-based understanding of the situation and needs, and approach each plan with humility and patience. Sadly, these last two criteria can be in short supply in many situations, owing to time and money constraints.

The bulk of our work in post-trauma communities can result in successful outcomes when we are willing to work from first principles. We will not always be successful, but that shouldn't mean that we don't try. It is useful to take a longer view. Post-trauma community rehabilitation is about the restoration of health and the expression of hope. Human progress has marched hand in hand with advances in hygiene and public health. Its absence leads to instability and war (Anon, 2020b). The long-term enabler of public health is infrastructure, and sometimes the most remarkable result in the planning process is to stimulate a local belief in the future and normalcy. The 2018 essential services infrastructure assessment in the Gaza Strip stimulated a local initiative to standardise their spatial data infrastructure, starting with a common datum. It provided the basis of a locally generated common reference.

7.8. Equity of access

It is curious that when we explore the effectiveness of different development initiatives and agendas, equity of access determines ultimate success. We discussed equity of access in Chapter 3. It would seem to apply to abundant access, quiet streets, complete communities, urban densification and green corridors. We see this most starkly during the transition of a post-trauma community from aid and reconstruction to development and normalcy. However, we also see it in urban and rural communities across the developed world. The collective benefit and successful outcome of development initiatives is when all community members have equitable access. Remember that equity of access is not the same as equality – recall the three children watching a football game. Equity is about opportunity defined by outcome, and wealth should not define each individual's ability to realise that opportunity. This is what Young warned of in *The Rise of the Meritocracy* (2008). When an institution has a shrinking base of beneficiaries, it can become exploitative of those not benefiting (Acemoglu and Robinson, 2012), and we create fissures in the fabric of our communities.

This social fragmentation is amply demonstrated by the migration from rural villages to urban centres in the Hejaz region of the Kingdom of Saudi Arabia, which happened over a decade. Following the country's education reforms, a new generation aspired to a professional life in the cities they could now access. The rural dynamic relied on this generation to maintain the agricultural routine and fabric of the community. Soon, the families of those successful in the cities followed. From a trickle of families to a sudden flood, and the rural villages became weekend cottage communities. Whether the sudden movement was a social dynamic, as Schelling (2006) describes, or simply because the village fell below a critical mass of labour remains unclear. What is clear is that few cities were prepared or planned for the sudden influx. When we look at al-Madinah, we see extensive areas that have developed without community structure. The elders, once used to gathering regularly, are now isolated in unfamiliar surroundings without their peers. The same has happened to spouses and, to a lesser extent, the children. New community relationships gradually form through the mosque and school, but the only community interaction is now the professional generation. The people in these developments are separated by generation and household, impeding social capital.

When we see infrastructure as the enabler of a service and integrated within the VSOS of the community and broader province, we see the implicit role that it plays in dealing with the consequences of other policies. When we take a more integrated approach, we might see the development of educational facilities and access going hand in hand with business centres and community foci. The community business hub is a facility enabled by broadband access and reliable data storage, adjoining an exchange where people can meet, exchange ideas and trade goods and services. It is little more than a technology-enabled medieval market, but highly effective nonetheless. These have been successfully introduced in Africa and the Middle East (Kelly and Firestone, 2016), providing the means to retain talent and community cohesion. Some commentators have referred to them as *oases of innovation,* which is a surprisingly apt descriptor. We can include sustainability and resilience in the design. The latest versions are offgrid capable for limited periods, sufficient to support offline working, and locally back up Internet-accessed data. As part of a broader scheme to slow the depopulation of Ontario counties, these are being proposed as a young professional generation heads to the Greater Toronto Area.

Equity of access is as much about providing access to opportunity locally as enabling that access. At one level, we might say that we should build the next generation of magistrates' courts closer to where their clientele live, making physical access to the law equitable. The legal cost of representation is another issue and part of the concept of equity of access. The concept is enshrined in the idea that we are all equal before the law and forms part of our social contract. When we dig into this idea a bit further, we see that we make planning decisions that isolate sections of the community rather than keeping them integrated. For example, care homes are rarely collocated with community foci. This means that the community doesn't benefit from elders' wisdom, and elders' mental and social well-being are discounted. The pandemic exposed the vulnerability of the elderly and the societal decisions that created that vulnerability. It also exposed the vulnerability of high-rise community housing residents and those living in food deserts, as well as those pushed far from where they work by the cost of housing. The less we support the physical, mental and social well-being of the vulnerable, the greater the cost to society of managing the consequences. The pandemic exposed that we are unwilling to meet that increased cost. So why is this relevant to infrastructure planning?

You will recall the example of a community grocer, Longo's, collaborating with Natural Resources Canada, demonstrating that the future grocery store could also be highly energy-efficient, a community hub and codeveloped with other community services. This example sustainable store is in Stouffville, Ontario. Aside from the improved performance efficiencies, the potential social value became apparent, stimulating interest among care home providers and residential developers to provide proximity developments to such community hubs. The hub retains functionality during a crisis and provides the necessities of the community. It is also configured as an exchange with elders, professionals, trades and young parents with children interacting at a human level. This community awareness feeds social capital and shared identity. It is also inclusive. This configuration is possible as a commercial initiative with municipal support. The shared recognition is that the community's enhanced social value will be reflected in a reduced burden on the municipal budget, improved real property values and possible enhanced revenues. The challenges arise when we apply this to housing; specifically, affordable housing.

The development of a community hub requires a shared vision and cooperation. These qualities are insufficient to deliver the affordable housing we need. The mention of affordable housing is enough to send most institutional investors elsewhere. The conventional models of residential development encourage cheap construction with few social features and are rarely sustainable. The driver of an immediate return on investment also encourages a densification approach that results in high-rise developments. Densification needn't mean high-rise construction and can be achieved with a more manageable seven to eleven storeys for apartment blocks. Ideally, we would look for four or five storeys. There are several reasons for this, not least the need to evacuate quickly in an emergency, even if the elevator isn't working. Fire tender ladders will reach the seventh storey, but no higher. Suppose we are to have affordable housing, typically for the more vulnerable and financially precarious community members. In that case, it still needs to be safe, comfortable and not create an additional burden during an emergency. Building affordable housing that is resilient, sustainable and does not create additional burdens on the municipality requires a new financial model and a different approach.

The approach is not so new, and we have several examples of inclusive housing developments around the world. Most are cooperatives, and charities and faith groups own many. The top two award-winners in the international Rethinking the Future Awards 2020 are inclusive residential developments that are community hubs. The second award in the 'Mixed use concept' category (Sustainable, 2020) is exciting because it provides social cohousing (affordable and inclusive) tuned to the surrounding community's needs and adjacent to a transit hub. When we look into the financing, it uses a through-life value approach instead of an estimate of value at the point of investment.

Within the designer's *people–planet–prosperity* approach, we see that investment in developing the property's social value and the land or market value of privately owned units. Private investors can realise a return on investment by selling off units at pre-agreed milestones, as the market value improves with the community value. Meanwhile, the social housing units (affordable, vulnerable persons, care-in-the-community, etc.) can remain at the original affordable housing revenue of 80% of the accepted market rate, or 30% of the household income, whichever is pre-agreed. This broader view of value and recognising a longer-term staged return on equity is attracting private finance keen to diversify asset portfolios. A shift in financing structure for the development can stimulate reliable and sustainable access to a more stable and equitable community.

The challenge in bringing equity of access back into community and infrastructure planning is the desire to persevere with familiar models that are not suited to a *health* outcome. This is harder to change than one might think. There is a natural community focus around transit hubs, which could be incorporated into inclusive mixed-used developments, if the transit authority is part of the development and willing to look forward. Changes of planning concepts and risk criteria can be threatening in institutions that are incentivised not to change. Borrowing from Queensland's approach to asset sweating, how much greater the value of school facilities if the school day reflected the parental working day? It would mean that working parents bring their children to school on the way to work and pick them up again after work. It could also incorporate early-years education with vaccinations and nutrition for all children, irrespective of background. The value of the infrastructure to the community is greatly enhanced, and the collective investment is in a more equitable future for the next generation. Conceptually, this would not be so different from the post-World War II world that delivered such extraordinary prosperity for a generation.

We have the capability, the resources and the need. We only have to want to make the changes to realise improved equity and population health. Political will is not enough, even when it exists. Technology and innovation that enhance efficiency rather than productivity must be managed. We need to think about how we plan our infrastructure to enable the next generation and how it can be delivered. We must be willing to work with evidence and select the right tools for the problems we identify, which means understanding and considering new and unfamiliar models and processes.

7.9. Information and communications technology (ICT)

In 2016, the International Telecommunication Union (ITU), a global telecommunications regulator and coordination agency of the United Nations, initiated

United for Smart Sustainable Cities (U4SSC). The project was remarkable in several ways, not least in what it takes to enable 'smart' capabilities in cities. While the project working group in which I was involved (Working Group 2: Connecting Cities and Communities of the United for Smart Sustainable Cities Project 2016/2017) focused on making these capabilities resilient and sustainable, the diversity of opinions about what a smart city is in practice remained at the core of the discussions. The U4SSC project had a clear mandate, to be '... a global platform for smart cities stakeholders, which advocates for public policies to encourage the use of ICT to facilitate the transition to smart sustainable cities' (UNECE, 2021). Finding a definition of smart cities was more challenging. It is one of those terms that has evolved out of an idea that each user interprets differently. This should come as no surprise. Each city is different. As we've discussed from a fundamental risk perspective, each city differs in location, culture and character, economy, demographics, hazard profile, and so on. The concept of being smart would similarly apply differently in each case.

The notion of a smart city appears to have started with IBM consultancy marketing in the 1990s and was best articulated in 2009, in the IBM Institute for Business Value's executive report *A Vision of Smarter Cities: How Cities Can Lead the Way into a Prosperous and Sustainable Future* (Dirks and Keeling 2009). Citing the increasing socioeconomic importance of cities, the report presses the need for cities to be more holistically and efficiently managed to keep pace with this change. Advances in technology provide an opportunity to function smarter, particularly around water and energy. This idea has an intuitive appeal and soon spurred technologies that enhance efficiencies in emergency services response way-finding through traffic, traffic monitoring and active management, and increased surveillance. We can also see the integration of different technologies in the same infrastructure, such as distributing Wi-Fi antennae with cameras at traffic lights and the expansion of public data connectivity through subway systems and all public buildings. However, is a smart city necessarily a technology-enabled one, or might it just be better operated?

The *Business Dictionary* (Sharman, 2016) defines a smart city as

> A developed urban area that creates sustainable economic development and high quality of life by excelling in multiple key areas: economy, mobility, environment, people, living, and government. Excelling in these areas can be done so through strong human capital, social capital, and/or ICT infrastructure.

From an infrastructure planner's perspective, this view of smart cities resonates. It is holistic and sees the population as a significant part of the solution. The investment in human capital creates an *oasis of talent* and the source of dynamic innovation. It reflects our understanding of the domains of the VSOS. There is an attractive simplicity in developing a new ICT system that monitors various city metrics for presentation to the municipal executive as a colour-coded dashboard. It provides the illusion of control, omitting the necessity to understand the city VSOS to know what needs to be monitored and what it means.

The Centre of Regional Science at the Vienna University of Technology, among others, has led the call for a holistic approach to smart city planning and development. New organisations are created each year, including, more recently, the University of Toronto's School of Cities. Writing in *Co.Exist*, an idea-sharing website, Boyd Cohen proposed a smart cities wheel that provides a holistic impression of how smart a city is (Cohen, 2012). More recently, ISO 37122:2019 (Sustainable cities and communities – indicators for smart cities) offers the possibility of comparing cities against a common metric. Together with ISO 37123:2019 (Sustainable cities and communities – indicators for resilient cities), it is part of ISO 37120:2018 (Indicators for city services and quality of life). These are part of an expanding suite of metrics that incorporate the SDGs and are used as the basis for green bonds and sustainable financial instruments. The challenge, as ever, comes with their application. As described with the LEED programme, do the metrics dictate development or measure progress? Metrics of performance cannot measure the capacity to recover, so the indication of resilience is incomplete. This issue is particularly acute in transitional economies (Borsekova *et al.*, 2015). If we plan to what will be measured, we can lose sight of what we are supposed to do (Muller, 2018).

What stands out in smart city development is the mitigation of inherent risk through development. When we understand how to mitigate these risks, ICT has a significant part to play. Technology, specifically ICT, is a capability amplifier when used to enable and not define. We see this reflected in the UK Environment Agency's 2020 *National Flood and Coastal Erosion Risk Management Strategy for England*. Similarly, initiatives such as the circular economy and the electric city are made possible through the intelligent application of technology. These place the social value, and specifically the city's human value, at the centre of the development agenda. The social value of infrastructure will determine its potential capital value.

7.10. Chapter summary

Infrastructure planning is complex but needn't be complicated. Nevertheless, a broader stakeholder reluctance to use evidence and select the most appropriate models, preferring to oversimplify an issue to suit a particular agenda, consistently complicates matters. This complication affects urban design and administration, the operation and maintenance of existing infrastructure networks, and the valuation of an infrastructure scheme for investment. Until recently, no amount of evidence to the contrary has persuaded much institutional change. The COVID-19 pandemic has forced a reassessment of many of these familiar planning and investment models. In part, this is due to the extraordinary socio-economic upheaval that has occurred in response to the pandemic, the reduction in the available public funds for development and broader uncertainty around how the world will function in the aftermath of the pandemic. The weaknesses inherent in many societies and economies are exposed, and citizens demand change. Some institutional investors have become more risk-averse and wait to see the nature of that change; others have called for clarity of purpose and vision in industry sectors. New finance structures for social infrastructure are emerging, attracting private investors who see opportunity and reliable long-term benefits, as well as an increased importance in green bonds and other instruments that enable change.

However, the impediment to outcome-based infrastructure planning has been a reluctance to diverge from the familiar. The tools for handprint construction have existed for decades. Yet, we have been unwilling to adjust our familiar designs and construction techniques. A consultancy dismisses existential risks for a manufacturer because it means designing with a different (unfamiliar) refrigerant. Sometimes, our acceptance of change is when it is legislated or becomes part of routine compliance. When we remain focused on the whole VSOS outcome of our plans, we can address the challenges of an uncertain future. Evidence in the common reference provides a handrail to demystifying the complexity. Each situation is different, and not all stakeholders wish to consider the future. Still, infrastructure is a statement of future capability and requires clarity in our vision of the world we wish our children to inherit. We need to consider more closely how our world is changing and where it may lead. If we are to deliver resilient and sustainable infrastructure, we must understand how infrastructure is affected by contextual change and how it changes prosperity, the planet and, above all, people. It doesn't mean that we need to be economists, political scientists, financiers, or any other profession. It means that we need a professional awareness beyond the narrow confines of our academically defined engineering discipline to a broader *engineering in society* understanding.

BIBLIOGRAPHY

Acemoglu D and Robinson JA (2012) *Why Nations Fail: The Origins of Power, Prosperity and Poverty*. Profile Books, London, UK.

Acemoglu D and Robinson JA (2019) *The Narrow Corridor: States, Societies, and the Fate of Liberty*. Penguin Press, London, UK.

Aghion P, Besley T, Browne J *et al.* (2013) *Investing in Prosperity; Skills, Infrastructure and Innovation*. London School of Economics and Political Science, London, UK.

Aldrich DP (2012) *Building Resilience: Social Capital in Post-disaster Recovery*. University of Chicago Press, Chicago, IL, USA.

Anon (2020a) A grey and stagnant land. *The Economist*, 15 Aug.: pp. 49–50. (North American edition.)

Anon (2020b) Pandemics and war: horsemen of the apocalypse. *The Economist*, 20 June: pp. 49–51(North American edition.)

Aristotle (2006) *Aristotle: In Twenty-three Volumes. 22: The 'Art' of Rhetoric* (Freese JH (trans.)). Harvard University Press, Cambridge, MA, USA. (Reprinted.)

Armitt J (2013) *The Armitt Review: An Independent Review of Long Term Infrastructure Planning Commissioned for Labour's Policy Review*. The Labour Party, London, UK. https://www.policyforum.labour.org.uk/uploads/editor/files/The_Armitt_Review_Final_Report.pdf (accessed 08/04/2021).

Ashley DB, Diekmann JE and Molenaar KR (2006) *Guide to Risk Assessment and Allocation for Highway Construction Management*. US Department of Transportation, Washington, DC, USA. Report FHWA-PL-06-032.

Beveridge W (1942) *Social Insurance and Allied Services*. His Majesty's Stationery Office, London, UK.

Boin A (ed.) (2005) *The Politics of Crisis Management: Public Leadership under Pressure*. Cambridge University Press, Cambridge, UK.

Borsekova K, Petrikova K and Vanova A (2015) Building of smart cities in specific conditions of transitional economies. *55th Congress of the European Regional Science Association: 'World Renaissance: Changing roles for people and places', Lisbon, Portugal*. European Regional Science Association (ERSA), Louvain-la-Neuve, Belgium.

Carrol L (1872) *Through the Looking Glass and What Alice Found There*. Macmillan, London, UK.

Chambers R (1997) *Whose Reality Counts? Putting the First Last*. Intermediate Technology Publications, London, UK.

Cohen B (2012) What exactly is a smart city? *Co.Design* 19 Sept. https://www.fastcompany.com/1680538/what-exactly-is-a-smart-city (accessed 11/08/2016).

Crudgington A and Kitching R (2020) *A Systems Approach to Infrastructure Delivery: A Review of How Systems Thinking Can Be Used to Improve the Delivery of Complex Infrastructure Projects*. Institution of Civil Engineers, London, UK. https://www.ice.org.uk/getattachment/knowledge-and-resources/briefing-sheet/a-systems-approach-to-infrastructure-delivery/ICE_Systems_Report_final.pdf.aspx (accessed 12/04/2021).

Cutter SL, Barnes L, Berry M *et al.* (2008) A place-based model for understanding community resilience to natural disasters. *Global Environmental Change* **18**:598–606.

Dennis C and Fentiman A (2007) *Alternative Basic Education in African Countries Emerging from Conflict; Issues of Policy, Coordination and Access*. Department for International Development, London, UK. DFID educational paper no 67.

Dirks S and Keeling M (2009) *A Vision of Smarter Cities: How Cities Can Lead the Way Into a Prosperous and Sustainable Future*. IBM Global Services, Somers, NY, USA.

Environment Agency (2020) *National Flood and Coastal Erosion Risk Management Strategy for England*. Environment Agency, Rotherham, UK.

Flyvbjerg B (2006) From Nobel prize to project management: getting risks right. *Project Management Journal* **(37)3**: 5–15.

Gartner (2020) *Top 10 Emerging Risks of 2Q20*. Gartner, Stamford, CT, USA.

Girod DM (2015) *Explaining Post-Conflict Reconstruction*. Oxford University Press, Oxford, UK.

Haver K (2011) *Haiti Earthquake Response: Mapping and Analysis of Gaps and Duplications in Evaluations*. Active Learning Network for Accountability and Performance in Humanitarian Action, London, UK.

Hooghe M, Marien S and de Vroome T (2012) The cognitive basis of trust: the relation between education, cognitive ability, and generalized and political trust. *Intelligence* **(40)6**: 604–613.

Infrastructure Risk Group (2013) *Managing Cost Risk & Uncertainty in Infrastructure Projects: Leading Practice and Improvement*. Institute of Risk Management, London, UK.

ISO (International Standards Organization) (2017) 15686-5 Buildings and constructed assets. Service-life planning. Part 5: Life-cycle costing. ISO, Geneva, Switzerland.

ISO (2018) 37120 Indicators for city services and quality of life. ISO, Geneva, Switzerland.

ISO (2019a) 37122 Sustainable cities and communities. Indicators for smart cities. ISO, Geneva, Switzerland.

ISO (2019b) 37123 Sustainable cities and communities. Indicators for resilient cities. ISO, Geneva, Switzerland.

Jacobs J (2000) *The Nature of Economies*. Random House, Toronto, ON, Canada.

Kahneman D (2013) *Thinking, Fast and Slow*. Anchor Canada, Toronto, ON, Canada.

Kelly T and Firestone R (2016) *Digital Dividends: How Tech Hubs are Helping to Drive Economic Growth in Africa*. World Bank, Washington, DC, USA. World Development Report 102957.

Kirsch T, Sauer L and Sapir DG (2012) Analysis of the international and US response to the Haiti earthquake: recommendations for change. *Disaster Medicine and Public Health Preparedness* **(6)3**: 200–208.

Kreye ME, Goh YM and Newnes LB (2009) Uncertainty in through-life costing within the concept of product-service systems: a game theory approach.

International Conference on Engineering Design, ICED '09, Palo Alto, CA, USA, pp. 57–68.

Lawrence TE (2008) *Seven Pillars of Wisdom: A Triumph.* Vintage Books, London, UK.

Muller JZ (2018) *The Tyranny of Metrics.* Princeton University Press, Princeton, NJ, USA.

Nie T and Ye K (2017) Demystifying the barriers to transport infrastructure project development in fast-developing regions: the case of China. *Sustainability* **9(10)**: 1915.

Plush T (2013) Challenges for participatory development in contemporary development practice. *Development Bulletin* **75**: 55–58. The Development Studies Network, Australian National University, Canberra, Australia. https://crawford.anu.edu.au/rmap/devnet/devnet/db-75.pdf (accessed 08/04/2021).

Queensland Government (2016) *State Infrastructure Plan, Part A: Strategy.* Department of Infrastructure, Local Government and Planning. Queensland, Australia.

Rangongo T (2020) Going beyond the traditional investment matrix. *Finweek*, 4 June: pp. 32–37. https://www.news24.com/fin24/finweek/investment/going-beyond-the-traditional-investment-matrix-20200604 (accessed 13/04/2021).

Rethinking the Future (2021) https://awards.re-thinkingthefuture.com (accessed 09/04/2021).

Schelling TC (2006) *Micromotives and Macrobehavior*, new edn. Norton, New York, NY, USA. (With a new preface and the Nobel Lecture.)

Sharman J (2016) *Smart Cities, Future Cities, Sustainable Cities.* NBS Enterprises, Newcastle upon Tyne, UK. https://www.thenbs.com/knowledge/smart-cities-future-cities-sustainable-cities (accessed 13/04/2021).

Sustainable (2020) *Sustainable Receives International Recognition in the 2020 Rtf Competition.* Sustainable, Toronto, ON, Canada. https://www.sustainable.to/news-recognition/2020/2/27/sustainable-receives-international-recognition-in-the-2020-rtf-competition (accessed 13/04/2021).

UNECE (United Nations Economic Commission for Europe) (2021) Sustainable Smart Cities. https://unece.org/housing/sustainable-smart-cities (accessed 09/04/2021).

UN Environment Programme (UNEP) (2020) *Global Industry Standard on Tailings Management.* UNEP, Nairobi, Kenya.

WEF (World Economic Forum) (2021) *The Global Risks Report 2021*, 16th edn. WEF, Geneva, Switzerland.

Young MD (2008) *The Rise of the Meritocracy.* Transaction, Piscataway, NJ, USA.

FURTHER READING

The distinction between an idealised solution and what works can be counter-intuitive. It is not a question of producing the perfect strategy and then detuning it to suit what will become adoptable. It has more to do with understanding the social value associated with the work. An interesting read is *Maximising Social Value from Infrastructure Projects* (Dobson *et al.*, 2020), commissioned by ICE.

A consistent issue with capital infrastructure, particularly *sustainable* and *resilient* infrastructure, is that in recent years we seem to consistently overrun in time and cost. In this book, I have argued that we need an integrated strategy that is based on a fundamental evidence-based systems understanding of the operations or services, and their context and enabling requirements. Andrew Crudgington's (2020) review for ICE of infrastructure project overruns provides a useful perspective, focusing on SAID (a systems approach to infrastructure delivery). It is worth reading, particularly as the SAID model will now be developed. I sense that SAID will feature in the UK's future infrastructure planning and practice.

The subject of smart cities becomes more complicated the more I read on it. In 2017, Arup published a report on how different cities are becoming smart (Future Cities Catapult, 2017). It raises the issue of surveillance and perception of control. Is that what makes a city smart; is a smart city what the purveyors of the enabling technology say it is? If so, does that mean that the denizens must surrender their freedoms for efficient urban function and municipal services – equity for efficiency? Is it similar to the relationship that they have with the police and the balance of freedom and security? I do not think that there will be a clear answer anytime soon, but the debate is fascinating. Ellie Cosgrove raises some of these considerations in her 2018 paper, while others (Futurecapetown, 2021) are concerned that smart cities benefit a minority. Deciding what they mean in practice and delivering real social value will be unique to the situation. The 2020 OECD report on smart cities and inclusive growth provides a useful summary of the potential benefits and concerns.

Cosgrove E (2018) The smart city: challenges for the civil engineering sector. *Proceedings of the Institution of Civil Engineers – Smart Infrastructure and Construction* **170(4)**: 90–98.

Crudgington A and Kitching R (2020) *A Systems Approach to Infrastructure Delivery: A Review of How Systems Thinking Can Be Used to Improve the Delivery of Complex Infrastructure Projects*. Institution of Civil Engineers, London, UK. https://www.ice.org.uk/getattachment/knowledge-and-resources/briefing-sheet/a-systems-approach-to-infrastructure-delivery/ICE_Systems_Report_final.pdf.aspx (accessed 12/04/2021).

Dobson J, Behar C, Ramsden C, Crudgington A and Heulin CA (2020) *Maximising Social Value from Infrastructure Projects*. Useful Projects, London, UK. https://usefulprojects.co.uk/wp-content/uploads/2020/01/Maximising_social_value_from_infrastructure_projects_v1.1.pdf (accessed 12/04/2021).

Futurecapetown (2021). Africa's future cities: a new utopia for Africa? *Smart Cities Dive* https://www.smartcitiesdive.com/ex/sustainablecitiescollective/africa-s-future-cities/1021606/ (accessed 12/04/2021).

Future Cities Catapult (2017) *Smart City Strategies: A Global Review*. https://www.arup.com/perspectives/publications/research/section/smart-city-strategies-a-global-review (accessed 12/04/2021).

OECD (Organization for Economic Cooperation and Development) (2020) *Smart Cities and Inclusive Growth: Building on the Outcomes of the 1st OECD Roundtable on Smart Cities and Inclusive Growth*. OECD, Paris France. http://www.oecd.org/cfe/cities/OECD_Policy_Paper_Smart_Cities_and_Inclusive_Growth.pdf (accessed 12/04/2021).

ICE Publishing

Hay, Alexander H
ISBN 978-0-7277-6562-8
https://doi.org/10.1680/pris.65628.193

Chapter 8
2020s and beyond: future considerations

With Sanjay Khanna

According to Klaus Schwab, executive chairman of the World Economic Forum, and Thierry Malleret, cofounder of Monthly Barometer, the 2020 global pandemic should trigger a 'great reset' of globalisation (Schwab and Malleret, 2020). They make a moral case that this reset requires a clear shift to stakeholder capitalism, something that needs to materialise now because unprecedented circumstances of inequality demand it. The debate about shaping the future with a stakeholder approach that is inclusive of communities – or a shareholder approach that prioritises business profits potentially at the expense of communities – is at the heart of an increasingly tense debate about how to build resilient societies against a backdrop of 'converging crises'. Given the impact of the pandemic, a massive recession, sociopolitical volatility, psychological vulnerability, geopolitical fragmentation and the climate crisis, however, the built environment and infrastructure can play a substantial role in supporting resilient societies, even without a great reset.

Conversations about the future that shape business and government leaders' thinking can be a barrier to problem solving. It is common to hear, for example, that major global challenges will be addressed by industry innovation and humanity's infinite potential and genius at adapting to change. Unfortunately, the comprehension, know-how and sociotechnical capacity to address various aspects of the future that are coming towards us – and catching up with us now and later – are unequally and unevenly distributed across human societies (Ramirez and Wilkinson, 2016).

It is quite plausible that our societies do not have enough human resources to tackle predictable repercussions that today's actions ought to address. Without exception, the professions and trades – accounting, architecture, construction, design, engineering, law, management consulting, medicine and public health – are not ready for converging crises. Individually and together, professions and trades need to build and scale the intellectual, operational and cross-disciplinary capacity to tackle this contextual challenge. Today, given that individual and cross-disciplinary capacity is unevenly and inequitably distributed, there is a chance to embed foresight and longer-term thinking into the planning of resilient infrastructure systems. On a global basis, governance systems and community engagement are not prepared to mobilise in response to a world with fewer resources to divvy up among more people – or to identify where there is human capacity to improve health and lessen suffering, given the convergence of a pandemic (the greatest global economic shock since World War II) and environmental, biocultural diversity and climate crises.

Adding to these wicked problems, imbalances between capital and labour constrain the freedom of various societies to address these issues. Few investors deploy capital for the common good, that is, for outcomes that improve population well-being, including disaster risk reduction and public health measures. Conversely, institutional investors and asset managers, such as Larry Fink, CEO of BlackRock, decry a lack of purpose in many industries, especially oil and gas (Fink, 2020). Unfortunately, international efforts that purport to be in the interests of stakeholders remain tied to Bretton Woods' economic and financial architectures and superstructures. Today, there is pressure on leaders to intelligently work within or reimagine these structures, considering what the key issues are and what can be done to address them.

As civil engineers working alongside allied professionals and stakeholders, collective thinking is constrained by familiar processes. Hence, it is no small task to plan resilient infrastructure systems, even without the many crises that surround us. The resilient infrastructure systems envisaged in this book exist where top-down governance and bottom-up understanding of communities' needs for health and well-being meet.

This chapter aims to help engineers to gain perspective on what is known, unknown and unimaginable – and to develop insight and knowledge drawn from understanding global change. The chapter is grounded in the theory expounded in this book that evidence-based analysis and a common reference can make it possible to turn an understanding of risk into sound decisions. The chapter reminds engineers that, in a world where each year brings new unprecedented risks and opportunities, not one profession has 'figured out' the global change environment. As a result, the process of collaboration within and across disciplines is more urgent, necessary and complex – as is developing a mastery of the emerging art and science of building social capital through the use of strategic foresight methods that make it possible to have the right conversations among stakeholders.

8.1. What is known

Humanity is living through an unprecedented transition from a postwar twentieth century of relative stability to a twenty-first century described by the Oxford Scenario Planning Approach (OSPA) as one of turbulence, uncertainty, novelty and ambiguity (TUNA). This is the new strategic planning context for organisations (Ramirez and Wilkinson, 2016). It is not that we haven't seen tumultuous change in the twentieth century, it's just that the accelerating rate of change of the Earth system, resource competition, the breakdown of civil and multilateral institutions, technological acceleration and its consequences (intended and unintended), risks of declines in population health (physical and mental) on a global scale, wealth and income inequality within and between nations, and extreme weather and the associated climate crisis all pose risks to the continuity and stability that human civilisations need to thrive and prosper (Khanna, 2016).

The era of disruptive change that we inhabit is throwing into disarray the very elements of stability and continuity that societies need to ensure proper education, health and well-being, and social and community services. Global change can be divided into five key megatrends to make the change context easier to comprehend.

- *Geopolitical fragmentation*
  The globalisation era may be ebbing (Irwin, 2020). We are entering a long period of retrenchment, with global and regional tensions rising as power blocs centred around the United States, the European Union and China reorient from cooperation and multilateralism to increasingly fierce competition, whose underlying cause is scarcity of natural resources, environmental degradation, homogeneous economic development approaches and rising unrest tied to lessened opportunities to provide equality of opportunity to governed populations. As global power relations change, as decision-makers' psychologies change, as societal conditions change, and as planetary conditions for trade and commerce change, geopolitical fragmentation is the result. The probability of diplomatic and military conflict increases in this interconnected context.
- *Socioeconomic reordering*
  Writ large, governments and businesses are increasingly indebted, as are consumer-citizens. The postwar middle class is being reordered as the upper middle class strive to maintain close relations with the upper class and the socioeconomically vulnerable endeavour to survive economic ructions. The Western middle class doesn't see what's coming – some in the middle class will hang on, while others may face destitution. In developing economies, there is a risk that the middle class that grew during the key period of globalisation will be a short-lived phenomenon.
- *Physical and mental health declines*
  Commercial entities appear to favour the instigation of disruptive change to markets. This is especially relevant and significant because too much uncertainty correlates with greater unease among many consumer-citizens, who will find they have less control of their own destinies. The perennial concern is that human societies require stability and continuity in order to remain healthy. Increased disruptive change anticipated this century promises to affect physical and mental health at a population scale.

- *Technological acceleration*
  From a technological perspective, the scaling of networks, and the manipulation of information towards mostly malign ends, means that more bad decisions can be made more quickly and at greater scale than at any time in human history. The other aspect to this is that consumer-citizens are accustomed to technology addressing immediate problems and now expect it to solve big issues as well, including the climate crisis and the destabilising mass dissemination of fake news. In fact, technological change doesn't remove risk, it simply shifts it elsewhere. Engineering's method of understanding a problem and using the most suitable tools available to solve it has traditionally been how to address risk and remains so today. However, the erosion of engineering and design more generally in favour of technology must be reckoned with. We fear and sometimes even reject evidence because it distracts from our political or institutional view, amplifying our emphasis on technology as the saviour.
- *Extreme weather and climate change*
  Human civilisation is firmly ensconced in the climate crisis era, which has also been dubbed a 'planetary emergency' by distinguished scientists such as Johan Rockström, codirector of the Potsdam Institute for Climate Impact Research, and climate activists such as Greta Thunberg. As of March 2021, the average monthly level of atmospheric carbon dioxide recorded at Mauna Loa Observatory, National Oceanic and Atmospheric Administration (NOAA), is 417.64 ppm, which reflects an increasingly dangerous accumulation of atmospheric carbon dioxide that fuels global heating. The level of atmospheric carbon dioxide will continue to rise in coming decades, helping to fuel more extreme weather and climatic change that will test the suitability of infrastructure across geographies for more challenging emergent environmental and planetary conditions (Rockström *et al.*, 2009). These conditions will test virtually all aspects of planning resilient infrastructure systems, especially enabling services that support human health, well-being and social cohesion.

These known knowns are, for all intents and purposes, implausible to reverse, making clear the increasing instability of the global commons.

8.2. What we know that is unknown

It is easier today to understand global context more clearly and accurately than ever before. Evidence can be used to properly map an organisation's or a project's risk profile, identify fragilities and pinpoint opportunities. Yet, while arriving at an understanding of these risks and opportunities is eminently doable, there is a pernicious habit of rejecting evidence and denying science when it conflicts with commercial or political interests (Burchman, 2020).

To address this serious challenge, it is essential to explore how known megatrends may interact to create plausible circumstances demanding a fundamentally different strategic or operational response to a changing world. Depending on the specific context, intersections of geopolitical fragmentation, socioeconomic reordering, physical and mental health declines, technological acceleration and extreme weather and climate change are likely to play out in unique ways.

For example, consider Black Lives Matter (BLM) protests in the United States. These social protests occurred at the intersection of geopolitical fragmentation, socioeconomic reordering, physical and mental health declines and technological acceleration. Coinciding with a global pandemic that affected Black and Latinx populations disproportionately, BLM protests grew in response to racist violence by police and white supremacists and a social media environment that amplified political tensions between those supportive of and those antagonistic towards Black and Latin Americans' civil rights.

Physical and mental health declines became part of the BLM story, too. The disproportionate impact of COVID-19 correlated with longstanding health and economic inequities faced by Black Americans, associated with an increased incidence of pre-existing conditions. Climate-related disasters occurring alongside COVID-19 in southeast and southwest USA held additional implications for US society, including a loss of natural capital and increased disease transmission, largely in Black and racialised neighbourhoods, where housing and infrastructure were inadequate. Trade tensions between the USA and China distracted from US domestic politics and added to the rising unemployment of poor and racialised Americans.

The confluence of these issues with a new US presidential administration may have further significant impacts on US democracy, potentially affecting the ability to address health through planning resilient infrastructure systems. The converging crises era demonstrates that there are limits to the capacity of human and natural systems to adapt to a wide spectrum of rapid, shocking change happening concurrently. This may include limitations on the capacity to think and act rationally, a major concern given the need for clear and effective action in the face of converging crises.

Similar unpredictable, interrelated confluences of events and circumstances will emerge in the TUNA (turbulence, uncertainty, novelty and ambiguity) era. The nature of the interaction of various factors will contribute to uncertainty, the 'U' in TUNA.

8.3. What is potentially unimaginable

It's important to consider what is potentially unimaginable in terms of emerging scenarios. It is not inconceivable, for example, that cities and regions whose relative stability have made them a fount for innovation, finance, trade and commerce will be fewer in number. It is well-documented that major world cities, such as Bangkok, Beijing, Hamburg, Hong Kong, Jakarta, London, Miami, Mumbai, New York, Paris, Rio, Shanghai, Singapore, Tokyo, Toronto and Washington (DC), are threatened by converging crises (Mora *et al.*, 2013).

This implies that key cities we expect to be oases of strategy, planning and governance innovation may not remain the urban centres of stability that are required for interdisciplinary teams of professionals to think through planning resilient infrastructure systems. Depending on the shocks they face, some key cities and their knowledge capital could be lost during this century. This calls into question what sorts of personal, professional and community mindsets and praxis are needed to successfully navigate complex planning, design, engineering and stakeholder engagement activities, which are part and parcel of planning resilient infrastructure systems.

This also implies that civil engineers will be developing resilient infrastructure systems during periods of heightened psychosocial distress at the community level and will need to maintain working environments of great clarity, focus and disciplined mindfulness, particularly as societies face greater socioeconomic, environmental, public health and intergenerational challenges associated with converging crises. The latter could include the need to engage with older voters, some of whom may feel that their interests do not coincide with those of younger generations who – in their lifetimes – will face perpetual consequences of shocking change.

8.4. Integrated strategic planning

Strategic planning encompasses scenario planning, forecasting, capabilities-based planning and many other methodologies. Scenario planning, in particular, is designed to address the TUNA context by enabling the development of plausible scenarios set up to 10 years in the future (Wilkinson, 2017). Given concerns about shocks such as the COVID-19 pandemic making prediction much more challenging, the development of plausible scenarios set 6, 12 or 18 months ahead is now becoming more commonplace in practice. Scenario planning is particularly compatible with planning resilient infrastructure systems because the development of alternate stories set in the future allows many aspects of infrastructure to be incorporated into the scenarios, including relevant political, economic, social, technological, legislative and environmental (PESTLE) elements that stakeholders should consider.

According to RAND Corporation (Samaras and Willis, 2013), capabilities-based planning enables central planners to ‘identify program needs, allocate resources, and track activities and outcomes’ against a background of uncertainty where various potential scenarios are taken into consideration. One can see therefore that scenario planning and capabilities-based planning complement one another and are useful to include as part of strategic planning related to resilient infrastructure systems.

In this era of socioeconomic uncertainty and associated social volatility, stakeholder and community engagement must reduce its emphasis on investors’ needs to the extent that this focus threatens life-affirming and life-giving interdependencies among members of society with very different means. Such supports foster both survivability and healthy human resilience at community and regional levels. The planning of resilient infrastructure systems should maintain a substantive focus on meeting community users' needs with a wide and respectful view of users, which could encompass substantive, non-coercive engagement with marginalised communities.

One example of how *not* to conduct stakeholder engagement (Mann *et al.*, 2020) is Sidewalk Labs' effort to influence Toronto communities with the objective of winning over the public to the idea of developing a smart city neighbourhood in what could have become a trendy district and international showcase for a BigTech smart city (by way of background, Sidewalk Labs is, along with Google, part of the Alphabet holding company). Sidewalk Labs hired an exhaustive array of lobbyists, public relations firms, event organisers, community influencers, privacy advocates, and so on. The result was 'stakeholder engagement theatre', where the desire of the company not to budge on data governance and data privacy issues was masked by elaborate, creative, inspiring and costly public engagement and lobbying efforts. While COVID-19 was the excuse for the collapse of the Sidewalk Labs project (Cecco, 2020), communities saw through the public relations and engagement exercise and contributed mightily to its demise and to increased parliamentary and regulatory scrutiny. The expensive 18 month effort ended in failure – a lose–lose for the city and for the company.

As indicated in the Sidewalk Labs example, regulatory and compliance elements must also be taken into account when it comes to strategic planning related to infrastructure, particularly when large, publicly listed entities are contributing to infrastructure planning, design and development, engineering, community engagement and construction. Whether it is voluntary disclosures, encouraged by the Taskforce on Climate-related Financial Disclosures (TCFD), or an increased call for greater assurance in investing, lending or underwriting (Eccles and Krzus, 2018), it is critical to demonstrate that you are doing everything reasonable to ensure your continued value in an uncertain future.

8.5. Resilience

Resilience is a poorly understood concept. Technically, it means that individuals, communities, organisations or cities have developed the capacity to adapt to change and bounce back from a shock so that they can ultimately function at similar efficiencies and performance to those before the shock. The challenge is that a perpetual TUNA environment may mean that the definition of resilience may need to be revised. Resilience may mean that individuals, communities, organisations or cities have developed the capacity to adapt to change and bounce *partially back* so that they can restore capacity at a later time, when post-shock circumstances are amenable to capacity rebuilding.

In other words, given the converging crises context, bouncing back *below original capacity* is also a form of resilience. As such, it is essential to remember that resilience is a continuous journey that demands a living dialogue among society, economy, environment and infrastructure. It is never wholly achieved but, with balance, increased stability and resilience are possible. Conversely, when instability is a feature, adaptation becomes impossible, as does the capacity to bounce back to any state that offers enough stability for capacity rebuilding.

The massive Beirut port blast of 5 August 2020 is a case in point (Devi, 2020). The explosion of 2750 t of ammonium nitrate improperly and neglectfully stored in port facilities was a 'black elephant', a well-understood massive explosion risk that lay in wait for an accidental or deliberate spark to ignite it. For documented reasons, the grave risk was not heeded by relevant authorities. When the explosion did occur, it met a Lebanese and Beiruti society whose resilience had already been hobbled by corruption, rising prices, an employment crisis, a refugee crisis, regional infighting, a central banking crisis – a joint economic, financial and fiscal crisis that sparked social protest on a regular basis. In concert, these converging crises impacted healthcare capacity and delivery prior to the blast. The blast worsened everything, causing billions of euros in damages to the city, creating post-traumatic stress disorder (PTSD) at the population scale, negatively affecting acute, preventative and rehabilitative healthcare services in hospitals and clinics. From a resilience standpoint, Beirut is not in a position to bounce back or bounce forward; the best it can hope for now is the resilience to wait until circumstances are more conducive to capacity rebuilding so that when rebuilding occurs the new infrastructures are able to respond resiliently to shocks that may come in the years and decades ahead.

One key to Beirut's rebuilding will be on the human scale of developing novel communities of practice focused on open innovation and, to a greater or lesser extent, healthy cognition, mental wellness, knowledge sharing and community-centred values. This means that when planning sustainable and resilience infrastructure, process is as important as what is accomplished. In Beirut, or any other place, people (communities, municipalities, politics, markets, social licence, etc.) will ultimately define the value (use and adoption) of any infrastructure over its life.

For engineers, a broad, deep and nuanced understanding of resilience-related issues is critical because resilience, like sustainability, has become a buzzword that can signify many different intentions and meanings, some that could contribute to resilience and others that could detract from it. It is important to be able to understand which is which and to put that knowledge to work in planning resilient infrastructure systems along with allied disciplines and a wide range of stakeholders.

8.6. Technology

Accelerating change is romanticised today, as is the concept and the reality of 'disruptive change' that can ensue. Unfortunately, human psychosocial and community development takes time and evolves in common, but differentiated, cycles, rhythms and patterns. Human psychosocial development follows painstakingly described milestones, where healthy development can be thwarted or encouraged. No method has been found to accelerate healthy maturation or the development of wise leaders and thoughtful citizens. Technology moves fast, typically without engaging with a community of wise users that could contribute to developing calm, slow technology interventions and user interfaces.

Converging crises mean that planning resilient infrastructure systems will involve thoughtful solutions that prioritise maintenance, repair and replacement in a local or regional context, even of relatively advanced technologies, such as novel materials. In planning resilient infrastructure systems, considerations of appropriate technology will be a critical aspect of maintaining and expanding societal resilience.

8.7. Ethics and law

Commercial practices in engineering need to be rethought and the guild model re-energised to properly mentor promising young architects, designers, engineers, planners, sociologists and artists during a time of accelerating and disruptive change.

This is a non-trivial issue. Planning resilient infrastructure systems for an unprecedented global context requires an approach that is less wholly transactional because the local context of infrastructure has become lost as transactional approaches have become templatised. Assumptions that underlie various contracts need to be rethought – from the long-term value of assets to the services that infrastructure provides to the nature of ownership and of stewardship.

It follows that the goal of planning resilient infrastructure systems and building long-lasting habitation for a TUNA world will require a new symbiotic ethical, cultural and contractual approach that is ruthlessly pragmatic and borne of innovative economic and financial arrangements that embed trust and equitable risk-sharing deeply into party and counterparty relations. The very nature of the TUNA environment means that these emerging ecosystems will develop in a fragmented, unequal and inequitable way, even as holism, equality and equity are embedded into the cultures and subcultures of human advancement through infrastructure. These will be deep, challenging and conflicting shifts, given the stakes for humanity's future.

8.8. Concluding remarks

Some people argue that the future is wholly unpredictable or, conversely, that it is so predictable that one should carry on living, building, consuming and socialising as usual. Even though we have rarely been able to predict what will happen in 10 or 15 years, much less 40 or 60 years, it is possible to apply disciplined methodologies to help us understand how a failure in a supply chain or market system will impact our operations. In other words, by building an objective and evidenced understanding of our current situation – and the trends about us – we can gain a strong appreciation of how changes in the future will impact our capabilities. Understanding today helps us know what is possible.

Strategic foresight's role is to explore plausible futures and usefully inform how we prepare our organisations and ourselves for them. When strategic foresight is combined with supposition and bias about the existing situation, however, a lack of purpose, value and credibility often results. Today, we are inhabiting a new geological and social age, within which we are building infrastructure. In this age of human-caused change, we know that the biosphere, including the atmosphere, land and oceans, is being irrevocably altered as the climate crisis unfolds. We also know that social relations are facing upheaval as a result of large-scale inequities across the world and within nations, regions and urban centres. The inevitability of mass migration to escape the consequences of environmental degradation and climate change are also part of the calculus, as is the rising burden of mental illness and physical and mental ill health at the scale of population health.

Arguably, we are crossing the threshold into a new geopolitical era of trade and conflict, informed by a fracturing of the postwar order, a massive shift in trading relations and an equally transformative and threatening change of planetary conditions that underpin the relative stability of human civilisation. Circumstances are such that technology platforms can enable the instrumentation of human habitation in ways that support or forestall community development.

Consideration of these various aspects and their confluence is important to understand the context within which infrastructure and human beings will function. In comprehending the nature of infrastructure in specific contexts, we note that aspects of infrastructure attuned to protection from a changing climate – and the ability of localities to ensure infrastructure supports the development of trusted relationships amid greater socioeconomic, sociocultural and psychological upheaval – need to be core objectives.

It will be difficult yet necessary to support balanced thinking in an unbalanced, less stable, global operational and cognitive context. A new commercial, social and cultural vision – borne of clarity of values, vision and purpose animated by health and well-being *as a pragmatic end* – will be needed to support planning resilient infrastructure systems. The penultimate outcome, whatever the approach that animates it is ultimately called, will need to be an infrastructure plan that is part of and in step with a social, economic and population health plan. It cannot be stand-alone.

BIBLIOGRAPHY

Burchman S and Jones B (2020) How boards can plan for the disasters that no one wants to talk about. *Harvard Business Review*, 4 Sept. https://hbr.org/2020/09/how-boards-can-plan-for-the-disasters-that-no-one-wants-to-think-about (accessed 12/04/2020).

Cecco L (2020) Google affiliate Sidewalk Labs abruptly abandons Toronto smart city project. *The Guardian*, 7 May. https://www.theguardian.com/technology/2020/may/07/google-sidewalk-labs-toronto-smart-city-abandoned (accessed 12/04/2020).

Devi Sharmila (2020) Lebanon faces humanitarian emergency after blast. *Lancet* **396(10249)**: 456, 10.1016/S0140-6736(20)31750-5.

Eccles RG and Krzus MP (2018) Why companies should report financial risks from climate change. *MIT Sloan Management Review* **59(3)**: 1–6.

Fink L (2020) Larry Fink's Letter to CEOs. BlackRock. https://www.blackrock.com/corporate/investor-relations/larry-fink-ceo-letter (accessed 20/09/2020).

Irwin DA (2020) *The Pandemic Adds Momentum to the Deglobalization Trend*. Peterson Institute for International Economics, Washington, DC, USA. https://www.piie.com/blogs/realtime-economic-issues-watch/pandemic-adds-momentum-deglobalization-trend (accessed 20/09/2020).

Khanna S (2016) This is the world our children will inherit, and it's not looking good. *Broadview*, 5 Jan. https://broadview.org/this-is-the-world-our-children-will-inherit-and-its-not-looking-good/ (accessed 13/09/2020).

Mann M, Mitchell P, Foth M and Anastasiu I (2020) #BlockSidewalk to Barcelona: technological sovereignty and the social license to operate smart cities. *Journal of the Association for Information Science and Technology* **71(9)**: 1103–1115.

Mora C, Frazier AH, Longman RJ *et al.* (2013) The projected timing of climate departure from recent variability. *Nature* **502**: 183–187.

Ramirez R and Wilkinson A (2016) *Strategic Reframing: The Oxford Scenario Planning Approach*. Oxford University Press, Oxford, UK.

Rockström J, Steffen W, Noone K *et al.* (2009) Planetary boundaries: exploring the safe operating space for humanity. *Ecology and Society* **14(2)**: 32.

Samaras C and Willis HH (2013) *Capabilities-Based Planning for Energy Security at Department of Defense Installations*. Rand Corporation, Santa Monica, CA, USA.

Schwab K and Malleret T (2020) *COVID-19: The Great Reset*. World Economic Forum, Geneva, Switzerland.

Wilkinson A (2017) *Strategic Foresight Primer*. European Policy Strategy Centre, Glasgow, UK.

Wilkinson A and Kupers R (2013) Living in the futures. *Harvard Business Review* **91(5)**: 118–127.

Zambakari C, Lipsitch M, Ioannidis JPA *et al.* (2020) *The Great Disruption: COVID-19 and the Global Health Crisis*. The Zambukari Advisory, Pheonix, AZ, USA.

FURTHER READING

Some, but not all, futures-related reading that I value is written by journalists with an informal skill of understanding strategic foresight; or by artists, architects, designers and technologists who are insightful about potential future worlds.

Simon Kuper, for example, is a *Financial Times* journalist. He wrote a superb article about Dutch engineers striving to protect cities from rising sea levels (Kuper, 2020).

Designer Bruce Mau's recent book *MC24: Bruce Mau's 24 Principles for Designing Massive Change in Your Life and Work* (2020) describes important design principles for the twenty-first century.

Architect Rem Koolhaus, a former collaborator of Mau's, produced *Countryside: A Report* (Koolhaus, 2020), a companion book to his Guggenheim Museum exhibition. The book highlights investments in the countryside in agriculture, innovation, distribution centres and much more, demonstrating how the countryside is a countercurrent to urbanisation in the Anthropocene.

The Slovenia-based artist and architect Marjetica Potrč (2015) has produced visionary visual art and writing that highlights various symbioses and interdependencies among cities, people, politics and nature.

And the prolific artist and engineer Natalie Jeremijenko got me thinking about future cities. One interesting project of Jeremijenko's is *Environmental Health Clinic and Lab* and I recommend reading about it (Rich, 2009).

Koolhaus R (2020) *Countryside: A Report*. Taschen, New York, NY, USA.

Kuper S (2020) Can the Dutch save the world from the danger of rising sea levels? *Financial Times*, 30 Jan. 2020. https://www.ft.com/content/44c2d2ee-422c-11ea-bdb5-169ba7be433d?shareType=nongift (accessed 02/03/2021).

Mau B (2020) *MC24: Bruce Mau's 24 Principles for Designing Massive Change in Your Life and Work*. Phaidon, New York, NY, USA.

Potrč M (2015) *Self-Organization in Communities Where the State Has Withdrawn*. https://designforthelivingworld.com/self-organization-in-communities-where-the-state-has-withdrawn/ (accessed 02/03/2021).

Rich S (2009) Natalie Jeremijenko's MOMA lecture. *Dwell*, 20 Mar. https://www.dwell.com/article/natalie-jeremijenkos-moma-lecture-48b56380 (accessed 02/03/2021).

ICE Publishing

Hay, Alexander H
ISBN 978-0-7277-6562-8
https://doi.org/10.1680/pris.65628.205

Index

Page numbers in *italic* refer to figures.